DESI LAND

DESI LAND

teen culture, class, and success in silicon valley

SHALINI SHANKAR

Duke University Press

Durham and London 2008

© 2008 Duke University Press

Printed in the United States

of America on acid-free paper ∞

Designed by Katy Clove

Typeset in Quadraat by Keystone Typesetting, Inc.

Library of Congress Cataloging-in-Publication Data

appear on the last printed page of this book.

CONTENTS

PREFACE AND ACKNOWLEDGMENTS

In 1998, when I first landed in Silicon Valley to survey my field site, it was a very different place than it is today. I had arrived at the height of the tech bubble, when Internet stocks were soaring, venture capital was flowing, and talk about start-ups and IPOS was inescapable. The events, personalities, and institutions presented in this ethnography reflect the energy of this newsworthy moment. When the dramatic crash of the tech market occurred in April 2000, it took months, if not years, to gauge all of the collateral damage. Although some locals joked about the inevitable fall of "dot-communism," most Silicon Valley residents hoped it was a temporary setback rather than a more enduring end to the frenzy of growth and profiteering. My subsequent visits in 2005 and 2007, however, indicated that this time had indeed come to a close. The optimism for advancement that underpinned this era, however, has not disappeared altogether.

The chapters that follow focus on the lives of Desi youth whom I met as teenagers in high school. They examine select aspects of Desi teen life, and while they foreshadow teens' transition into adulthood, they treat teenage years as important in their own right. Throughout, I foreground youth voices, perspectives, and stories as teenagers. My discussion of this pre-9/11, tech-centered period analyzes aspects of class and community formation as well as of success and upward mobility. It is particular to this time period but also contextualizes these processes in broader debates of race, class, and diaspora in America. My account of this dynamic era concludes by revisiting teens years later and looking at how the calamitous events of 2000 and 2001 have changed life for Desi teens and their communities.

The Silicon Valley teenagers and families in this ethnography have my unending gratitude. Their generosity exceeded all of my expectations. My deepest thanks go to Aman, Amandeep, Amar, Amun, Amber, Amrit, Annie, Archana, Arsh, Ashdeep, Bicky, Chinni, Chirag, Derek, Dhana, Dicky, Farhana, Fatima, Happy, Harpreet, Inderjit, Japneet, Jeffery, Jessie, Jessie, Kabeer, Kamalpreet, Kiran, Kiran, Kiren, Kiron, Kishan, Kunal, Lakshmi, Mandeep, Mandeep, Manjot, Manpreet, Minal, Nafisha, Natasha, Natasha, Neelam, Neera, Navjit, Nilofar, Parijat, Pooja, Punam, Rahul, Rajney, Raman, Raman, Rehana, Robby, Ruby, Runa, Samir, Shalini, Sharia, Shireen, Shirima, Shivali, Shivani, Shraddha, Sim, Smita, Spandan, Sukhi, Sumeiya, Usha, Vasanta, Vanya, Zahed, Zayba, and their families and friends. To the families who adopted me as a daughter, thank you for your boundless generosity; it meant the world to me. Numerous school faculty helped make this project a reality, and I am grateful to Allison, Ben, Bruce, Chris, Chris, David, Fred, Jan, Jim, Jim, Josh, Lata, Marilyn, Marta, Michael, Mike, Paul, Rashawn, Ray, Sandie, Sandra, Stuart, Terry, Tim, Virginia, and, in fond memory, Aida. I would also like to thank those in the Bay Area who helped me to establish this project, especially Ved Vatuk, Vishal Ramani, James Freeman, Sam Rao, Ray McDermott, Raka Ray, Raba Gunasekara, and the staff of the South Asia Archive at UC Berkeley.

At New York University, my greatest debt of gratitude is to Bambi B. Schieffelin, who continues to be a tremendously supportive and intellectually generous colleague and friend. I have also benefited greatly from working closely with Faye Ginsburg and Fred Myers, both of whom have provided invaluable commentary and longer term insights on my research. I also thank Andrew Ross and Arvind Rajagopal for their close reading of the dissertation on which this manuscript is based. My colleagues at Binghamton University, especially Jean-Pierre Mileur, Charlie Cobb, John Chaffee, Lisa Yun, Pamela Smart, and Douglas Holmes, have been very supportive of my work, and I thank them for their generosity.

Support for this research was provided by a Social Science Research Council (SSRC) International Migration Program Dissertation Research Fellowship. Write-up funds were provided by a Spencer Foundation Dissertation Fellowship on Research Related to Education, New York University June E. Esserman Dean's Dissertation Fellowship, and a Binghamton University Dean's Semester. Thanks also to the American Institute of Indian Studies for funding a Hindi Intensive Summer Program in Udaipur, India, and to SSRC for a Predissertation Workshop Fellowship. In its initial stages, this research was influenced by my work at Education Development Center / Center for Children and Technology, where I developed a more nuanced understanding of how youth become invested in their education and use the tools available to them. This research is also shaped by my time as a volunteer at SAYA! (South Asian Youth Action) in Elmhurst, New York, and I thank the youth at SAYA! and Sayu Bhojwani for sharing their time and perspectives.

I am thankful to Ken Wissoker for being a thoughtful and encouraging editor, and to Courtney Berger and Mark Mastromarino for their editorial assistance. I am also very grateful to Purnima Mankekar for her intelligent, insightful review of this manuscript, as well as to the anonymous reviewer who offered helpful suggestions. Special thanks to Jillian Cavanaugh for reading and commenting on numerous versions of this work, coining the title phrase "Desi Land," and being a fantastic colleague and friend since the day we met. Tejaswini Ganti offered very thoughtful feedback on this manuscript and other work and has been supportive throughout this endeavor. I also thank Susanna Rosenbaum for her close engagement with this work in its dissertation form and her companionship while I was writing it, as well as Matt Durington for commenting on an earlier version of this manuscript. Portions of this work have been presented at conferences, published in journals, and discussed at length with numerous colleagues. My deep appreciation goes to all who engaged with the research presented here, especially Lila Abu-Lughod, Patricia Baquedano-Lopez, Don Brenneis, Robert Culp, Josh de Wind, Yen Le Espiritu, Steven Feld, Nancy Foner, Donna Gabaccia, Susan Gal, Steven Gregory, Webb Keane, Aisha Khan, Madhulika Khandelwal, Don Kulick, Jayati Lal, Karen Leonard, Adrienne Lo, Owen Lynch, Sunaina Maira, Daniel Miller, Raza Mir, Robin Nagle, Kirin Narayan, Kent Ono, Vijay Prashad, Angela Reyes, George Sanchez, Helen Schwartzman, Michael Silverstein, and Jack Tchen. Any oversights, errors, or omissions are my own.

This work has also benefited from feedback from my dissertation writing group, Maggie Fishman, Melissa Checker, Wendy Leynse, Peter Zabielskis, Jessica Winegar, and Steve Albert; and the Spencer Fellows cohort, Eileen Anderson-Fye, Rebecca Zarger, Lance McCready, and Jennifer Cohen. I also thank Nitasha Sharma, Omri Elisha, Ananya Mukherjea, Kathe Managan, and David Valentine for their generous comments on my work. Cheryl Furjanic, Jennie Tichenor, Robin Barron, Heidi Kenyon, and Fran Goldman have been wonderful support and company. Special thanks to Gita, Bharat, and Arjun Baliga-Savel for wonderful San Jose hospitality, and Eileen Juico, Bill Knauer, and Emiliana for providing great companionship and a space to write in New York City.

Like the teens in this ethnography, my family is foremost in my life, and their unconditional love and support has been invaluable. Throughout my work and especially during this project, my parents, Shyamala and Ratnaswamy Shankar, have showered me with encouragement and enthusiastic support. I also thank my brother Ravi for being such a good listener and friend. To my grandmother Paati and in memory of my grandparents Pattuamma, Swayambu Thatha, and Ratnaswamy Thatha, thank you for your involvement in and openness to my pursing this career path. To my extended family, especially Linda and Jim Mueller, Karen, Mark, Amy, Lili, Dan, all my cousins, mamas, chittis, chittappas, periammas, and periappas, thanks for taking such an active interest in what I do. Finally, to my love, Kurt, and my sweet little Roshan, thanks for your creative suggestions, unending patience, and love.

A note on the usage of non-English terms in this book: I have included the translation and transliteration of Hindi and Punjabi terms in text as well as in a glossary. Pluralization in Hindi, Urdu, and other languages follows common teen usage rather than standard rules of Hindi/Urdu grammar. For example, the plural of "bindi" is noted as "bindis" rather than "bindiyan." As language use generally varies in diasporic contexts, I here preserve this speech and do not correct any deviations from standard usage.

Versions of parts of this book have appeared previously and are reprinted with permission of the publishers, for which I am grateful:

"Digitally Speaking: Languages of Youth Connectivity," SAMAR (South Asian Magazine for Action and Reaction), fall/winter 2001: 44–48.

"FOBby or Tight? 'Multicultural Day' and Other Struggles in Two Silicon Valley High Schools." In Local Actions: Cultural Activism, Power and Public Life, edited by Melissa Checker and Maggie Fishman, 184–207. Copyright © 2004 Columbia University Press. Reprinted with permission of the publisher.

"Reel to Real: Desi Teens' Linguistic Engagements with Bollywood," *Pragmatics: Quarterly Publication of the International Pragmatics Association* 14, no. 2/3 (June/September 2004): 317–35. International Pragmatics Association.

"Metaconsumptive Practices and the Circulation of Objectifications," *Journal of Material Culture* 11, no. 3 (November, 2006): 293–317. Sage Publications.

Introduction

WELCOME TO DESI LAND

In 1981, when I was in grade school, I heard four words that changed my world: "I want my MTV." Now, a quarter of a century later, MTV finally wants me. That is, MTV Desi wants me. This subscriber-based channel that launched in 2006, like a slew of other new products eager to capture the small but lucrative market share of the South Asian diaspora, caters to an emergent demographic: Desis. At first glance, the term Desi, the Hindi word for "countryman," is simply the newest in a long line of names used to refer to South Asians living outside the Indian Subcontinent. Upon closer examination, however, Desi marks the inception of a particular type of diasporic, racially marked, generationally influenced consciousness at the beginning of the millennium. The emergence of the term signals a defining moment in the South Asian diaspora, during which a population that has steadily grown is emerging as a strong public presence. As a new generation of Desi teenagers comes of age, several questions arise: How do meanings of race, class, and immigration contribute to the emergence of this distinctive category? How are Desi teens of different socioeconomic backgrounds positioned in their neighborhoods and schools? In what cultural and linguistic ways is Desi teen culture signified and practiced, and how is it shared across generations? How do all these processes shape what it means to be Desi in different diasporic locations?

This ethnography examines these questions in Silicon Valley, California, during the high-tech boom of the late 1990s. At that time, Desi teens faced the mixed blessing of coming of age in a California marked by inflated narratives of success about Asian Americans and the economic promise of the high-tech industry. Although they are all interested in success, how they define this term and the goals they pursue can vary significantly. Over the past few decades, Desis have been widely heralded as "model minorities" who are thought to be upwardly mobile and socially integrated and raise academically high-achieving children. Such a stereotype, however, obscures inequalities that are deepening with this generation.

The title Desi Land acknowledges these rifts as part of the visible and varied presence of Desis in Silicon Valley. Desi Land evokes two compelling yet dramatically different landscapes that both characterize Silicon Valley life. In one sense, Desi Land resembles Disneyland, a constructed space of imagination and wonder. During the high-tech boom when I conducted research, Silicon Valley projected a sense of awe and endless possibilities. The promise of technology dangled dreams of success within every person's reach. An indefatigable spirit of entrepreneurship and prosperity emanated from this industry, and in this contained universe of dreams and venture capital, anything was possible. In this context, Desis established a strong presence in Silicon Valley by forming tightly knit communities, participating in public culture, and excelling in the high-tech industry.

On another level, Desi Land is reminiscent of Dixieland, a place of tremendous creativity and talent but also deep-seated racism and prejudice in the American South. This side of Desi Land harkens back to the early twentieth century, when immigrants from the Indian Subcontinent were lumped under the category "Hindoo" and denied citizenship, civil rights, and family reunification. By contrast, Desis in Silicon Valley have benefited greatly from postwar immigration laws that have actively recruited well-educated professionals. For these Desis, the model minority stereotype, which suggests that they have the social and moral character to excel in American society, makes their lives very different from their California predecessors'. Beneath this veneer of promise, however, lie dynamics of inequality that suggest that the racial and class standing of Desis is anything but equitable and secure.

Desi Land is located somewhere between Disneyland and Dixieland and is inflected both with a spirit of wonder and enthusiasm as well as immense obstacles of class and race for those who are not well positioned to realize their dreams. The types of expectations Desi Land places on teens and their families, and the ways they are able to manage them, is a constant reminder that the land of opportunity is still one of inequality. In Desi Land, the "*Amrikan* Dream" stands in notable contrast to the color-blind, utopic American Dream and its promise of upward mobility. In *Amrika*, or "America" in Hindi/Urdu, cultural difference is fraught with tense intersections of power and positionality. Everyday dynamics of race, class, language use, and gender intersect with immigration histories and local places to make being Desi an active negotiation. Unlike the American dream in Silicon Valley, where every teenager can become a dot-com millionaire, the Amrikan dream underscores the complexity of such a promise for Desi teens whose parents work on assembly lines and as janitorial staff at the same companies where other Desis are thriving in upper management.

Such a predicament calls into question the very nature of success and what it means to succeed in Amrika. The ways Desi teens negotiate the race- and class-based politics at their schools, manage the social and academic expectations of being a model minority, and engage in particular types of language use and displays of materiality are valued alongside, and sometimes even instead of, success defined as economic mobility and academic achievement. While these latter aspects are widely used as benchmarks of success in immigration and diaspora studies, community-specific meanings of loyalty, reputation, style, and other signifiers that elude quantification also inform Desis' own ideas of success. Socioeconomic background shapes how Desi teens form social cliques and engage in peer-exclusive as well as cross-generational cultural and linguistic practices. Everyday arenas of consumption, media, and language use as well as more formal spaces of multicultural performances, orientation toward school, and ideas about dating and marriage all contribute to what success means to Desi teens at the beginning of the millennium. The ways Desi teens relate to these narratives of success, how they craft their own meanings of what it means to be successful, and how they aim to achieve their goals in Silicon Valley are the core concerns of this book.

The future of Desi Land and whether it can and will continue as it is discussed here, lies in the hands of Desi youth. Their time in high school affects their lives afterward and leaves them differently able to manage the new socioeconomic dynamics of Silicon Valley as they enter adulthood after 9/11 and after the high-tech bubble. The opportunities offered by their communities and Silicon Valley, as well as their loyalty to these people and places, shape their present and future. In what follows, I elaborate on these key issues, including the development of the category "Desi," the distinctive nature of Desi teen culture, the configurations of class and community that shape it, and the broader historical and social context of race and the model minority stereotype.

DEFINING DESI IN THE SOUTH ASIAN DIASPORA

The emergence of the category "Desi" is a significant moment for South Asian diaspora studies, for it signals the shift from South Asians as immigrants longing to return to a homeland to public consumers and producers of distinctive, widely circulating cultural and linguistic forms. "Desi" is an inclusive category that supersedes potentially divisive categories of nation, religion, caste, ethnicity, language, and numerous other differences (see Mukhi 2000). Although these important social markers are relevant in Silicon Valley, teenagers also participate in a more unified diasporic consciousness that at times transcends them. As "Desi" is a generationally specific term, teens tend to use it far more than their parents. "Desi" has come into wider usage in the past two decades, and I use this term to refer to anyone of South Asian descent even when I discuss adults or early immigrants because teens use this term.

Desi teens in Silicon Valley encompass a wide range of religious, linguistic, and ethnic backgrounds, including Punjabi Sikhs, Pakistani Muslims, Gujarati Hindus, Indo-Fijian Hindus and Muslims, Bangladeshi Hindus and Muslims, and a handful of Tamil, Telegu, Malayalee, Khannada Hindus, Sri Lankans, and Nepalese. My inclusion of teens from all these groups poses different limits and possibilities than analysis of a smaller, more homogeneous sample would allow. Staying true to the definition of this term, I believe, has enabled a rich and varied ethnography that a narrower focus may have precluded.

For these Desis, Silicon Valley is more than a diasporic location; it is a home that has shaped the dreams and aspirations of adults and children alike. While these diasporic residents maintain ties with South Asia, Fiji, Canada, the United Kingdom, and other places, California resonates in their past, informs their present, and promises a desirable future. In this sense diaspora studies has called for a refocusing that underscores the significance of space, place, and identity (Appadurai 1996; Axel 2004; Basch, Glick-Schiller, and Szanton-Blanc 1994; Brah 1996; Braziel and Mannur 2003; Chow 1993; Clifford 1994; Gilroy 1993; Grewal and Kaplan 1993; Gupta and Ferguson 1997; S. Hall 1990; Lavie and Swedenburg 1996; Ong 1993; Tololyan 1991). In this sense, South Asia is decentered as an idealized homeland and emphasis is instead placed on local places of settlement (Bhatia 2007; George 2005; Khandelwal 1995; Niranjana 2006; Raj 2003; Shukla 2003; van der Veer 1995; Vertovec 2000).

Desis today are making an impact on the Silicon Valley landscape in ways distinct from early post-1965 immigrants, who felt displaced and longed for their homeland (Conner 1986; Drew 1987; Safran 1991). Studies of early post-1965 South Asian immigrants in North America describe how these Desis settled into neighborhoods dominated by other racial and ethnic groups and had limited opportunities to be Desi in public (Jensen 1988). Although these Desis were financially successful, they nonetheless remained socially marginal (Gibson 1988; Helweg and Helweg 1990). Later studies of Desis chronicle the emergence of a more pronounced South Asian public presence in the form of parades, festivals, social organizations, places of worship, and ethnic grocery stores (Bacon 1996; Bhattacharjee 1992; Jacobsen and Kumar 2004; Joshi 2006; Karamcheti 1992; Mankekar 2002; Mukhi 2000). Although studies occasionally mentioned them beginning in the late 1980s (Agarwal 1991; Gibson 1988), Desi youth have now emerged as a site of focus in their own right. Much of the earlier work on diaspora understandably focused on the adult generation, but studies in the past two decades have turned their attention to a new generation beginning to come of age.

BEING AN AMRIKAN DESI TEENAGER

The complex social cliques and dynamics of style and success of Desi teens in Silicon Valley underscore the obsolescence of terms such as "ABCD," or "American-Born Confused Desi." This term, most often used by first-generation Desis to describe second-generation youth, is rarely used or even acknowledged by Desi teens in Silicon Valley.[1] The term reflects Desi adults' characterizations of second-generation youth as culturally and intergenerationally conflicted (Bacon 1996; Helweg and Helweg 1990; Rangaswamy 2000; Rayaprol 1997). In these accounts, youth are "American" at school, "Indian" at home, and "caught in limbo" between these two worlds (Rangaswamy 2000: 167; see also Agarwal 1991; Purkayastha 2005).

The feature film *American Desi* from 2001 epitomizes this common depiction of the Desi youth experience and offers a useful foil to my approach. The film examines what it means to be an ABCD, the acronym from which the film's title is presumably derived. The film presents familiar narratives of ethnic identity formation as a process of losing and then finding one's culture and connecting to one's heritage through music, dance, and food. These tropes play out in the form of an upper-middle-class, ethnic coming-of-age story set in college, where a male protagonist embarks on a soul-searching journey to go from being American "Kris" to Desi "Krishna." Instrumental in this transformation is the good Desi girl Nina, who disciplines Kris in all matters, ranging from the Hindi language to Indian food. Narrative resolution is reached with minimal struggle, and the film quickly restores the proper American immigrant cultural order: Krishna will remain Kris but has learned to incorporate select aspects of his Indian heritage into his life. Having resolved the contradictions that mildly plagued him, college-educated Kris can now have the best of all worlds, and may even succeed in winning over Nina, if he can execute what she has taught him.

Desi teens in Silicon Valley exhibit a far more nuanced consciousness about what it means to be Desi. Rather than finding their heritage while they are in college, they live it throughout high school. Their schools feature a mix of races, ethnicities, and languages; Desis are one of many racial groups rather than a lone minority in a White majority. Indeed, these Desi teens are "masters of code-switching" (Narayan 2004) and seamlessly move between Bollywood and hip-hop, high school and the *gurd-wara* (Sikh temple). Moreover, they feel a sense of ownership and belonging in all these realms and are able to negotiate different cultural contexts and identities (see Ahmad 2003; K. Hall 2002; Maira 2002; Puwar 2003).

As Desi teens move among several different worlds, terms such as "hybridity" and "authenticity" speak to their experience but do not fully capture its complexity. For this reason, I use teen terminology for describing their worlds, which I discuss in detail below. My approach is certainly informed by insights about hybridity that address the complexity of cultural negotiation in diaspora. Homi Bhabha (1994) identifies a "third space" that acknowledges that diasporic culture is different from both original and mainstream culture (see also Werbner and Modood 1997). Along these lines, Lisa Lowe (1996) notes the uneven dynamics of power in which immigrant communities must negotiate the state and society. She asserts, "Hybridity is not the 'free' oscillation between or among chosen identities" (82). The idea of hybridity is itself reliant on a series of polarities, in which marked aspects of Desi life stand in opposition to an unmarked American mainstream.

Questions of authenticity surface routinely in the lives of Desi youth. Not only are teens faced with myriad cultural options, but they must also defend their choices in the face of static, orientalist expectations of school peers and faculty about what it means to be from the Indian Subcontinent. R. Radhakrishnan (2003: 27) astutely asks, "If a minority group were left in peace with itself and not dominated or forced into a relationship with the dominant world or national order, would the group still find the term 'authentic' meaningful or necessary?" Authenticity draws attention to the unequal power dynamics of those who produce cultural representations and others who validate or critique them. Indeed, when White Americans or Europeans cross borders they are seldom considered hybrid, or if they are, they do not pose a threat to nationalism or a White hegemonic world order (Hutnyk 1999–2000; Kalra, Kaur, and Hutnyk 2005). By contrast, Desis in the United States are subject to scrutiny and judgment about their cultural and linguistic choices.

Desi teens create styles that defy simple classification. In this ethnography, I use their terminology to describe their world. To differentiate what is fashionable from what is not, Desi teens use the terms "tight" and "FOBby," derived from "Fresh off the Boat," respectively. FOBby does not simply signal all things South Asian while tight signals everything American. Rather, Desi teens continually define these terms according to context. How they organize themselves into different types of cliques, create distinctive styles, and order and evaluate their world defies polarities of "American" and "South Asian" or even "first generation" and "second generation." Desi teen culture in Silicon Valley is informed by social class, material culture, and modernity far more than it is by generational categories. A second-generation middle-class Desi teen from San Jose is not necessarily more hip than an upper-middle-class Desi teen who just arrived from cosmopolitan Bombay. California is marked by a strong Latino and Asian American history and a wide range of local and global cultural forms. These teens have been raised on MTV, Bollywood films, and California culture. "Desi bling," a distinctive diasporic style that I discuss in chapter 3, for example, draws on this wide range of elements.

In these ways, locally defined and deployed meanings of Desi terms such as "FOBby" are a lens through which to understand how class-coded values operate in a diasporic context. Desi teens use the term FOB to index their particular judgments and stances toward a class-based youth culture that transcends a simple East-West binary. Signifiers of tight—be they from Bollywood, California, or elsewhere in the world—all share the common attribute of being cosmopolitan and chic by youth standards. In contrast, what is FOBby could include that which is unhip, unattractive, and generally undesirable from India or elsewhere. Such contextually defined social categories underscore the importance of local places in defining youth culture. Indeed, even a small and seemingly homogeneous category such as Desi teens can vary from Desi youth of other ages as well as from Desi youth elsewhere.[2] The heterogeneity of this population is reflected in such social and aesthetic judgments.

Desi teens "kick it," or spend time together in their cliques, for the majority of their school social time. At times, the type of clique they belong to is salient, and I refer to them as well-liked "populars," studious "geeks," or "FOBs," who are marginalized for their lack of cultural and linguistic capital. In other instances, their middle-class or upper-middle-class status shapes their dispositions and tastes in significant ways. Also important are their religious, national, linguistic, and caste backgrounds, which surface in particular contexts. All of these groupings, however, transcend the binary of being American or being "other" and characterize the complex nature of Desi teen culture.

Such dynamics are magnified during high school. Desi teens are invested in staying in Silicon Valley and remaining connected to their communities. This time, marked by various types of peer-exclusive and intergenerational relationships, is notably different from life in college, away from home. Studies of upper-middle-class Desi youth in college, night clubs, or living independently show that they have far greater freedom to explore and express identity (Maira 2002, N. Sharma 2004). Desi teenagers in high school, however, generally have limited freedom and purchasing power and are subject to numerous forms of surveillance. Some practices are cross-generational, others are peer-exclusive, and both of these together inform how diasporic identity and community are formed. What is shared, what is kept exclusive, and how this plays out in day-to-day life is integral to understanding Desi teen identities, as well as how diasporic communities are maintained and reproduced generationally.

While there is much confluence between generations, teenagers are rarely in complete agreement with the rules to which they are subject. In their everyday cultural and linguistic practices, they contest constraints and occasionally change them in the process. Such quotidian acts, or "micropractices," as Michel de Certeau (1984: xiv–xv) calls them, underscore the significance of "the clandestine forms taken by the dispersed, tactical, and make-shift creativity of groups or individuals already caught in nets of 'discipline.'" Micropractices are found nearly everywhere in Desi teen life. Although these less noticeable actions may not break rules or openly challenge authority, they are significant nonetheless. In these ways, Desi teens exercise agency that is circumscribed: their ability to transform their communities is within reach but bounded. How these teens orient themselves to the cultural and linguistic values of their communities, the narratives of progress that abound in Silicon Valley, as well as the popular culture in their lives all shape their ideals of what it means to be a Desi teen.

COMMUNITIES AND SOCIAL CLASS IN DESI LAND

In Silicon Valley, constellations of community and class are particular to the high-tech economy at the end of the twentieth century. Desis there actively create and maintain communities that provide social support, linguistic continuity, and contexts for display, gossip, and value. To refer to the large population of South Asian Americans in the Bay Area, I use the term Desi Community with a capital "C." Like Benedict Anderson's (1991) "imagined" community, these residents acknowledge being part of this larger group whether or not they interact personally with one another. By contrast, community with a lowercase "c" acknowledges the multiple, smaller groups that make up the Desi community; this is the most meaningful unit in the everyday lives of teens and their families. Akhil Gupta and James Ferguson (1997a: 13) assert that such constructions are premised on forms of exclusion and constructions of otherness, and Desi communities in Silicon Valley emphasize these boundaries among themselves as well as with other racial and ethnic groups. Desi communities are self-selected groups that organize around kinship, class, religion, nationality, spoken language, and ethnic group. Families who form these social groups consistently work to maintain the bonds that initially connected them. Such communities are significant because they are the arenas in which Desis define success, style, and other values and in which intergenerational change and aspects of social reproduction occur.

Social class has a tremendous impact on community as well as everyday life for Desi teens. The ways they orient themselves toward their schools, how they define their values and beliefs, and what they consider to be successful can vary significantly for Desi teens of different class backgrounds. Class is an important dynamic in shaping life in the South Asian diaspora in general, as there can be great disparity between Desis of different classes (Abraham 2000; Das Gupta 2006; Matthew 2004; Mohammad-Arif 2002; Rudrappa 2004; Visweswaran 1993). Such differences largely correlate with immigration history. Early post-1965 immigrants who answered America's call for highly skilled laborers tend to be more upwardly mobile than Desis who came with a mixed skill set as part of family reunification or other measures in the late 1970s and early 1980s (Khandelwal 2002; Lessinger 1996). In spite of these seemingly clear-cut distinctions, class categories are not simple to define. Sheba George's (2005) study of female nurses who immigrated from India before their husbands illustrates how class mobility must be understood according to specific occupations and conditions of migration. Although Desi families in Silicon Valley do not openly discuss class, the unending focus on homes, cars, jobs, and all other markers of wealth underscores the centrality of class in their communities.

In Silicon Valley, as in other regions, class is defined by local social and economic contexts (Devine and Savage 2005; Halle 1984; Liechty 2003; O'Dougherty 2002; Skeggs 2005). I identify Desi teens as either middle class or upper middle class according to the type of work their parents do, whether both parents work, and their parents' level of education, English proficiency, neighborhood, home, cars, and lifestyle. In Silicon Valley, upper-middle-class teens are usually the children of skilled professionals, especially engineers and doctors, while middle-class teens are the children of unskilled or semiskilled workers, most often assembly line workers, truck drivers, and custodial staff. Scholars of social class will likely balk at my calling assembly line workers middle class, so please allow me to explain.

One of the unusual aspects of Silicon Valley life during the 1990s for this Desi community is the impact of high growth and opportunities during the high-tech boom, as well as the equity afforded by the rapid appreciation of homes they have owned since the late 1970s. Such conditions have inflated standard class categories and complicated trajectories of class mobility.[3] During the late 1990s, Silicon Valley flaunted unending reserves of venture capital, job security, and property appreciation. Families of assembly line workers who bought homes for $38,000 two decades earlier saw their homes soar in value to half a million dollars and more. I am aware that my usage of "middle class" is somewhat unconventional, but so too is the potential for class mobility in Silicon Valley. In any other economy, these Desis would be working class, and upper-middle-class Desis would perhaps not be as prosperous.[4] That both middle- and upper-middle-class Desis purchased real estate and situated themselves in the high-tech industry well before the dot-com boom of the late 1990s, however, has enabled an unusually high degree of wealth and accumulation. This fateful confluence could be characterized as what Marshall Sahlins (1984) has called "the structure of the conjuncture." Indeed, being in the right place at the right time has not only improved their assets, but also positioned them to take advantage of new opportunities presented by the high-tech industry. Jobs such as systems operators, network professionals, and other "grey-collar" positions require short stints of postsecondary training but can confer status and recognition in their communities that Desi teens' parents could rarely attain through their assembly line jobs. Although the long-term promise of such positions is unknown, it nonetheless shapes how middle-class Desi teens relate to their schooling and how class reproduction between generations may unfold. Such opportunities underscore how economies of late capitalism can destabilize traditional trajectories to class mobility and create new opportunities that complicate existing class categories (Ortner 2003).

By the same token, wealth alone does not elevate one's class status, as Pierre Bourdieu and others have argued. Bourdieu's (1985) concept of cultural capital draws attention to the types of social knowledge and resources parents are able to instill in their children and how these affect children's lives and outcomes as they enter adulthood. For Desi teens, cultural capital is informed by their parents' educational background, occupations, English-language proficiency, and class status. Such factors shape how teens are able to form relationships in academic and school activities, how they conduct themselves linguistically, and the paths they pursue after high school.

Although class background informs cultural capital, the latter can never be reduced to class alone. Middle-class youth whose parents have profited from the high-tech industry rarely gain more cultural capital from this windfall, though the types of opportunities they can provide to their children may change as a result. Likewise, some middle-class youth are able to succeed in the educational system despite not having the same advantages as upper-middle-class youth. Thus, I use cultural capital as an illustrative but limited analytical tool that draws attention to how youth predispositions play out in school settings and beyond. Especially when their Silicon Valley high schools are overenrolled and fiercely competitive and the model minority stereotype suggests that all Desi teens should be stellar students, cultural capital contextualizes the plight of individual teens in the broader socioeconomic forces at work in their lives.

RACIALIZING DESIS IN AMRIKA

Desis have been able to integrate into upper-middle-class America in ways that they had previously been unable to earlier in the twentieth century (Prashad 2000). Upper-middle-class Desis have been able to take advantage of the model minority stereotype to settle into wealthy neighborhoods with Whites and other Asian Americans and send their children to high performing schools; in so doing, they have furthered the expectation that the next generation of Desi teens will do the same. While this could certainly be the case for upper-middle-class teens, middle-class teens contend with a different set of racialized, class-based options. Upper-middle-class and middle-class Desi teens are differently able to negotiate the cultural and linguistic dictates of their schools and accordingly find potentially different places for themselves in the racial order. Indeed, as class differences bifurcate this population, Desis' status as a model minority comes into question. Race and ethnicity are often reformulated at unstable moments in a capitalist economy, though they may otherwise appear to be static, bounded entities (Brodkin Sacks 1994; Ignatiev 1996;

Omi and Winant 1994; Sollors 1986). I use "race" to refer to broad classifications such as Asian American, African American, White, and Latino, and "ethnicity" to denote differences of nation, language, religion, and regional specificities within these groups. In California, as in other parts of the United States, racial and ethnic groups have had drastically different experiences with economic and political success depending on the time and conditions under which they emigrated (Leonard 1992) as well as the variety encompassed within ethnic groups (di Leonardo 1984).

Scholars note the racial ambiguity that surrounds the category of Asian Americans (Okihiro 1994), and South Asians in particular (Kibria 1998; Prashad 2000; Visweswaran 1993). Much of this uncertainty arises from the dramatic recasting of Asian Americans during the twentieth century. Despite the rampant anti-Asian discrimination during the early part of the century and the atrocities of the internment of Japanese Americans during World War II, these prejudices have been redirected in the postwar era. Asian Americans were named a model minority in 1966 when both the *New York Times* and later *U.S. News and World Report* lauded Japanese Americans and Chinese Americans respectively for succeeding without government support, by relying on their families. By praising the success of some minorities, these reports indirectly blamed others for not advancing in what was touted as an open society. The racist dynamics that govern structures of opportunity were neither acknowledged nor taken into account (Prashad 2000).

Within the category "Asian American," differences of race, class, and ethnicity are obscured by the model minority stereotype but are absolutely crucial to understanding the specific subjectivities that make this collective heading meaningful. Scholars have noted stratifications of race, class, and ethnicity contained within this group and how discourses of whitening and darkening have differently positioned those of varying social capital (Ong 1996). Indeed, the socioeconomic positioning of some Asian American refugees from Laos, Cambodia, and Vietnam can be far lower than that of professionals from China, Korea, and Japan. Youth especially bear the burden of managing a model minority stereotype that not only denies racism and class inequality, but also deters Asian American solidarity with other oppressed racial groups, such as Blacks and Latinos (S. Lee 1996, 2005; see also Omatsu 1994; Reyes 2006; Tuan 1998).

For Desi teens in Silicon Valley, the uncertainty of what it means to be of

South Asian decent is evident in how they align themselves with the culture of their school and with other racial groups, as well as how they are positioned in neighborhoods and communities. On the one hand, it is far more socially desirable to be Desi now than it was at the start of the twentieth century. Rather than having to downplay their culture and religion, Desi teens today are encouraged to express their cultural heritage and display their ethnicity, although in controlled ways. With the support of ideologies of multiculturalism, they celebrate aspects of their cultural background through food, dance, and costume and speak their heritage language in socially sanctioned spaces. Yet when they cross these lines by engaging in cultural or linguistic expression that challenges the hegemonic codes of their schools and communities, they cease to be model and their status becomes more ambiguous. What happens to these Desi teens in school socially, academically, and otherwise greatly impacts their transition into adulthood. The ways Desi teens use language, perform their ethnicity, and orient themselves to the school environment all shape their place in the Amrikan racial order.

All of these dynamics underpin identity politics and processes of racialization. Desis are no longer another ethnic group among many under the "American umbrella," where differences are erased and all hyphenated identities are made to appear homogeneous and equal (Prashad 1998: 108; see also Purkayastha 2005; Radhakrishnan 2003). Arjun Appadurai (1993: 808) has commented that in the United States, the "right side of the hyphen can barely contain the unruliness of the left side." Desis teens seek to live beyond the hyphen, be it literal or figurative. Whether they are creating cultural expressions that confound local expectations of authenticity or disregarding the unspoken high school dynamics of English monolingualism, Desi teens seek new parameters for cultural and linguistic expression. Indeed, as Desi teens come of age, visible class differences and racial ambiguity may pose a threat to the homogeneous depiction of the model minority.

In this defining moment, some Desis will continue to seek a place in upper-middle-class society alongside Whites and other upwardly mobile minorities, while others share more economic, academic, and professional similarities with working-class Latinos and Whites and with other working-class Asian Americans.[5] Processes of racialization for Desis in the United States have been productively examined by studying encounters between Desis and local populations of Whites, African Americans, and Latinos (Bhatia 2007; George 1997; Leonard 1992; Prashad 2002; Raphael-Hernandez and Steen 2006; Sharma 2004). In the ensuing chapters, examinations of Desi teens and how they negotiate school and community contexts offer a multilayered portrait of what it means to be Amrikan in a transforming Silicon Valley. I situate my analysis of teenage life within these broader parameters because identity means something only when it is connected to these larger social and economic forces. Although these Desi teens and their communities may seem insular, they are not unaffected by institutions such as schools and workplaces. Meanings about them are constructed through media and pervade their high schools and communities. Racial definitions are further complicated by the aftermath of 9/11, which has left some Desis even more invested in separating themselves from others who may be mistaken for enemies of the state. Although much has changed in the Silicon Valley economy since the high-tech bubble burst, the underlying narratives of progress that existed for Desi teens in high school continue to resonate into their young adult lives as they search for success in Desi Land.

ETHNOGRAPHY IN DIASPORAS

Ways of being a Desi teen are articulated through competing regimes of value, challenged through everyday practices, and reinstated by local institutions in the context of globalization. Such processes draw attention to dynamics of power that impact and position teenagers as they struggle with their own ideas about their lives and futures. I regard culture and language not as variables to be lost or retained, but as dynamics that are shaped and reshaped through practice. Stuart Hall (1996) argues that in diaspora as elsewhere, identity cannot simply be given or lost, but is actively constructed. When I discuss the Desi teen culture, I am interested not only in marked aspects of their cultural heritage, but in other elements that are equally important to them. Likewise, I am not simply concerned with whether they *can* speak their heritage language, but *how* they speak it, with whom, and in what contexts and the types of things they say. By contrast, many studies of immigrant youth examine aspects of culture and language in static, homogeneous ways through sociological models of assimilation and acculturation (De Wind and Kasinitz 1997; Levitt and

Waters 2002; Portes and Rumbaut 1996; Zhou and Lee 2004). These studies focus primarily on second-generation and "1.5"-generation youth who immigrated during early childhood rather than looking at multigenerational peer groups. I found these analytical categories to be less relevant than the cliques and communities that youth themselves create.[6]

Race, class, gender, and community formation, as well as cultural and linguistic identity, are best examined through long-term, systematic observation in situ. While quantitative studies of migration and diaspora certainly offer some insight into these areas, they tend to distill the messiness of life into narrow lines of inquiry by using statistical methods and controlled selection of research participants. Indeed, they overlook the texture of everyday life in which such processes occur as well as what their findings actually mean to people in their studies. De Certeau (1984: xviii) insightfully notes that

> Statistical investigation grasps the material of these practices, but not their form; it determines the elements used, but not the "phrasing" produced by the bricolage (the artisan-like inventiveness) and the discursiveness that combine these elements, which are all in general circulation and rather drab. Statistical inquiry, in breaking down these "efficacious meanderings" into units that it defines itself, in reorganizing the results of its analysis according to its own codes, "finds" only the homogenous. The power of its calculations lies in its ability to divide, but it is precisely through this ana-lytic fragmentation that it loses sight of what it claims to seek and represent.

Drawing on this insight, I present a combination of ethnographic participant-observation, open-ended interviews, and an inclusive sample of teens by focusing on daily and longer-term aspects of diasporic life. By foregrounding their own stories and lives, this approach illustrates that being a Desi teen is as much about narratives of success that communities create and circulate as it is about actual material wealth individuals can accrue; it is as much about how teens express identity in highly specific and differentiated ways through their everyday cultural and linguistic practices as it is about how they are regarded by their community and society; finally, it is as much about how they articulate and pursue what they consider to be meaningful in their lives as it is about belonging to a racial and ethnic category renowned for its success.

The community settings and three high schools in which I conducted research from September 1999 through August 2000 and February through May 2001 feature a truly diverse cross section of Desi teens. When I conceived of this project, I intended to use Mercer, Greene, and Waverley public high schools primarily as a starting point from which to meet a wide variety of Desi students. After daily spending time there with students, I realized that my investigations of language use, consumption, media, and, more broadly, success would be made much more complex by including time spent in school. I became especially interested in how schooling is not simply a neutral or external part of their identity in and attachment to their community; but rather, how it integrally shapes them. Especially in the case of diasporic youth, identifying with and being attached to their school may be opposed to family- or community-based agendas (Gibson 1988). When regarded as a place in conflict with family and community, schools can be overlooked as a site in which Desi youth build relationships and worldviews toward the formation of adult identities and relationships. As a space of seclusion from their families, this four-year prelude to adulthood is central to shaping how youth become adult members of their communities. I look at school and community together because they are interlinked; school success means little without community success, and much surveillance about dating and sexual activity occurs through extensive peer policing and impression management in school. Considered together, these school- and community-based cultural processes provide deeper perspectives on how teens become successful adults.

KICKIN' IT WITH DESI TEENS

"Why do you come to school if you don't have to?" was the thoughtful query posed to me by one sophomore in the beginning of the 1999–2000 school year. At times, I absolutely dreaded meeting teens in this environment. Being an anthropologist offered little immunity from the insecurity and fear of rejection that circulate like airborne diseases in high schools. It was far less difficult than I had imagined to locate groups of Desi students kickin' it together; it was far more intimidating to actually approach them. From a distance, I watched groups of vibrant teens engage in lively conversations. One by one, almost in slow motion, their conversations halted and activity ceased when they realized I was approaching, and they turned to stare at me walking toward them. Immediately I knew I had violated

17

some kind of code, for teens simply do not walk up to unknown cliques the way I did. But it was always too late to turn back. Facing a sea of expectant faces, I choked back major queasiness and began to spit out my introduction. Time and time again, I was pleasantly surprised and grateful that I had mistaken their cliquish nature for snobbishness and their wary countenance for antagonism. Once I settled into school, I never wanted to miss a day, because with high school, the second time is the charm.

Being a second-generation Desi not only eased my transition into social groups, but also provided a basic foundation for understanding the nature of Desi teen culture. While teens and their families were exceedingly kind and open in sharing their lives with me, I did not consider myself an insider to any group. Kirin Narayan (1993) insightfully cautions that "native" anthropologists still need to understand and be accepted by their communities, and I soon realized that Desi teens in Silicon Valley live in a world starkly different from my own. Aspects of my background, including growing up in New York and speaking Hindi, Tamil, and a little Punjabi most likely enhanced my ethnographic cachet. Because I was older than them and an outsider to the Bay Area it was easier for them to trust me, and because I am a Desi it was easier for them to share some experiences and viewpoints. My high school experience in the 1980s in a predominantly White middle-class high school in suburban New York with Jews, Italians, and Irish friends offered no comparison to their racially and linguistically diverse schools in an era of multicultural discourse. I had never seen schools with so many Asian American students, especially those in wealthy, suburban neighborhoods.

Some aspects of Silicon Valley community life were quite familiar to me, such as belonging to a South Asian community where families kept up with each other's lives, gathered for social events, and encouraged their children to socialize with one another. My home life in high school was similar to these teens', although I probably faced fewer constraints. I was raised in a media-saturated home, where my mother watched Bollywood films and my father occasionally glanced at them over his periodicals. As a spiritually minded, upper-middle-class Hindu, my mother routinely told me to be less fixated on material things, which no doubt contributed to my complete fascination with them.

Over the course of my fieldwork, several families warmly welcomed me as a daughter, and I called these adults Aunty and Uncle, a common referential practice in Desi contexts. Aunties spared no discretion in telling me I should have already been married and had children. To uncles, I appeared a bit wayward in the career department, especially given the lucrative opportunities in the high-tech field.

Desi teens were quite curious as to why I chose to base my study in the Bay Area, why their school was selected, and how Desi teenagers here might be different from those in New York, where I lived. After a battery of questions about these topics and being assured that I was not a school faculty member in disguise, Desi teens were by and large very welcoming. Most settled on defining me as the college student from New York doing a report. I was permitted to move between cliques of kids that did not get along, and many teens shared confidential information without fear of my spreading gossip across groups. Some Desi teens conveyed to me that they were not "authentic" enough to be included, as they did not kick it or spend time only with other Desis or speak their heritage language well. Other Desi students told me that they disagreed with researching just one group, saying that such an approach was exclusive, discriminating, and singled them out. Likewise, several of the non-Desi kids I got to know well were puzzled as to why they were not asked to participate more substantially in my study. I found these to be valid criticisms for which I had no satisfactory answer. If anything, it increased my already abundant respect for teenagers because they rarely held back their probing, blunt questions. To borrow their lexicon, they kept it real and expected me to as well.

Although faculty at all three schools were exceedingly welcoming and offered to introduce me to students, I chose to approach students on my own to avoid being regarded as an authority figure, to gain their trust, and to ensure that they spoke to me out of their own will, rather than through the coercion of faculty or because they thought it might enhance their grades. Their not having to compete with me or fear me as a disciplinary figure placed me in an excellent position. I always put their academics, privacy, and safety first. I did not take students out of class to interview them, access their academic records, or discuss information they told me with their teachers, parents, or other students. Such practices limited my access to some types of information, but it enabled me to collect the type of data that most interested me: teenagers' everyday opinions, activities, aspirations, and transgressions.

The general awkwardness endemic to adolescence made it far easier for me to interact with girls than with boys. I got to know a number of boys well and even visited their homes when their parents were present, but did not spend the type of extended time alone with them that I was socially sanctioned to do with girls. I was nonetheless able to speak with and keep in close contact with numerous Desi boys. As I completed my fieldwork, one boy I had gotten to know well warmly told me that he and his friends would miss me, and exclaimed, "You were totally like one of us. Not that we're much or anything. We're crap, but you're, like, the God of crap." At that moment, I felt I truly belonged.

As fieldwork wore on, I sought to help teenagers in ways that might be beneficial to them. I offered to tutor teens in preparation for tests, SATs, and college applications. Only upper-middle-class teens availed themselves of my offer. In retrospect, I wish that I had been more proactive about helping middle-class teens academically. Despite my attempts, we only interacted socially. One possible reason is because middle-class Desi teens tended not to be assertive in asking for academic assistance or taking advantage of school resources and saw my offer in this vein. Another possibility is that they did not consider my academic help to be relevant or useful to their lives. In school, I occasionally helped teachers in classes I attended regularly, such as setting up lab tables, returning papers, or watching the classroom if the teachers had to step out. Some teachers asked me to present my research project to students and explain the process of getting a PhD. In one of the schools, the librarian routinely asked me to promote reading, books, and the library and to participate in book talks and talk about the significance of Asian Heritage Week. By and large, however, I simply sat with students as they sat in their classes, noting how they engaged with their studies and how they passed the time.

There were certainly challenging incidents during fieldwork. Teenagers can be quite unreliable when it comes to making and keeping appointments, executing plans, and giving accurate directions. A handful of students found my presence unwelcome and kept their distance from me during my school visits. Some of their friends informed me that they did not trust sharing their secrets in front of me, as I was there to write everything down and "expose" them. To this day, a few are convinced that I was an undercover FBI agent. One family I interviewed was highly wary of my questions and refused to be tape-recorded during their interview. Teens occasionally put me in awkward positions by asking me to call the school in an Indian accent and pretend I was their mother to cover for their cutting school, forge notes for unexcused absences, get them out of class under the pretense of interviewing them, drive them places when they were cutting class, or buy them alcohol or drugs. I did none of these things, and in the end, I believe I earned the respect of some teens while frustrating others.

Despite such moments, I deeply enjoyed the time I spent with the youth you are about to meet. I felt their contagious excitement about life, laughed at their jokes, and took great pleasure in their company. I was struck by the overwhelming optimism with which they regarded the world and the boundlessness of their future plans. Not only did such observations enrich my life immeasurably, but they lend color and depth to the topics I discuss.

OVERVIEW OF CHAPTERS

The chapters are organized around topics that emerged as significant in Desi teen life. True to the nature of the term "Desi," you will meet Muslim, Hindu, Christian, and Sikh teens who have moved to Silicon Valley from Fiji, South Asia, Canada, the United Kingdom, Africa, and other diasporic locales. Although you will meet only a handful of the teens I got to know during my fieldwork, their words, actions, and lives will directly convey the ideas, frustrations, and hope that they embody. The words and stories of additional teens are presented throughout the ethnography. Family details are provided for teens I discuss frequently, names are used for those who appear more than once, and the rest remain unnamed for clarity's sake. Pseudonyms are used throughout for all teens, families, schools, and school faculty, but San Jose, Fremont, and other California place-names are real.

Each chapter begins with a profile of a Desi teenager compiled from extensive participant observation and interview excerpts. Here especially, teens elaborate on the complicated nature of their social lives, the frustrating aspects of having cliques of Desi friends, and the difficulties of balancing all that is asked of them. In these reflections, Desi teens often express their exasperation at the insular, dramatic nature of Desi cliques and their desire to find more diverse groups of friends. Such viewpoints are especially telling because they indicate how Desi teens would like to see their social worlds and the intensive efforts they must engage in to form Desi social alliances. Indeed, although Desi cliques seem homogeneous and natural, they are actually fraught with dynamics of social tension and belonging, making these alliances anything but easy. The types of negotiations that teens undergo with their Desi social circles are not unlike those that their parents perform in their communities. Such dynamics are quite telling of the efforts and concessions Desi teens make toward building a social world similar to that of their parents.

Desi families and teens have established a visible presence in Silicon Valley neighborhoods and schools. Chapter 1 chronicles how meanings of "Desi" have shifted over the past century and how current Desis arrived in Silicon Valley and created thriving communities for themselves in California at the start of the new millennium. This region has undergone tremendous shifts in population, landscape, and economy with the rise of the high-tech industry. The promise of technology, as I call it, has brought the Amrikan dream of making it big in the high-tech world into the Desi imagination and shapes goals and aspirations for adults and youth alike. Chapter 2 traces the emergence of a distinctive diasporic youth culture. I examine how this category has come into being, its hallmark characteristics, and its global and local influences. Style is defined through Desi teen culture and emerges in ways of dressing, speaking, and being. Desi teens use their own cultural logic of the world to create categories of evaluation, form social cliques, and kick it with one another. In these social worlds, Desi teens claim spaces in their school and manage the confluence of life across high school and communities. They use new media technologies to stay connected, especially when social constraints in their lives preclude them from interacting in person.

Desi teen cultural and linguistic practices signify identity, community, and success in a wide range of contexts. Chapter 3 examines the types of relationships individuals form with material objects, from how shopping and commodities are significant to teenagers to how verbally mediated relationships with objects enable particular types of status and display within communities. "Desi bling" is the ruling aesthetic of these style-making practices, and I discuss its significance in peer-exclusive as well as cross-generational contexts. Chapter 4 examines language use in diasporic contexts. Focusing on family-based as well as peer-based language use, I present ways in which language use is instrumental in social cliques and interactions within them. More than a way of communicating, language use can be a basis of social judgment, both by peers and by school administrators. Different types of language practices, including those excerpted from spontaneously occurring conversations, are analyzed here. Chapter 5 situates Desis among other racial groups in high school. I analyze how dynamics of race, class, and gender are unmade and redefined during school multicultural day performances and provide a behind-the-scenes look at the complex politics of negotiation that underlie seamless, celebratory performances. Questions of tradition, authenticity, representation, and identity are in active contestation in these forums, and Desi teens must manage competing expectations about the character and purpose of public expression.

Desi teen relationships with their school and community set the stage for adulthood. Chapter 6 draws attention to how discourses of success are constructed and circulated in high schools. Expectations of high performance place great pressures on upper-middle-class and middle-class Desi teens alike and push them to carefully consider their own goals and aspirations in relation to the standard accomplishments expected of them. While upper-middle-class teens manage this stereotype, middle-class teens have an exceedingly difficult time and often fall short of the expectations placed on them academically as well as socially. For these teens, being bilingual in their monolingual high school can bring about a spate of unforeseen consequences. I discuss how youth are positioned in high schools and the ways they conceive of success in their communities, especially in the context of the high-tech industry. Chapter 7 examines how Desi teens are subject to numerous social codes imposed by their families and communities. While these rules vary according to class and religion, most Desi teens are concerned with maintaining their family's reputation in their closely knit communities. Proscriptions are enforced through peer surveillance at school as well as in community settings, and youth who do not want to follow these rules do so on the "DL" or "down low" to avoid becoming the subject of unwelcome gossip. Their opinions about arranged marriage underscore their widespread interest in reproducing the types of communities in which they have been raised as they enter adulthood.

The final chapter returns to broader questions of race in a post-9/11 America, as well as class in a Silicon Valley no longer benefiting from the high-tech boom. I analyze how class differently encodes racial meaning for middle- and upper-middle-class Desis and trace the lives of several youth into this period. The book concludes with updates on the youth, their communities, and the perceived future of Desi Land.

Like most ethnographies, this one could continue indefinitely, with ongoing updates of youth as they enter adulthood. In a postscript, I note a few recent events and observations from my final visit in July 2007. I include these more recent details because so many ethnographies of youth seem to start and end with the teen years. While I am most interested in this time period, the way teens transition into adulthood and how they begin to integrate into and form new communities speak not only to Desi teen culture, but also to diasporic identity and community formation on a broader level. How they negotiate questions of race, class, and gender from youth to adulthood contextualizes insights about Desi Land and the nature of diasporic communities.

CALIFORNIA, HERE WE COME,

RIGHT BACK WHERE WE STARTED FROM

Umber has an unfortunate knack of getting into trouble at school and home. She kicks it with other Desis at school, but often finds herself at the center of gossip and arguments that place her outside of the social circles of which she desperately wants to remain a part. Although she continually promises to be more mindful of her parents' rules, she ends up spending a lot of time alone in her room. Here, she has covered the back of her wall with glossy clippings of her favorite Bollywood stars and confides her secret ambition to make it onto the silver screen. Umber's family was landed gentry in Punjab but moved to Nairobi in the 1940s, where her father was born. From Nairobi they moved to Yuba City, California, in the 1970s to do farm work and stayed until 1983, when they came to San Jose. At first Umber's father worked as a farmer with his brothers in Yuba City, but then went to Chico State University and now has a job in management information systems. He loves to tell Umber and her younger brother stories from his teenage days at Yuba City High School, where he belonged to a bhangra dance troupe.[1] On his family room wall, he proudly displays a portrait of his dance troupe in full costume from the 1970s. Although he wants a bigger house, he and his wife like this neighborhood and want to remain within walking distance of their relatives. Like many Desi families, Umber's grandparents live with them and take care of the children when they get home from school, which has helped their parents save money on child care. "You really need an education these days," her father reflected. Gesturing to his three-bedroom tract home, he remarked, "If you want a house like this, it is already over half a million. You have to work for it." Umber shrugged indifferently as she asked her parents for the fourth time if she might go to the mall with her friends.

Desi families like Umber's have helped to establish a strong Desi Community in Silicon Valley. They have created a space for themselves in residential neighborhoods, the retail landscape, public culture, and especially the high-tech industry. Over the past few decades, the surge in high-tech jobs has made Silicon Valley an attractive place for families like Umber's, who are in search of lucrative careers as well as steady, well-paying nonskilled labor positions. Of all the influences in this region, technology reigned supreme in the late 1990s. The development of the high-tech industry and its pervasive narratives of progress, innovation, and success have had an indelible impact on Desi migration to Silicon Valley. This industry has drawn thousands of people with what I call "the promise of technology," and it continues to shape the lives and aspirations of its Desi residents. From the beginning high-tech labor has been polarized into an exceedingly wealthy professional class and a struggling laboring class that has had to cope with the industry's cyclical nature. This configuration has primarily attracted upper-middle-class professional Desis in search of white-collar tech work, as well as working-class Desis who gradually became middle class and have high hopes that their children are upwardly mobile as well. Such socioeconomic differences shape neighborhoods and social life for Desis as they transform the landscape and population of this region.

Desi families flocked to Silicon Valley from South Asia and other parts of the United States, as well as other diasporic locations in the United Kingdom, Canada, and Fiji, and established supportive communities that they work hard to maintain. Large, visible Desi communities settled into neighborhoods with religious places of worship are ubiquitous in Desi Land, but were barely a possibility until the past few decades. Over the span of a century, Desis have moved up in status, from being undesirable, racially non-White immigrants to sought after residents whose ambiguous racial status skews closer to White. Changes in immigration policy, victories of the civil rights movement, the emergence of the model minority myth, and the rise of multiculturalism all contribute to these changes.

Yet all is not sunny in California. The title of this chapter, which fans of televised teenage drama may recognize as lyrics from The OC show opening, emphasizes that while Silicon Valley is indeed more diverse than predominantly White, wealthy California communities such as those in Orange County, it is nonetheless plagued by discrimination against race, class, and gender. Although many Desis have prospered in ways that early Punjabi settlers could not have imagined, dynamics of inequality still exist among Desis and become increasingly apparent during times of social and economic difficulty. During these times especially, community support is paramount.

Desi communities generate ideas of success and create intergenerational connections. These social formations set the stage for Desi teen culture and shape how teens relate to their family, school, and California. As is true for other immigrant groups in this region, notions of Desi success, progress, and mobility are community-specific and locally defined (Freeman 1989). In Silicon Valley in the 1990s, high tech held great promise for quick wealth without traditional educational qualifications. With stories of teenage millionaires circulating, Desi teens looked to high tech with great hopes. Such aspirations are addressed intergenerationally as adults in Desi communities try to help youth achieve their goals. How communities create ideas of success and how success can be achieved vary according to class. Both middle- and upper-middle-class Desis, however, turned toward the high-tech industry with their aspirations of achieving the Amrikan Dream.

THE RISE OF SILICON VALLEY HIGH TECH

The high-tech industry has brought about myriad changes in the population, landscape, and narratives of progress. Silicon Valley burgeoned from what, as recently as the 1950s, were agricultural lands into a major player in the global economy. Silicon Valley begins about thirty-five miles south of San Francisco and encompasses fifteen hundred square miles extending through San Jose (S. Cohen and Fields 2000). Santa Clara is the heart of Silicon Valley, and the wider boundaries encompass Palo Alto to the north and San Jose to the south. Santa Clara County was instrumental in the Gold Rush in the 1850s because it was home to one of the first mining corporations and the largest quicksilver (mercury) mine, an element essential to extracting gold and silver from raw ore (Pellow and Park 2002: 34–35). Once a bountiful stretch of agricultural land, the urban sprawl now known as Silicon Valley once went by a collection of other names, including "The Valley of Heart's Delight" and the "The Prune Capital of America" (Khanna 1997: 67).

The birth of Silicon Valley is generally traced to the establishment of Shockley Superconductor in 1956, though some mark 1939—the year William Hewlett and David Packard formed their partnership—as its true start (Kenney 2000). "Silicon" refers to silicon dioxide, the material used to make semiconductor chips through an elaborate and expensive process. "Valley" refers to flat Santa Clara County, which is flanked by the Diablo Mountain Range on the east and the Santa Cruz mountain range on the west (Khanna 1997). Silicon was used by William Shockley and two others to invent the transistor at Bell Laboratories in New York in 1947. Silicon soon began to replace germanium, and the transistor industry took root in Santa Clara when a former employee of Shockley left to form his own enterprise (G. Matthews 2003). Silicon Valley was thus named in 1971, when the journalist Don Hoefler wrote a three-part series on the history of the semiconductor industry for *Electronic News* (Khanna 1997: 67). Other Silicon Valley articles appeared in the early 1970s in *Fortune* magazine, and by 1975 the place had become a location in the public imagination (Kenney 2000).

The high-tech industry flourished in this California landscape (C.-M. Lee et al. 2000). Land was affordable and builders faced few initial bureaucratic constraints; moreover, parcels of undeveloped land were ideal for business parks and campuses (Li and Park 2006). During the 1950s and 1960s, Stanford University played a key role in high-tech innovation, as start-ups and companies gravitated toward the semirural land around the campus (Saxenian 1985). From its early days, Silicon Valley has been a production hub in what Manuel Castells (1985: 25) has termed the "Warfare State," a term used to refer to the growth of military-related production and the corresponding development of certain urban regions in the United States. Electronics production for military use, such as microwave tubes for aerospace and satellite use, flourished in this region shortly after World War II in companies such as Lockheed-Martin and computer companies such as Sun Microsystems (Leslie 2000). Silicon Valley has also been a leader in television, radio, and other electronic innovation (Sturgeon 2000). A handful of other industries have also established themselves in this area. For example, in 1955, the Ford Motor Company opened a plant in Milpitas, a town sandwiched between San Jose and Fremont, and remained active until the 1980s.

In recent decades, Silicon Valley has seen several cycles of rapid growth and decline. The 1970s were eventful venture capital years. Steve Jobs and Steve Wozniak produced the first microcomputer in a garage and in 1976 launched Apple Computers (Castells 1996). By the mid-1980s, over 70 percent of residents worked in high tech and a significant portion of the remaining 30 percent worked in service or support, a trend I saw during my research a decade and a half later. The 1980s began with major successes, but the late 1980s saw a downturn in the stock market. Though the region then went through a decline, this was reportedly due to external forces rather than a lack of entrepreneurial enthusiasm. The next decade continued the 1980s slump but picked up by the mid-1990s, a time when the stock market was more receptive to initial public offerings (IPOs; Kenney and Florida 2000: 19). Such ebbs and flows, perhaps most dramatically in the bubble of the late 1990s and its subsequent burst in 2000, suggest that the high-tech industry is cyclical in its growth but persists despite setbacks.

High-Tech Globalization and Flexibility • Flexibility of capital and labor imbue Silicon Valley with its global character. The rapid development of this region coincided with, as well as contributed to, the restructuring of capitalism that occurred in the late twentieth century (Castells 1996; see also Harvey 1990; Jameson 1991; Lash and Urry 1987). Like the postwar growth of other regions of the United States, such as Route 128 in Massachusetts, Silicon Valley has played a pivotal role in transforming society from the industrial to the informational age (Saxenian 1985: 82).[2] Fordist mass production has been replaced by advanced capitalism, and the shift from product- to process-oriented economies has flourished in Silicon Valley (Angel 2000). Such new economies modify urban areas and position Silicon Valley as a powerful player in the world economy. Saskia Sassen (1991) terms these dynamic metropoles "global cities" and notes the rise of informational industries that have transformed the nature of urban spaces and are central to globalization. Venture capital has been critical to the growth and development of technological and entrepreneurial projects, as well as the continued growth of Silicon Valley (Kenney and Florida 2000).

Labor is also flexible in Silicon Valley. Although since 2001 the region has been experiencing the latest wave of outsourcing to South Asia and other regions of the world in the form of data processing and call centers, the practice of outsourcing labor is not new in Silicon Valley. As early as 1963, Fairchild, a founding firm of Silicon Valley, built an assembly plant in Hong Kong (G. Matthews 2003: 230). The flexibility of labor arrangements is perhaps most stark in the practice called "body-shopping," in which workers are solicited from other countries to live and work in the United States on temporary visas (type HI-B). The quota of HI-B temporary workers rose dramatically during the late 1990s. Of those who were body-shopped, nearly half came from India to work in computer-related occupations (Aneesh 2006).[3] These body-shopped laborers reported glass ceilings at work and racial tension in society (Prashad 2000). These decades of growth in Silicon Valley have initiated both growth and diversification of local populations.

Of all these periods, the late 1990s and 2000 are the years for which Silicon Valley is most renowned for its international power and status. By 1993, the region had once again picked up, and the United States began to outproduce Japan in microchip manufacturing (G. Matthews 2003). The area had added about 200,000 jobs since 1997, and average annual wages during this time were $46,000, compared to the U.S. average of $29,000 (S. Cohen and Fields 2000). Silicon Valley had a population of about 2.3 million in 2000 and about 1.2 million jobs. By 2000, the region was reported to be 150 percent more prosperous than the national average (S. Cohen and Fields 2000). At the height of the high-tech industry, Chinese and Indian engineers were running one-fourth of Silicon Valley's high-tech businesses and their companies had accounted for over 58,000 jobs and $16.8 billion in sales (G. Matthews 2003).

TRANSFORMING LANDSCAPES AND POPULATIONS

During several decades of rapid transformation, technology swiftly established an economic and cultural hegemony over this region, so much so that it has earned the name "technoburb" (Li and Park 2006: 121). In stark contrast to its bucolic past, contemporary descriptors of the region emphasize its modernity and international qualities. In the late 1990s, billboards on the strip of Highway 101 that connects San Francisco to San Jose via numerous towns in between that make up Silicon Valley attested to the centrality of technology in this region. Rather than including a smattering of the usual products—movies, drinks, airlines, banks—nearly every bill-

board advertised something related to technology. From must-visit websites to promises of superior networking infrastructure, there were barely
any signs of life outside the high-tech industry. When I began my fieldwork in 1999, there were but a few remaining patches of former farmland
waiting to be converted to corporate parks and housing.

Such dramatic commercial and residential growth has brought about a
spate of problems, including environmental concerns, poor public planning, and an exceedingly high cost of living (Khanna 1997). Pollution due
to toxic waste from semiconductor chips as well as defense production
has been so menacing that it has earned the former "Valley of Heart's
Delight" the unfortunate moniker "The Valley of Toxic Fright" (Pellow
and Park 2002: 19). Transportation problems, congestion, and auto-
emission pollution routinely violate EPA standards. While residents of the
foothills can distance themselves from these problems to an extent, the
less wealthy residents are unable to escape it. Even in the 1970s and 1980s
job development far outpaced housing, causing a constant shortage of
living space (Rogers and Larsen 1984). In order to avoid residential overcrowding while still raising much-needed tax revenue, extensive tracts of
land were rezoned for industrial use, and this further exacerbated the
housing shortage. Even worse, most places were zoned for single-unit
rather than multiple-unit dwellings (Saxenian 1985).

San Jose is now the largest and most densely populated city in the Bay
Area, overshadowing the nearby cities of San Francisco and Oakland. Real
estate developers who continue to build at a furious pace have colonized
areas of San Jose that were previously farmland or bare. Luxurious gated
communities of multimillion-dollar homes in the surrounding foothills
that had been sparsely populated before the high-tech boom began to
flank small, modest homes built on flat expanses. Brand new developments of identical, boxy, supersized McMansions have cropped up all over
the foothills in San Jose and Fremont and make the older tract houses in
the flat regions of the valley look even more diminutive. The newness of
these communities is apparent everywhere, from the newly seeded lawns
and recently planted trees to the pristine streets and sidewalks.

From the 1970s until the present, the high-tech industry has drawn
waves of immigrants into this region. Glenna Matthews (2003) notes the
fateful confluence of the 1965 Immigration Act with the evolution of
Silicon Valley as a high-tech center: San Jose's foreign-born population

went from 7.6 percent in 1970 to 26.5 percent in 1990 and continues to grow as family reunification further expands these numbers. In the past two decades, particularly between 1990 and 2000, California in general and Silicon Valley in particular have experienced tremendous population expansion, most of which is due to high numbers of Asian immigrants. Thousands have arrived from Mainland China, Taiwan, Hong Kong, Vietnam, Philippines, and South Asia to work in Silicon Valley (Li and Park 2006; Wong 2006). Unlike earlier waves of European immigrants, who entered the United States in the Northeast, contemporary immigrants have been disproportionately concentrated in the West. California edged New York out of the distinction of being the highest receiving state by accounting for over 33 percent of legal immigrants while New York accounted for only 14 percent (Portes and Zhou 1995: 38).

This growth of Asian Americans in Silicon Valley is the latest in a long history of dramatic demographic shifts. Santa Clara County, in which Silicon Valley is located, has experienced waves of settlers over the centuries. Initially settled by Ohlone Native Americans, the area saw the arrival of the Spanish explorer Gaspar de Portolá in 1769, gold diggers during the Rush, Chinese who came to build railroads in the same period, Mexican laborers who came to work in the fields, and European cannery workers in the 1950s and 1960s. During the heyday of the U.S. automobile industry, Portuguese farmers primarily tended to the agriculture in the region while Ford employed Mexican, Filipino, and African American autoworkers who settled in Milpitas and the surrounding areas of San Jose and Fremont. Mexican Americans, whom I also refer to as Latinos or Chicanos, have had a strong, long-standing presence in the South Bay (Pitti 2003; Zlolniski 2006).[4] This region was further diversified by the arrival of a wave of Vietnamese immigrants after the fall of Saigon in 1975 who came in search of work and affordable housing.

This trend has continued, as the 2000 census indicates that California's overall population grew 13.8 percent to 33.9 million over the past decade, and its Asian American population has grown 55 percent since 1990. At 4.2 million, Asian Americans now constitute 12 percent of the state's population, outpacing the growth of all other groups. California has the largest South Asian population in the United States, 143,206 of whom live in the San Francisco Bay Area (Zhou 2004). Within the Asian category, Silicon Valley now hosts the state's largest Desi population, a distinction held by Los Angeles a mere decade ago. Asian Americans are concentrated in San Jose, which is 28.8 percent Asian American, while Fremont reported 39.8 percent.[5] Overall, Silicon Valley's high-tech employment boom contributed to a 97 percent increase in the Desi population, which grew to 314,819. San Jose has experienced a 149 percent increase, and Fremont's Desi population shot up 272 percent, which, along with increases of 318 percent in Santa Clara and 528 percent in Sunnyvale, accounts for most of Silicon Valley.

Thus, a region formerly dominated by European American immigrants who were integral to fruit picking and packing is now home to a massive influx of immigrants from Asia as well as Asian Americans. In these diverse, ethnically saturated residential "ethnoburbs" (Li and Park 2006), Asian Americans have built a strong residential and retail presence. Hong Kong developers have transformed small retail complexes into shopping meccas (G. Matthews 2003). Entirely Asian shopping centers, Asian-owned banks, and distinctive places of worship, among other markers, signify a shift toward a far more ethnically diverse region. The 1997 opening of Ranch 99 in Milpitas distinguished itself as the largest Asian American shopping area in the United States, containing stores, restaurants, bookstores, and grocery outlets. On opening day, over 95 percent of the shoppers were Asian American, including a sizable Taiwanese population (Chang 2006: 104–5). In this retail flurry, the Ford Motor plant, which closed in 1983, received an extreme makeover when it was bought by Chinese businessmen and transformed into The Great Mall, featuring restaurants, arcades, and designer outlet stores.[6] In this transforming landscape, Desi Land has taken root and continues to grow.

CREATING DESI LAND IN CALIFORNIA

Changes in immigration policy enabled Desis to form close-knit communities that have created a fertile setting for the emergence of Desi teen culture. The ability to create such a visible and rooted presence is a notable shift from earlier Californian Desis. Desi immigrants who arrived before 1965 lacked basic civil rights and were unable to achieve a critical mass that Desis today take for granted. The first lone immigrant from India arrived in Salem, Massachusetts in 1820 (Helweg and Helweg 1990: 46). During the remainder of the nineteenth century, fewer than 700 people from India entered (Jensen, cited in Rangaswamy 2000: 3). Between 1901 and 1910, more than 3,000 men came to take advantage of California's agricultural opportunities (Leonard 1992). Although most of these early arrivals were Sikhs from Punjab, along with some Muslims and Hindus, they were lumped under the category of "Hindoo" (Song 1998). Between 1907 and 1920, approximately 6,400 Indians entered (Hess 1976), a relatively modest number compared to the influx of 380,000 Chinese, 430,000 Japanese, and 150,000 Filipinos (Bhardwaj and Rao 1990). The Immigration Act of 1917, also referred to as the Asiatic Barred Zone Act, effectively ended immigration from Asia between 1917 and 1946 (Leonard 1997).

Although they were far fewer in number than other Asian immigrants at the time, early "Hindoos" were especially reviled. Termed "the Hindoo invasion," these immigrants were socially isolated and subject to all manner of discrimination as well as less pay than their fellow Asian laborers (Hess 1976). Their turbans and beards elicited more prejudice than the Japanese immigrants experienced, and their illiteracy did not help matters (Leonard 1997). Numerous headlines appeared in local California papers that fueled existing ill will toward this group.

In 1907, violence erupted against Indian immigrants in Washington State. They, along with African Americans, were considered social and economic liabilities, so much so that in 1913 in Port Angeles, California, real estate brokers agreed not to sell real estate to "Hindoos or Negroes . . . [because they] have depreciated value of adjacent property and injured the reputation of the neighborhood, and are generally considered undesirable" (quoted in Hess 1976: 161). A 1909 federal Immigration Commission report describes this group as unable to assimilate, and a 1920 report by the California State Board of Control similarly states, "The Hindu is the most undesirable immigrant in the state. His lack of personal cleanliness, his low morals, and his blind adherence to theories and teachings so entirely repugnant to American principles make him unfit for association with American people" (quoted in Leonard 1992: 24).

In the constant struggle over who is and is not to be considered White, Desis, like other "nondesirable" but necessary immigrant groups, were consistently left in the blind spot of racial definition or fell subject to its aberrant nature. Citizenship was premised on race, but little had been established regarding racial categories and meanings. "Asian" was an especially ambiguous category. Chinese and Japanese were both deemed

"Asiatic," making the Chinese ineligible for citizenship and barred from immigration after the 1882 Chinese Exclusion Act. Japanese settlers continued to immigrate but were denied citizenship after the U.S. Supreme Court's ruling in 1922 in *Ozawa v. United States*. Indians, however, presented a curious case because they were not clearly defined as "Asiatic." Yet their brown skin tone and other phenotypic features precluded them from blending in with Whites. Several Desis were able to make early successful cases to individual judges that Indians were of Aryan descent and therefore "White" (Helweg and Helweg 1990: 54).

A landmark decision, however, clarified early racial ambiguity for Desis. In the 1923 case of the *United States v. Bhagat Singh Thind*, Indians were declared ineligible for citizenship because they are not White (Prashad 2000). Before this case, sixty-nine members of the "Hindu race" had been naturalized (Leonard 1992: 84). In the realm of citizenship, Hindoos struggled in court to be seen as White persons; the *Thind* case denied claims that Indians shared the same Aryan heritage as those from northern and western Europe. (Hess 1976: 170). This case set into motion shifting and arbitrary parameters for the racial status of Desis and what Whiteness means in the United States. Under these conditions, maintaining an ethnically exclusive community was out of the question. Laws now prohibited Hindoos from sponsoring spouses or brides for immigration, owning land, or marrying Whites. Their most available recourse was to marry Mexican American women and place their assets in their wife's and children's names.[7]

In the mid- to late twentieth century in America, several immigration acts contributed to a rapid growth of Desi communities (Brown 2006). The U.S. government repealed the Chinese exclusion laws in 1943, passed the 1945 War Brides Act, and relaxed the Asian exclusion laws in the early 1950s. After 1946, naturalization became possible and quotas of 100 people per year were allowed to emigrate from India (Helweg and Helweg 1990: 46). Between 1946 and 1965, nearly 6,000 immigrants moved to the United States (Hess 1976: 158), many of whom were students, businessmen, refugees, and "twice migrants."[8] It was only in 1965 that the quota system that had limited immigration from certain countries was finally eliminated. The Hart-Cellar Act, as it was known, set a new quota of 20,000 from each country. It also established a system of preferred categories for immigration, including highly skilled labor that the United States needed, and allowed family unification. This resulted in a rapid and substantial growth of immigration from Asia, nearly 7 million between 1970 and 2000. Desis first appeared in the U.S. Census in 1980 under the category "Asian Indians," prior to which they were in the Asian "other" category. They have grown from 361,531 in 1980 to 815,447 in 1990 to 1,899,599 in 2000 (Zhou 2004). By 2000, they constituted 16 percent of the total Asian American population of 11,906,680. Though Asian Americans (Asian alone or Asian in combination) are only 4.2 percent of the reported 281.4 million U.S. population, they are one of the country's fastest growing population (Ong 1996: 740).

Desi Communities in Silicon Valley • Over the past two decades, Desi communities in Silicon Valley have grown from small, often socially isolated sets of families to large, bustling entities. Both middle-class and upper-middle-class Desis organize themselves into communities based on shared religion, language, nationality, class status, geographical proximity, and sometimes caste. Upper-middle-class families live in the San Jose hills and in Fremont. They are predominantly Gujarati Hindus and Pakistani Muslims, as well as some Sikh Punjabis and Hindus from South India and Maharashtra. In most of these families, one or both parents are well-educated professionals who immigrated after 1965. The main earner, usually the father, has a graduate degree, a stable job with benefits in a white-collar profession, and speaks English fluently. Often the mother has a comparable occupational status, and the family owns a large home in a recently built development.

During the early 1990s, upper-middle-class families that lived in older homes around Fremont and San Jose used their profits from the technology boom to buy homes in newly built gated communities. By high school, upper-middle-class teens lived in large, well-appointed homes with luxury automobiles that they frequently upgraded. These children attend high-performing public schools with other wealthy Asian American and White youth and are often bound for competitive four-year colleges. They aspire to make their mark on the high-tech industry, medicine, or some other professional field.

Middle-class families in this study are primarily Sikh Punjabis or Hindu and Muslim Indo-Fijians and reside in East San Jose. Many of these families moved to San Jose from Yuba City and other parts of California within the past twenty-five years, when they left farming to seek work in the high-tech industry. There are also a number of Malayalee Christians as well as Indo-Fijian families who moved for economic reasons as well as to escape the growing hostility toward those of Indian descent in Fiji. Most middle-class Desi adults are employees of local Silicon Valley technology companies and work on assembly lines, as janitorial and cafeteria staff, and as local delivery people. Some parents have worked at the same company for over a decade and have advanced in the roster of assembly line tasks. Occasionally they are partners in small businesses and co-own convenience marts, liquor stores, or similar outlets. Most middle-class youth live with their nuclear family and sometimes a live-in grandparent in a single-family home in diverse neighborhoods populated with Asian Americans, Latinos, and African Americans of a similar class status.

There are notable commonalities and differences between the schools that upper-middle-class and middle-class Desis attend and how they are able to position themselves in these institutions. The high-tech boom of the 1980s and 1990s contributed to a general overcrowding, and as of 2000, Mercer, Greene, and Waverly high schools were all enrolled at 75 to 125 percent over their capacities. This predicament has reprioritized administrators' agendas and led them to focus primarily on basic tasks of discipline and curriculum; such a move places the onus of getting what one needs from the school squarely on the student. These faculty and administrators, who are largely White or Latino, have also had an exceedingly challenging time dealing with the religious, linguistic, and cultural diversity of their changing student bodies. This influx includes South Asian and East Asian teens, asylum cases from Iran and Afghanistan, Vietnamese who arrived after the end of Vietnam War, and a growing population of Hmong refugees from Laos. Coupled with the increasingly diverse needs of a Latino community that has long been underserved by California school districts, the character of this region has changed dramatically and rapidly.

Most upper-middle-class Desi teens attend Mercer High School and, to a lesser extent, Greene High School. Located in South Fremont, Mercer High School has 2,249 mostly upper-middle-class youth in ninth through twelfth grades; the school's racial composition is 54 percent Asian American (about one-third South Asian American), 41 percent White, 3 percent Latino, 1 percent African American, and less than 1 percent Native American. Mercer is ranked as a top public high school according to California State standards, and families scramble to enroll their children into its feeder schools and acquire a legitimate address in the area.[9] Those who have learned of the reputation of the best school in Silicon Valley come from as far away as Tokyo, Mumbai (Bombay), London, and other parts of the United States.

Class-based tension is intense at Mercer. Newer Asian American arrivals purchase homes costing more than a million dollars, while White and Latino families watch homes they have occupied for at least a generation soar in value. Angela Shen, the only Asian American teacher at Mercer, commented, "The poor kids almost inevitably are White or Hispanic. They are the ones that can afford to live here because theirs is a house passed down by a grandparent, whereas almost all the people who are moving have to have money because the property values are so high." The struggle to find residential real estate within the school zone is as fierce as the competition among students to succeed. The declaration of twenty valedictorians in the class of 2000 was, according to some school faculty, a promise of even grander successes to come.

Middle-class youth attend either Waverley or Greene High School in southeast San Jose. Greene had 2,648 students during the 1999–2000 school year and a racial composition of 53 percent Asian American, 28 percent Latino, 12 percent White, 6 percent African American, and less than 1 percent Native American. Here, the tension between middle-class and upper-middle-class students is most pronounced. Middle-class students live in the small, single-story homes surrounding the school, while upper-middle-class youth drive down from posh new gated communities in the hills. Of the three high schools, Waverly had the fewest Desis. During the 1999–2000 school year, Waverly High School had 2,154 students and a racial composition of 51 percent Latino, 39 percent Asian American, 5 percent African American, and 5 percent White. It is known locally as a problem school, rife with gang-related incidents and at-risk students. While some kids used the adjective "ghetto" to describe it, most admit its reputation has improved through a mandatory "common dress" code and other adjustments. My initial assumption about Desi kids who attended Waverly was not entirely accurate. A number of them attend because they live in the low-income neighborhoods surrounding the school, but many others do so because it is a "magnet school" for those planning to study medicine.[10] Those who elect to attend Waverly are especially motivated, but the growing numbers of Desi teens who live in the Waverly attendance area tend to participate less in school activities and struggle with their studies. Regardless of the school they attend, these teens and their families are active members of their communities.

Settling into Neighborhoods • From building places of religious worship to supporting one another in business, politics, and social endeavors, community networks are especially invaluable during times of economic, political, and social instability. Families relied heavily on one another when they first moved to this area and continue to do so. Settling into residences close to a place of worship is especially important to Sikh and Muslim families. Proximity to a musjid (mosque) or gurdwara (Sikh temple) eliminates the need for transportation and enables elderly relatives and others to regularly attend prayer services. Many Pakistani Muslim families in Fremont as well as Fijian Muslim families in San Jose live close to and worship at a musjid with other members of their community. While Hindu families mention their routine visits to temple, many pray at homes on a daily basis and so are less likely to prioritize living close to a temple.

Over the years, the streets around the San Jose gurdwara have become saturated with Sikh families. One teen's grandfather, whose family has been in San Jose since the late 1970s, explained the inception of the gurdwara in the 1980s: "When we first came to San Jose, there were not so many people of Indian origin. There were only twenty-five Punjabi families here in 1980. We had no resources to buy land for the gurdwara. Slowly we made commitments and now there are thousands of families and due to their efforts, we have a gurdwara here, which is worth $2.2 million. We also bought forty acres of land for a new gurdwara that is also worth $2 million. Within a year or two it will come up.[11] This is a great progression of our community." Middle-class teens and their families from both Waverly and Greene regularly attended this gurdwara. On a walk around this neighborhood, Umber, the middle-class girl whom you met at the start of this chapter whose family has lived on the street next to the gurdwara for about a decade, divulged to me the names and personal information of at least a dozen Indian families who live within a three-block radius. Although all the homes in this tract are nearly identical, the overwhelming aroma of masala wafting down the street quickly differentiated her aunt's house from the other three- and four-bedroom homes that surround it.

Regardless of their class status or religious background, families settle near one another and socialize regularly to maintain their close and supportive networks. Ananya, an upper-middle-class girl, describes how her family's Oria community network initially lived in Massachusetts, where her father was working at MIT. She reports that her father was the first president of the Oria Society of America and that a number of those families decided to move to California en masse. As this group keeps growing, the original group has taken to calling itself "senior citizens of the Oria community, all those old families. There are new people that come, a few families that come every month. There must be two hundred families in the Bay Area." When communities grow to be as large as Ananya's, families rarely socialize with Desis outside of their ethnic groups.

Seeing friends and family is a daily occurrence for Desis, and seldom do days go by without social calls and casual get-togethers. Mrs. George, middle-class mother of Deepa, recalls when there were so few Malayalee Christian families that everyone knew each other and continually gathered in each other's homes. Now there are so many families, each large and extended, she exclaimed, "You can't have everyone in the house! Like my one family, if I invite them, this house is full already." Mrs. George conjectured why these parties remain so ethnically insular. She has a lot of friends from work that she would like to socialize with more, but, she remarked, "It's boring for them. For example, you feel left out, even if I invite you with the group. I have to ask you every minute if you are okay, and still you feel left out, because you don't understand the language and food and culture. I have a lot friends from other groups, Filipino and Americans, but I don't call them." As Mrs. George notes, Desi families enjoy commonalities of language and cultural background within their own ethnic and linguistic community. Feroze, a middle-class boy, asserted, "My family has become the socialite elite among the Bangladesh community. We know everybody, so we get invited to everybody's houses. At least once a month, there's a seventy-person party at our house. So it's insane!" As Feroze suggests, communities can become so large and established that people barely have time to fulfill their own social obligations of weddings and graduation and dinner parties, let alone routinely venture outside of their circle.

Reciprocity and social and economic support are the backbone of these relationships. Mrs. Malik, the mother of Taahir, explained, "Every other weekend there's a Desi party, on Sunday or Friday or Saturday night. I think when you go to people's parties all the time, you have to have an excuse for giving one. Like two months ago, people were coming back from hajj and there were parties every weekend." Mrs. Malik affirms that leaving some families out is not an option. This can make gatherings for established families exceedingly large. Umber reflected that her family has grown over the past three generations of living in California. Her father noted that getting the entire family in one home is no longer an option and joked, "We have too many relatives [here]—at least five hundred—if you want to get everyone together you need a fairground!" He quickly added that he greatly values this preponderance of relatives, and that he is very lucky that he and his brothers have helped each other with down payments for their homes. For Desis, socializing is not a frivolity or simply a leisure activity; rather, it is a central part of how bonds of community are forged and maintained.

While numerous families laud the support and comfort afforded by their social networks, there are drawbacks, especially when families do not get along well. Janvi, a middle-class Sikh girl, expressed her disillusionment with her extended family and community. As we sat in a Wendy's restaurant in San Jose, she picked at her fries while recounting that her family had a hard time since they moved from India to Yuba City and then San Jose. Her mother, the only daughter-in-law in her husband's family, was given the responsibility of cooking, cleaning, and taking care of their entire extended family when they lived in Yuba City in one large house and the men worked on farms. Even through her relatives have moved with them to San Jose, her parents have felt alienated from the rest of the family. "My dad feels very lonely out here—he has no allies," she lamented.

Other teens feel protective of their parents and are careful that people do not exploit their trusting nature. Preeti, a middle-class Sikh girl, explained, "When me and my sister were young, they used to be close to other people, but as we started growing up, they realized that they can't trust a lot of other friends. My uncle's wife used to steal from my mom, and now that we're older, she knows better than to do anything mean to my mom." Other families, too, report problems such as stealing, betraying trust, and asking for help without offering it to others. Such families are still invited to all gatherings but are often the subject of gossip afterward. Desi teens and their families note these downsides to community as problematic, but such breaches rarely cause complete breaks from family.

From childhood, Desi teens are included in and inculcated into extensive family and community interaction. In family contexts, many Desi youth are socialized to participate in intergenerational rather than peer-exclusive interaction. They enjoy attending family and community events and readily interact with adults and peers alike. Abhijeet, a middle-class boy, described how he spends a lot of his leisure time: "On the weekends we chill with our grandparents in Yuba City, or with aunts in Sacramento, or in San Jose. We visit family a lot, I have lots cousins, some are older and done with high school. But we all kick it together." This sense of ownership and pride in spending time with family and community is a commonly expressed sentiment among these middle-class Desi teens. Upper-middle-class Desi teens are also invested in their communities. Mr. Patel remarked about his daughter Tara and his son, "They come to cultural events not because we force them to. Around age ten or eleven, Tara discovered boys and she started going with us. Same with my son, they go to the *garba* [a Gujarati group dance] because they want to do it, because it is a social place to see other kids." At community events, both peer and intergenerational connections are maintained.

For middle- as well as upper-middle-class teens, there is significant social continuity between school and home, as community networks spill over into schools. Although teens experience a great deal of peer policing at school—a place usually free of parental surveillance—there is also a sense of solidarity and shared cultural and linguistic practices. Mrs. Malik explained that she has known many families in her Muslim community since she was a girl in Karachi, Pakistan: "There is a community sense here, everybody pretty much leaves each other alone because everybody has her own life, but there is always something to fall back on. We are very lucky in that sense. Taahir benefits because a lot of my friends' children are in school with him, so if he is going to their house, I know where he's going." Although youth express ambivalent feelings about being watched at school and admit that there are downsides to this type of closeness, such as gossip and little or no privacy, they by and large welcome community support networks and are invested in being a part of them.

SEARCHING FOR SUCCESS IN SILICON VALLEY

Middle- and upper-middle-class Desis have settled into neighborhoods and socialize within their growing communities. Such communities are largely organized by class lines, where upper-middle-class Desis are professionals and middle-class Desis are assembly line workers. In the high-tech industry, these two poles can be quite disparate and the rift between them large. Anna Lee Saxenian (1985: 83) notes that the semiconductor industry has a distinctive corporate structure, in which "the industry . . . employs an unusually large proportion of professional and managerial employees alongside an equally large, but minimally skilled, production workforce. This top-heavy and bifurcated labor force fundamentally shaped the social structure and urban geography of Silicon Valley." This dichotomy has led to a spate of well-paid professional managerial jobs that require a bachelor's degree or higher, alongside low-paid assembly line and clerical jobs characterized by poor pay and benefits and less than satisfactory working conditions, especially for unskilled assembly line work.

On the whole, the high-tech industry pays higher wages than the national average (Rogers and Larsen 1984) and provides a greater number of assembly-line and wage-labor positions to women than non-high-tech industries, though they offer less than the union wages offered in cannery work in this region (G. Matthews 2003: 141). In these lower echelons, Asian women dominate the blue-collar rungs of the high-tech industry, and numerous mothers of middle-class teens held such positions.[12] During the boom, work was plentiful and these employees were offered job security, competitive wages, and sometimes even stock options and bonuses. During slower periods, however, they are the first to be laid off from assembly line jobs and have great difficulty finding other jobs, as production is increasingly outsourced (Pellow and Park 2002: 65).

Even Desis who are excelling in this industry face difficulty in a White-dominated upper tier. The 1995 Glass Ceiling Commission report indicates that Asians are not advancing despite their high qualifications. Historically, Asian Americans have been paid less than Whites for various types of employment, and this trend continues. Even in the late nineteenth and early twentieth centuries, Whites were paid higher wages to do less grueling work, leaving the more intensive labor and lower compensation to Asians and Mexicans (Pellow and Park 2002: 35). Bernard Wong (2006) reports a similar finding in his study of Chinese Americans in Silicon Valley, and notes that while most are engineers, some become entrepreneurs because of the glass ceilings to advancement that they face. As recently as 1990, Asians who are better educated than Whites were paid 14 percent less and promoted less frequently for entry-level tech jobs, and this trend continues a decade later (Wong 2006: 31). Indeed, despite stories of those who have beaten the odds, even those who are doing well are not doing as well as their White peers.

A top-heavy housing structure mirrors the top-heavy employment structure of the high-tech industry. While the large and wealthy professional upper-middle-class workforce lives in the northern and western regions as well as in South Fremont, the lower income production workforce is concentrated in the flat "south side" of San Jose (Rogers and Larson 1984). Within San Jose, the northern and western regions of the city are far more desirable than the eastern and southern sides and have been called "bedroom communities of less educated minorities" (Saxenian 1985: 87) although even this region has gentrified significantly over the past decade. Middle-class Desi families who moved into these areas in the late 1970s and early 1980s have benefited from this property appreciation. For newcomers, however, settling in takes tremendous capital. Despite the ongoing growth, zoning laws and prohibitively high housing prices have made this area especially challenging for newer middle-class residents. Bidding wars over residences have displaced lower income residents to cheaper housing in the southern and eastern corners of San Jose as well in outlying cities. In this economy, even previously undesirable areas of San Jose have become attractive. Steve Dinh, an administrator at Waverly High in East San Jose, has lived in Silicon Valley for over twenty years. He described the rise in desirability of East San Jose, where many middle-class Desi families live: "I remember these homes up and down Capitol Expressway. When we bought our home there, it was $120,000. They just built the home in about 1980. While the same homes today are going for about $450,000 or $500,000." Such growth has now been accepted as commonplace and has created a class-divided society in Silicon Valley.

When Desi families who are now middle class first arrived in Silicon

Valley in the late 1970s and early 1980s, even the lower income portions of San Jose were out of their range. After initially renting apartments, two or three families—usually kin—pooled their resources to buy a home to share until they could help one another amass enough capital to buy their own homes. For example, Mrs. Kapoor, the mother of Meru and Jasbir, teenage girls, explained how her family and her husband's four brothers all moved from Yuba City in search of more regular and profitable work than the peach orchards where their family had worked for the past twenty years. The five brothers initially bought and shared two homes in San Jose and eventually purchased three more homes nearby. Middle-class families like the Kapoors have created a neighborhood out of what seems like undifferentiated tract housing by dropping by each other's homes daily and being intricately involved in each other's lives. Every afternoon at 3 o'clock, when she returns from her 6 a.m. shift as a quality inspector at a microfilm company, Mrs. Kapoor makes chai and samosas for the steady flow of family members that begin appearing. Mrs. Kapoor talks about wanting a bigger house, but that would mean moving out of this area in which so many family members are within close walking or driving distance, and it does not seem worth the trade-off.

Lower-income residents of Silicon Valley have felt the effects of an exceedingly high cost of living, especially those working in the lower echelons of the high-tech industry.[13] In 1999, before the bubble burst, dot-com hopefuls and "Y2K" specialists occupied every available rental, and desperation for housing was at an all-time high. Mrs. George commented that she even had to unlist her telephone number because Desis in search of housing kept identifying her Indian name in the phone book and asking to rent out her garage as a living space. Noting this trend, Greene's assistant principal, Mr. Lopez, reports an influx of both wealthier Desi students whose parents are high-tech professionals and middle-class youth whose parents relocated from other regions of the United States or directly from South Asia to seek blue-collar employment during the fertile economic period of the mid- to late 1990s. Commenting on the changing socioeconomic character of the San Jose area, he remarked, "Silicon Valley is getting richer. People on subsidy can't afford to live here any more. Some of our kids' families overcome that by doubling or tripling up on homes or converting garages into rooms."

While upper-middle-class families have steadily moved into larger, newer homes in gated communities, most middle-class Desis still occupy the same modest homes they bought twenty years ago, when they moved to Silicon Valley. Although residents in these areas could profit substantially from selling their home on the current market, they concede that this same pattern of real estate appreciation would preclude them from affording a larger home. Thus, while home prices have risen dramatically in this and other parts of San Jose, populations in these areas have not changed significantly. Homes bought for fifty thousand dollars that are now worth half a million and more still have iron security bars on their windows and doors and old cars raised up on cinder blocks in the front yard. Most middle-class Desis are reluctant to leave their jobs, schools, and communities in San Jose and opt instead to stay in their current homes. Even families that have earned significantly more by shrewd investments and business ventures choose not to move out of their neighborhoods and instead remain close to friends and family despite their ability to aspire to join a wealthier social circle. As will become clear, this type of loyalty is paramount to meanings of community and defines the values and aspirations of Desi teens.

These shifts have pushed some long-time residents who are not homeowners farther and farther out of the Bay Area. This was especially the case for high school faculty and administrators, some of whom commute one to two hours each way to live in affordable communities. Monique Albert, an African American teacher who grew up in the Bay Area, declared in frustration that she can no longer afford to rent an apartment in South Fremont near Mercer High School, where she teaches: "Housing in the South Bay is too expensive. You don't have much choice if you don't have a lot of money." The area now draws wealthier, upwardly mobile professionals, many of whom are Asian or Asian American; they displace less wealthy Whites, African Americans, and Latinos. Angela Shen, an art teacher at Mercer who attended the high school as a student in the early 1980s, reflected on the drastic changes Fremont has undergone: "Back then there were a lot more [families with] Hispanic surnames. I think a lot of them have been pushed out in the meantime. The Asian population was somewhere around 27 percent, and it tended to be extremely high-end families—generally, not recent immigrants, not recent in terms of coming in the last five years." Overarching narratives of success, however, can often mask all of these deterrents.

The Promise of Technology and the Amrikan Dream • As families looked to the high-tech industry for opportunities, they were particularly interested in upward mobility and prosperity for their children. Especially as Desi teens weighed their options during high school in the 1990s, the promise of technology and narratives of progress in this region underscored differences of class while also suggesting means of class mobility. During the late 1990s, Silicon Valley was awash in stories of success, from fourteen-year-olds who had created portals from their bedrooms to twenty-somethings who had made millions overnight from dot-com ventures. Social events were abuzz with names of promising venture capitalists, IPOs of dot-com stock, and new opportunities in technology infrastructure. Being in any other industry meant missing out on what was arguably the second gold rush.

At the height of the dot-com boom, technology was a strong and pervasive force. Consider this conversation in a tenth-grade English class on a hot San Jose morning. In a packed classroom, fifteen- and sixteen-year-olds squirmed to keep from sticking to the plastic chairs and desks, perhaps from fear of becoming attached permanently. Reviewing vocabulary with his class, Mr. Suarez asked, "Who can tell us the meaning of 'aristocracy'?" Met with a silence broken only by the occasional rustling of a note being passed, he implored, "Can *anyone* name an aristocrat?" A lone hand went up and produced an excited "Yes, Stephanie!" from Mr. Suarez. "Bill Gates," she answered, with a confidence that inspired several students to nod in agreement and take note. For Stephanie and countless other teens, the promise of technology is the prospect of vast economic gain and social status to middle- and upper-middle-class youth alike. It has transformed the very idea of success into something ever more accessible, even for those whose opportunities are otherwise limited.

The high-tech field has especially shaped local notions of progress and contributed to defining values and aspirations for its residents (English-Lueck 2002). During the high-tech boom of the late 1990s, Silicon Valley presented Desis with the opportunity to achieve their Amrikan Dream: to make a fortune in a prestigious technology career, become flush with cash to satisfy material desires and help family, and to retire early. Careers in science, technology, and medicine are widely valorized and coveted in South Asia and among diasporic Desis. Internationally renowned branches of the Indian Institute of Technology (IIT) are highly competitive and

47

produce some of the most sought-after engineers worldwide. Indeed, seats in science colleges are prestigious and highly coveted. These values complement those in Silicon Valley well. Hundreds of HI-B workers from India have made IIT a household name in the Bay Area. The technology-saturated environs of Silicon Valley further this cultural preference for technology. Charles Darrah (2001) terms this phenomenon "technoculture," in which technology creates a worldview of assumptions, values, and practices from technology. Technoculture extends beyond machines and gadgets to "the nature of work in high tech industries and the location of Silicon Valley in a global system of production and consumption" (4). Technology pervades many aspects of economic and social life, and it is difficult to overstate its ubiquity in this area.

In the late 1990s, technology's overwhelming promise made it the obvious avenue for success. Abhijeet, a middle-class Sikh Punjabi boy, asserted, "There are lots of lucrative opportunities around here. If you're not going into computers, you're nuts!" Some youth do not aspire to enter the high-tech field, but the majority regard it as a strong possibility. To not consider it would be foolish, as I was told on numerous occasions by parents who kindly suggested that my time would be better spent actually working in the high-tech industry rather than asking them countless questions about it. Technology has been a part of their lives since childhood, and Desi teens are comfortable with the technology of video games, pagers, instant messaging, and more recently, cell phones and handheld communication devices. Even middle-class kids who do not have computers at home have grown up using them in school. In these ways, the high-tech industry has insinuated itself into the local imagination.

California itself has played a role in shaping local versions of success. Glenna Matthews (2003: 6) notes that "generations of Americans and those abroad have been schooled to believe that California is the place where dreams come true." Since its founding, Silicon Valley has encouraged original ventures rather than joining established ones. Hewlett-Packard began this trend, and stories of the first Apple computer being made in a garage only fuel this type of success. Indeed, the lore of companies born in basements disrupts conventional trajectories to success that rely on higher education, job experience, and gradual upward mobility.

The massive influx of venture capital into local businesses made these dreams loom large in the 1990s. For example, in 1993, the San Jose *Mercury*

News reported that three hundred new firms were funded by venture capital each year in Silicon Valley, including new start-ups and spin-offs from existing firms and "restarts" of previously floundering companies (quoted in Bahrami and Evans 2000: 173–74). Desis play a visible role as venture capitalists in the high-tech industry. Media accounts happily underscore this point in such features as *Fortune*'s cover story on South Asians in Silicon Valley (May 15, 2000). The article dubs this group the "Indian Mafia" and notes that they "invest in one another's companies, sit on one another's boards, and hire each other in key jobs. Many live in close proximity and hang out together" and have created companies that have a collective market value of $235 billion. With such stories from their own Community, it is not surprising that Desi teenagers consider themselves imminent millionaires.

In this innovative environment, even failure is met with aplomb. One of the tenets of Silicon Valley entrepreneurship is the absence of stigma for "honest failures," as well as the belief that this positive attitude toward failure has contributed to the ultimate success of many high-tech companies (Bahrami and Evans 2000: 177). Silicon Valley during the late 1990s was a self-contained space of unlimited possibilities; such an environment "allows people to celebrate risk taking and entrepreneurship, since the costs of failure are not viewed as catastrophic; new opportunities are just around the corner" (Darrah 2001: 4). There were no barriers to entry: "Like the first gold rush, all one needs in Silicon Valley is passion, commitment to hard work, and a little luck and imagination" (Pellow and Park 2002: 2). Skilled employees, venture capital, a fast growth rate, and an expanding market for products make the high-tech industry advance and develop at a much more rapid pace than other industries (Rogers and Larsen 1984: 29) and furthers the possibility of the Amrikan Dream for Desis.

Silicon Dreams • Stories of unimaginable wealth and advancement were commonplace in Silicon Valley in the late 1990s. Mrs. Malik has watched the booming prosperity of her Pakistani Muslim community. With her son Taahir nodding in agreement, she recited a local legend: "It's normal to retire in your early thirties over here." Noting my quizzical look, she elaborated, "I don't know about the East Coast, but over here you do these things. Every second car you see over here is a BMW, a Mercedes, a Porsche. The latest cars are on the street; it's just the economy! The economy is so amazing. It's good, it's job security." Lucrative opportunities in the high-tech industry have made this type of California lifestyle commonplace for upper-middle and even some middle-class families. Youth of all class backgrounds aspire to owning luxury automobiles and living lives filled with various material comforts. Especially in a place like Silicon Valley, where extraordinary wealth has become typical, pressure to display success to one's community is compelling. Even middle-class families are able to use their home equity and job security to acquire consumer goods not typically associated with middle-class living, such as luxury automobiles and high-end home electronics. The ability to make money as a means to acquiring these status-conferring items, whether temporary or long term, is a valued asset.

The potential of technology is evident to teens of all class backgrounds; the types of training they complete and the positions they are drawn to, however, can vary significantly. Upper-middle-class youth who study computer engineering at four-year colleges receive a high-quality education irrespective of the career they eventually pursue. Many of those who had gravitated toward medicine or business are considering computer science and engineering. Technology is also shaping the aspirations of middle-class youth who see it as an opportunity to succeed quickly and dramatically. Youth in middle-class families by and large aspire to be wealthy, but not necessarily through lengthy undergraduate and graduate programs that lead to long-term job stability or upward class movement. Unlike upper-middle-class Desi youth, success for middle-class youth is rarely articulated solely in terms of educational achievement or long-term career advancement. More often, parents define upward mobility in terms of their children having a better life than they do in terms of commodities, homes, material acquisitions, and job security.

During the high-tech boom of the 1990s, Desis were able to create opportunities for their children by encouraging them to explore new niches in the high-tech industry. New types of technology jobs offered middle-class Desi teens an inroad into the white-collar world. Between highly skilled engineering positions and grueling assembly line work emerged an intermediate category of technology workers: systems operators, Microsoft Windows administrators, and other "low-tech" entrees into the high-tech world.[14] More prestigious than assembly line work yet far less upwardly mobile than engineering jobs, such categories of work offer the distinctive title of computer professional as well as monetary benefits in an industry that signifies modernity and progress. Youth considered these "grey-collar" technology jobs to be a faster, easier, and more profitable path to getting ahead than the assembly line technology work of their parents. Accordingly, middle-class Desi teens set their sights on junior college and training institutes and degrees in specialized programs that can become obsolete. Indeed, these positions offer opportunities to achieve the Amrikan Dream in ways previously unimaginable.

Desis laud Silicon Valley not only for its economic opportunities, but also for its multicultural character and color-blind narratives of advancement. Mr. Shah, the father of Tara, an upper-middle-class girl, enthusiastically explained that he has no fear of glass ceilings based on his race. He has had no problem advancing at his company and noted, "Right now being an Indian in Silicon Valley is a huge plus. People would rather give money to an Indian than a White guy . . . maybe because I'm in the computer field where things are more progressive. It's basically what you do that counts, not who you are." Mr. Shah's assertion that being Desi could actually help rather than hinder one's advancement only bolsters the strength of the Amrikan Dream in the Desi mind. Like Mrs. Malik's comment, it underscores that the high-tech industry offers a chance to achieve greatness regardless of educational background, class status, and even ethnic and racial background.

As Mr. Shah reflects, the multicultural nature of Silicon Valley during this period seems to make it a place where Desis feel comfortable with being people of color. Mrs. Malik likewise remarks that while she has experienced discrimination here, it pales in comparison to her experiences elsewhere in the United States: "I think Silicon Valley is a very good place to live because if you go to other states or anything, you realize that there is discrimination." Being in a Desi-saturated area is regarded positively. Mrs. Oberoi, mother of Dilip, an upper-middle-class Hindu boy, explained, "I am glad we raised [our children] in the Silicon Valley. There are lots of Indian families, culture, musicians, and singers in this area, good exposure for them. Even in the school there [are] the multicultural activities." The diverse population of this area makes it easier for the Desi communities to maintain their exclusive social circles without seeming exclusionary.

The ways adults in Silicon Valley valorize not only the high-tech industry but also Silicon Valley creates a compelling case for their children to follow suit. Desi teens, along with other youth, expressed pride and loyalty to the area in remarks such as "It's so cool how we live in Silicon Valley—we control the world!" and "Why would you want to leave the Bay Area? It's the best place in the world!" Even those who do not consider this region particularly exciting nonetheless speak highly of it and note its transformation. Simran, a middle-class Sikh girl, related a conversation with visiting relatives about her perceptions of Silicon Valley: "They thought San Jose was really bad, that there are a lot of gangsters. I'm all, 'It's not even like that!' They're all, 'You can't walk outside in the middle of the night.' You can't because, like, there's nowhere to go." Like her peers, Simran is reluctant to even consider leaving this beloved area, despite any shortcomings.

CONCLUSION

Desis in California are in a far more advantageous position than a century ago, when they were barred from citizenship and land ownership. They have made a prominent place for themselves in the changing landscape of Silicon Valley. Establishing enduring ties to this location roots this Desi Community to this place and maps undifferentiated, generic suburban spaces into distinct neighborhoods with extended family and friends, places of religious worship, and ethnic stores and restaurants. Not only do adults participate in this model of community interaction, but children also see the value of it in their social lives.

The high-tech industry has shaped the aspirations and priorities of Desi teens in Silicon Valley. Nonetheless, widening socioeconomic gaps are only partially hidden in a region overjoyed by its own success. The types of futures that middle-class teens dream about can be quite different from those of upper-middle-class youth. For both, however, this industry provides narratives for success as well as specific material desires and informs their sense of style. In the next chapter I elaborate on this style as part of a broader discussion of Desi teen culture and examine how Desi teens orient themselves within their communities and schools and map campus space and activities according to their own cultural logics.

DEFINING DESI TEEN CULTURE

Rafiq has no particular allegiances with any of the cliques at his school, especially not with Desis. Charismatic yet approachable, Rafiq moves through Greene High School's cliquish landscape without having to affiliate with any one group. Rafiq's Bangladeshi Muslim family moved from London when he was six years old. His parents both have college degrees, but he has a far less affluent lifestyle than his friends' parents who work in the high-tech industry. Rafiq's father works for a medical records company and his mother at an elementary school. Rafiq aspires to become a lawyer or public defender. Although he is widely liked by the students who elected him student body president, he avoids being tied to a clique because he finds his way of being Desi to be different from the others at the school. After numerous attempts to dissuade me from interviewing him because he was "not very Indian," he relented and began by explaining that he was not "authentic" enough: "I don't kick it with all the Indian kids. The major reason is that they have a pride for where they came from. I got to talking to a lot of teachers telling me who I am, maybe I should learn more about the culture and find a reason to be proud of, instead of making up reasons. When I see that group of Indian students at the school, they have pride for Punjab or some area of India. I don't feel that and that's why I don't hang out with them." Rafiq's social life has not suffered from his choices, and he stands by them on a political and ideological level that few of his peers consider.

Desi teen culture is an emergent cultural form with distinctive stylistic elements. Like other youth cultures, it is time- and place-specific, is premised on constructed and perceived differences, and is constantly shifting. While its constitution and underpinnings vary from school to school, and certainly within schools, Desi teen culture is a prevalent force in Silicon Valley. As much as teens like Rafiq make the case that they are unlike the myriad Desi teens at their schools, they too contribute to defining what it means to be a Desi teen and how certain stylistic choices shape this aesthetic sensibility.

Perhaps the most remarkable aspect of Desi teen culture is its newness. Like the category of Desi itself, this emergent cultural form is only beginning to take hold in Desi as well as South Asian contexts. This is so because in the South Asian context as well, youth culture is an emergent category. Neoliberal globalization and satellite television in South Asia have brought waves of this youth culture to the region as recently as the 1990s. Meanwhile, Desi teens in America experience a youth culture that their parents missed altogether. Desi teen culture is constructed from a range of local and global influences, and Desi teens draw on stylistic elements from global media such as Bollywood as well as from local media such as hip-hop and pop music videos on MTV.

Race, class, gender, and intergenerational relationships all inform Desi teen culture. In shaping their culture, teens struggle to define what the term "Desi" means. They are aware of the nascent status of this term and discuss specific elements of what this category means to them. Youth ideas about race, ethnicity, skin color, and language use all define Desi, and class shapes these politics of representation. Even those who do not fully participate in Desi teen culture, such as Rafiq, nonetheless care a great deal about defining it. Desi teens are deeply invested in developing their own style but also see the value in considering their parents' opinions and their reputation in their community. Indeed, one of the most significant aspects of Desi teen culture is its intergenerational character. Rather than remaining peer-exclusive, some youth engagements with media, material culture, and language practices are shared with parents and even grandparents.

Such character, I argue, is crucial to how teens orient themselves toward their parents' values and become deeply invested in their closely knit communities. In this way, points I discussed in the previous chapter—how Desis have become a visible part of the high-tech industry and Silicon Valley neighborhoods and schools and have created extensive community networks—all contribute to the emergence of this Desi teen culture. As members of their communities, teens are concerned with finding ways of expressing their own style without alienating themselves from the social groups to which they express a deep investment and sense of belonging.

Like other teenagers at their high schools, Desi teens create cultural codes and social categories that reflect these meanings, and organize themselves in cliques accordingly. Desi youth classify themselves and one another according to social categories that are shaped both by the particulars of their class status and by the unique culture of their high schools. An intricate cultural logic governs the processes by which teens form cliques, claim space at their high schools, and "kick it," or spend time together. Such cliques consist of youth who bond together over common tastes and dispositions, as well as their positioning at schools. The nature of these cliques and their relative positioning in the school campus not only shape the category "Desi" but also teens' orientation toward their schools.

DESI TEEN CULTURE

Desi teen culture is a relatively new category in the diaspora as well as in South Asia. Prior to the 1990s, the years after childhood led either to student life at college or to marriage. Being a teenager was more of a precursor to these phases rather than a distinctive time unto itself. Scholars have chronicled the emergence of youth culture in western Europe and America after World War II and noted its coincidence with delayed entry into the workforce due to extended schooling, a rise in leisure activities, and youth income becoming disposable rather than integral to family economies (Brake 1980; Lave, Duduid, and Fernandez 1992). In South Asia, this development is still in its formative stages. While the teen years in America are popularly understood to be a time of transition, marked by exploration, rebellion, independence, and creative expression, such ideologies were virtually absent in South Asia until recently. The image of the young and rebellious teenager has certainly appeared in Bollywood films since the early 1970s,[1] but there were few social opportunities to partake in a youth-specific lifestyle for most teens.

Since India's neoliberal globalization in 1991 and the introduction of satellite television after the first Gulf War, new forms of consumerism and media have proliferated (Mazzarella 2003). STAR TV, a satellite provider operated by Rupert Murdoch, began importing a spate of programming from the United States and the United Kingdom, including news, sports, talk shows, soap operas, sitcoms, and Hollywood films. Other channels were launched specifically for the youth market, such as MTV Asia, MTV India, and Zee TV. Compared to the prior offerings of the state-run network Doordarshan and a second channel also operated by the state, television suddenly offered an entire world that was previously inaccessible.

A concurrent proliferation of consumer options, including international chains of retail stores and fast-food restaurants and the rise of local versions of these venues, is also integral to the emergence of youth culture. Alongside these, enormous new shopping malls rapidly appeared, replete with international and domestic stores for those who have benefited from neoliberal globalization. It is worth noting, however, that the vast majority of South Asians find these new lifestyle choices economically inaccessible, though they covet them nonetheless (Liechty 2003). Although their peers in South Asia are riding the youth culture wave as Desi teens in California experience it, Desi parents in Silicon Valley missed it altogether. In this sense, the current generation of Desi teens is among the first to engage in youth culture as a youth-specific domain of activity.

One of the most distinctive aspects of being a Desi teenager in Silicon Valley is the teens' orientation to their community. While many American teens tend to have limited interaction with their parents' friends and count the days until they can leave home, Desi teens can have a deep investment in maintaining ties with their community into adulthood. Madhu, a middle-class Punjabi girl, describes her position on her family and community in Silicon Valley and contrasts it to older cousins living elsewhere in the United States: "There are quite a lot of Indians here, and we have been following our Indian traditions and we are kind of attached to them, so we don't completely go away from it. Like going to gurdwara, *melas* [festivals (Punjabi)], wearing traditional *suits* [*salwaar kameez* or a similar Desi outfit (Punjabi)] when you have to do something around the house; going to cultural events; make sure you try your mom's *subzi* (Hindi—vegetable curry), you have to learn how to cook, clean. These other cousins are kind of spoiled. At our age they were 'free,' but now it's payback time . . . no connections, no communication. I don't want to see myself in the future like that." Like Madhu, most teens want to remain close to their communities and so they negotiate their parents' expectations rather than ignoring them outright.

Desi Teen Technology and Media • Desi teen culture is marked as well by particular styles and relationships to global and local technology and media. Visual media is especially instrumental in shaping teen culture, as it is "embedded in people's quotidian lives" (Ginsburg, Abu-Lughod, and Larkin 2002: 2; see also Abu-Lughod 1995; Anderson 1991; Askew 2002; Mankekar 1999; Spitulnik 1993). In sprawling Silicon Valley, Desi teen culture requires technology to staying connected (Marcus 1995). Many teens started using pagers when they became cheaply available in the late 1990s. While newer forms of technology have made pagers obsolete, the underlying purpose for which they were used remains relevant.[2] Cliques of friends create pager codes and ID numbers to identify themselves to others and send each other phatic notes such as "Hi," "What's up," and "Hello." Each participant in a clique has a numerical code that identifies him or her as the sender; only those with the codes can communicate with other members of the clique. I learned this the hard way, when my pages were met with no response or acknowledgment. I soon learned to append the requisite *55 (which represent my initials, "SS"), the code name given to me by a clique of girls who were baffled as to why I did not already have a code. Once initiated, I too could ask for the "411" (information) or let them that know my page was "911" (urgent) or that I was going to be "87" ("L8," the code for "late" upside-down).

An alternative to paging is instant messaging (IM), which is generally done late at night and can leave no record. In the suburban sprawl of Silicon Valley, IM provides a sense of togetherness and connectivity that is difficult for many Desi teens to achieve during the day. For youth who are allowed to meet with friends, the lack of adequate public transportation makes them reliant on parents or friends with cars. Given constant traffic jams, homework, and numerous other activities, speaking digitally is the next best thing to daily face-to-face interaction. For others, online time is the closest they will get to peer interaction outside school or community settings. Yet unlike the cheap and ubiquitous pager, IM poses issues and constraints around access. Youth who do not have networked computers at home or can log on for only short amounts of time are less participatory in online socializing and have to rely on pagers or their time in school to stay connected.

Desi teens watch generous amounts of MTV, especially videos, along with other television programs. Music videos by hip-hop artists such as Tupac Shakur, Dr. Dre, and Snoop Dogg, as well as pop stars such as JLo, Britney Spears, NSync, and Backstreet Boys, were popular choices in the late 1990s. Music, including bhangra, hip-hop, and pop, is also widely consumed. Umber, a middle-class Sikh girl, likes hip-hop, rap, and R & B. She adored the new Dre and Snoop CD, so much so that she screamed whenever she heard one of its hit singles. One day, as I drove her home in my car, Umber began to shriek even louder than the music she had cranked up. She exclaimed, "That's my favorite song! I don't know what it's called and I just love that song. If it comes on the radio, they say, 'Umber's song is on!' When we're in the car, I'm like, 'That's my song, Mom!' She's like, 'Yeah, whatever.' " Such excitement was hardly unusual. Desi teens integrate their favorite tunes into their everyday activities. They enjoy Bollywood and other Indian pop music around the clock on satellite dish service. The union of these Desi musical genres with hip-hop is under way: one such example is "Beware of the Boys" (popularly referred to as "Knight Rider bhangra" for its sample from the 1980s television show theme song), which has been overlaid with tracks by Jay Z.

Diasporic films in English, especially *American Desi* and *Bend It Like Beckham*, similarly resonate with Desi teen viewers. The social life of media in diasporic contexts has been noted to foster bonds of community and mediate identity while enabling connections to homelands and other diasporic locales (Appadurai 1996; Naficy 1993). Such films also feature coming-of-age narratives, which explore complex issues around relationships with parents, friendships, and especially romance in various diasporic locales. Although these films are primarily in English, characters do code-switch between English and other South Asian languages, an aspect that many teens immediately recognize and appreciate. Of all these media, the influence of Bollywood is perhaps most pervasive to defining Desi teen culture.

In the late 1990s in America, where discourses of multiculturalism and cultural diversity were the accepted cultural logic, Bollywood films were as much a part of living in America as the other media available to these youth. Bollywood is the world's most prolific film industry; its films are popular among Desi and non-Desi communities worldwide (Larkin 1997; Liechty 1995) and in Desi diasporic locations such as Fiji (Ray 2000), Great Britain (Gillespie 1995; K. Hall 2002), and Queens, New York (Shankar

2004b). Once a tongue-in-cheek name used by the English-language media in India (Ganti 2004), the term "Bollywood" is now widely used to refer to Hindi-language films made in Bombay (renamed Mumbai in 1995). Serving simultaneously as visual culture, a social institution, and a linguistic resource for many diasporic youth, Bollywood films have deeply affected the everyday social lives of South Asians in the Subcontinent and beyond.

Bollywood songs and styles have appeared in recent Hollywood films, such as *Moulin Rouge* and *Ghost World*, and in popular music by Shakira and various hip-hop artists. Indeed, the pervasive influence of Bollywood films, songs, actors, and narratives is undeniable in Silicon Valley. From watching new releases and following up on film star bios to acquiring Bollywood cell phone ring tones, Desi teens have made this media institution an integral component of their culture. With multiplexes screening these films, numerous stores renting and selling the movies and their soundtracks, and ubiquitous Internet sites offering movie clips and star gossip, most Desi teens consume Bollywood on some level.

Historically, Bollywood films had been made for South Asian audiences, but production has expanded since the 1990s to imagine the diaspora as a key source to increase overall marketability (Ganti 2002). There are many competing visions of modernity in Hindi films, but several recent films made in the 1990s and more recently seem especially relevant to these youth. The modern, hip youth culture and lifestyles portrayed in the recent hits *Dil To Pagal Hai* (The Heart Is Crazy) and *Kuch Kuch Hota Hai* (Something Is Happening) as well as the trend of featuring Desis in London, Los Angeles, and New York in such films as *Dilwale Dulhuniya Le Jayenge* (The Bravehearted Will Take the Bride), *Pardes* (Foreign Land), *Kal Ho Naa Ho* (Say This Is Love), and *Kabhi Alvida Naa Kehna* (Never Say Goodbye) have made the films immensely popular. Bollywood films portray a global youth culture replete with branded products from the United States and Europe. Moreover, they focus on Desi youth culture in locales such as the United Kingdom, the United States, and other regions with large diasporic populations.

Consuming Bollywood • Desi teens share Bollywood intergenerationally; most teenage Bollywood fans in Silicon Valley began watching Hindi films at home with their parents on the VCR. New films are now released simultaneously on DVD and in theaters. Film rentals are easily available at the local South Asian grocery stores at a low cost and with loosely enforced late fees. With mail-order DVD subscriptions such as Netflix, renting films is easier than ever. Many families taped their DVDs onto videotapes, creating a vast library of titles for repeat viewing. Neetu exclaimed, "We watch everything that comes out! My mom gets videos or DVDs from the Indian store and I sit there watching them." Her friend Madhu chimed in, "It was like whenever we had some free time," she paused and looked at Neetu, and they squealed in unison, "Let's go watch some Hindi movies!" Neetu added, "My house, we watched movies for my birthday. I started watching Hindi movies when I was three years old. . . . We like the clothes, the songs, the guys. . . . Hrithik Roshan is so handsome!" Other teens watch with some members of their family but not others. Simran described the frustration she and her sisters and mother feel toward their father: "I don't watch them with my dad because he talks through the whole thing: 'That's unrealistic, that can't happen!' We'd rather turn it off than watch with him." She added with a smile, "We taped over his army movies and he got kinda upset."

Desi families often make Bollywood films easily accessible to their children. Tara, an upper-middle-class girl, has been a fan of Bollywood since childhood. It is a love nurtured by her father, who remarked, "Hindi movies, she watches almost every one of them. *Kaho Naa . . . Pyaar Hai* (Say This Is Love), she practically knows every line, from beginning to end. We do watch together. I pause it, tell her the story if there are no subtitles. I am member of Netflix. We see four movies, DVDs, every week. Zee TV, TV Asia. . . . [We're] very serious about it." Whether at home or in the theater, Desi teens enjoyed watching a film with their parents, something their American peers might be less likely to do. In the Bay Area, the main cinema is Naz, which moved from a twin theater on a small main street to an eight-screen multiplex in a strip mall with a spacious parking lot. With a dozen screens at its disposal at any given time, Naz can show new releases in various Indian languages on multiple screens as well as classics sure to draw a crowd. Desi parents who have the means enjoy treating the family to a Naz outing, while others are content to settle on the sofa with a DVD for an evening; either way, such intergenerational film consumption solidifies teen relationships with their parents.

Seeing a film in the theater is a true spectacle. On a trip to Naz with Tara and her parents to see *Refugee*, we lingered in the parking lot as Tara's parents greeted friends and Tara chatted with Safina, a friend from school. Carloads of Desis continued to arrive. Moving through the lobby filled with the wafting scent of stale popcorn, which no one bought, and fresh samosas that everyone would want at intermission, we filed into the coveted rear of the crowded theater along with families with crying babies and large groups of young men. Lines of dialogue were punctuated with loud comments, potentially romantic moments were met with whistling, and the ultimate triumph of the hero was celebrated with applause. Songs caused upsurges of singing and humming throughout the theater, making the voices coming from the seats nearly as loud as the sound blaring from speakers. Over samosas and chai during the intermission, we browsed the selection of film CDs and DVDs for sale in the lobby. Tara and her father schooled me on the production details of the movie we were watching, and he narrated an impressive preview of upcoming films starring the same actors and actresses, courtesy of his favorite Bollywood websites.

Songs from films are well known and liked among Desis in Silicon Valley and are incorporated into a number of aspects of the teens' lives. The average film features at least six song sequences that further the narrative structure of the film by celebrating alliances or revealing hidden desires between characters. Prior to seeing *Refugee* in the theater with Tara, we stopped at one of several Indo-Pak grocery stores to pick up the film's soundtrack. She explained, "I need to hear the songs before the movie, at least to get a preview." After purchasing the CD, we sat in the strip mall parking lot and previewed a few minutes from each song. Wanting to familiarize herself with all the songs before seeing the film, Tara made fast work of the CD. Her father, who joined us at the theater, had similarly spent part of his workday downloading and listening to song clips from the film and noted the scenes in which they would be featured. Tara and her father were not the only ones singing along to this new release, indicating that other viewers had done the same or come back for repeat viewings. Outside of the film, songs contribute to the movie's appeal. Especially popular songs are heard in cars, on headphones, and at parties and are used in teens' own dance productions. They are viewed apart from films on DVDs whose menus are programmed for just such repeat screenings. Indeed, film songs are so popular that my 2004 viewing of *Kal Ho Naa Ho* at a Mumbai theater was repeatedly embellished by audience members' cell phones ringing loudly with the movie's theme song as the ring tone.

Desi teens idolize Bollywood actors and actresses. Among girls, popular actresses such as Aishwarya Rai, Karishma Kapoor, and Urmila Matondkar are admired Desi counterparts to the American teen idols Britney Spears and Jennifer Lopez. Having Desi role models, many of whom have dark hair and dark eyes, is important to their self-image. Although many of today's Bollywood actresses are exceedingly thin and fair-skinned, with light hair and eyes, they are nonetheless South Asian in their looks, speech, mannerisms, and values. Male actors are similarly respected by Desi boys, who are happy to have action heroes they can call their own. Avinash, a Hindi film fan, relates, "I used to be a Shah Rukh Khan fan, but this new guy, Hrithik Roshan, is off da' hook. He's built, he can act, *and* he can dance." Other youth idolize Hrithik for his chiseled good looks, muscular physique, and prowess on the dance floor. Adorning girl's notebooks, bedroom walls, and screensavers, photos of Hrithik are ubiquitous. As we shopped for a Hrithik poster to take with her to college, Tara explained that he is "the best-looking guy ever," and joked, "for all these White girls know, I can put up the poster and say he's my boyfriend."

Like stars everywhere, these actors and actresses take on larger-than-life personas. Gossiping about alleged transgressions of some film stars—which include smoking, drinking, drugs, incarceration, affairs, and wearing "hootchie" or revealing clothing—occurs alongside testimonials of those who can do no wrong. On a visit to Umber's house, I was confided in about her secret ambition to become a Bollywood star, and she closed her bedroom door to reveal her not so subtle obsession with Bollywood stars, demonstrated in a floor-to-ceiling collage of glossy pictures. Umber has transferred schools several times because of her unfortunate knack for getting into trouble. Her solace is Bollywood, watching the films and singing their songs. She explains, "I cut out all these pictures from magazines. This is the second time I changed it. I took them all down and changed them. I used to be really crazed over it but now I don't have [as much] time, but I still like it. Kajol [a popular young actress] is my favorite because her acting was good and I respected her because she didn't dress like a hooch, you know, like most of them do in those movies." Like Umber, numerous other girls bring *filmi* magazines to school, adorn their notebooks with glossy photos they cut out, and keep up with whatever gossip they can access.

In these ways, Bollywood is both everyday entertainment and a cultural trendsetter for Desi teens. The films shape not only Desi teen culture and intergenerational connections, but what it means to be Desi in the United States. Those films set in the United States are especially instrumental in examining issues of cultural difference endemic to diasporic encounters. What they do less of, however, is examine the real-life racial and class-based meanings for second- and third-generation Desi teens. The next section explores how Desi teens attempt to define these meanings in ways that articulate with the broader social dynamics at play in their lives at school and home.

Racial and Ethnic Meanings of Desi • Desi teens discuss what it means to be Desi in terms of group dynamics, inside jokes, and skin color. They define "Desi" based on shared humor and everyday commonalities. Janvi, a middle-class Sikh girl, described how her relatives greet one another: "They do the 'Desi hug'—the hands go around but you don't know where to grab." Similarly, one upper-middle-class girl raved about how much she enjoyed the Desi student show during her visit to UC Berkeley: "They were making jokes that only other Indians would understand. Other people wouldn't think it was funny, but because you can relate to it, it is really cool and funny." Some teens enjoy teasing each other about things that only other Desis would think were amusing. One day at lunch, when Ranvir, a middle-class Sikh boy, learned I had asked his friend to tape-record their spontaneous conversation, he proclaimed, "Let's conversate!" For Ranvir, this meant teasing all his female friends, including telling one of them, "Janvi stinks! She smells like roti (Indian bread) and daal (cooked lentils)." Janvi responded by whispering into the tape recorder, "Shalini, this guy is not an Indian, he's a Mexican," which sent her friends into peels of laughter. This inside joke is premised on the misrecognition that often occurs between Latinos and Desis in Silicon Valley. As these teens remark and I discuss in detail in subsequent chapters, middle-class Desi teens can undergo the same kind of treatment and marginal social positioning that Latinos are subject to in California high schools.

Skin color—a preoccupation in South Asia—is a concern that has only gained strength in diasporic contexts. Desi parents express their desire for their children to appear light-skinned, a quality generally thought to increase social prestige and cachet for marriage. Parents tell their children, especially their daughters, to avoid the sun and wear clothes that complement their coloring. Desi teens do not necessarily come to these judgments on their own, but are receptive to parental critique. Taahir, an upper-middle-class Muslim boy, recalled, "I got orange pants for my birthday, and my mother said I couldn't wear them, because they don't look nice. 'They don't suit your complexion at all, it doesn't make you look nice. It makes you look even darker than you are, and that's not a good thing.' So we got them exchanged." Not only do Taahir's parents play a role in shaping his tastes, they also dictate broader ideals about skin color and race that are commonplace in Desi culture. Similar to Bollywood ideals, light skin color is at a premium, and Desis are interested in appearing as fair as possible. Such judgments make Desi teens even more aware of their own skin color in comparison to the other shades of brown that surround them in Silicon Valley.

Feeling at ease with other Desi teens lays the foundation for exclusively Desi social circles. Madhu, a middle-class Sikh girl, thoughtfully remarked on why many teens have exclusively Desi circles of friends:

> People who started immigrating from India in the late '70s, as they came, our generation is one of the first that had to deal with being born here and trying to deal with Indian culture. Ours is totally different. We have to deal with community, culture, parents, school, religion. All the Indians that we see in San Jose, people our age: Where are we, like, supposed to go in this Indian society—with our family or with Americans? Our little cousins, brothers and sisters, they know a little more. We are the oldest, everyone born in the early '80s, they are experiencing the real stuff of getting along. Knowing that other Desi youth are going through the same thing, it is a sort of comfort. You don't say it, but you kind of know.

Many Desi teens enjoy having a primarily Desi social network. Although they each have at least a few non-Desi friends, by and large the close friends they kick it with every day are Desi.

For all these reasons, most Desi teens gravitate toward exclusively Desi social circles. Ranvir explained how he became close to the other Desi teens like him when he transferred to his school: "All the Indian people there are like family to me—it's like kickin' it with cousins. We are all together and do the same thing. Even if you are a new kid, they go up to you to find out who you are. You meet them in classes." This type of ethnic grouping mirrors the broader dynamic at their high schools. One upper-middle-class girl at Mercer remarked, "All Indians hang out with each other, so do Asians and Whites. Everyone seems to feel more comfortable that way." Her friend confirmed this: "You feel more comfortable with other Indians—you have stuff in common when you come together. It's also easier to relate to Asians. With White people, you have to search and try to find something in common, but with Indians it's understood." For Preeti, a middle-class Sikh girl, being Desi is closely connected with certain types of language use. She noted, "Most Indian people understand where you're coming from, you feel more comfortable with them. Plus, you can speak another language with them, and they'll understand. Most everyone [in my circle of friends] is Punjabi." This sense of belonging, much like that of their parents in their communities, is most often found among other Desis.

Some teens resist the urge to kick it only with Desis and instead choose a diverse group of friends. Rafiq, the upper middle-class boy at Greene whom you met at the start of this chapter, explained, "That's how our culture is . . . that Desis will accept you just because you are a Desi. I don't know how the history of it was . . . that's the nature of how Indians, Pakistanis, and Bangladeshis act. If they see you, you are from the area, suddenly this brotherhood comes to you." Even teens like Rafiq who try to avoid exclusively Desi social circles suggest that they could join one if they ever felt the desire to feel more included. Other teens remark that they wish they had a more diverse group of friends, and those who do find it more challenging, as groups tend so often to congregate by race and ethnicity. Along these lines, Kavita noted that she used to kick it with a more diverse group of friends at school, but now she kicks it only with Desis. Although she is still close to these other friends, they now talk on the phone instead of at school. Charanpal, who had a lot of Latino and African American friends at his previous school, remarked that his circle of friends shifted when he transferred to Greene: "I don't know why I made only Desi friends. I got to know them and now they are my good friends." Yet moving outside this circle seems less feasible and, at times, a less desirable option for many kids when they enter high school.

Another reason Desi teens stick together is because, although racism is not reported to be a source of overt tension at their schools, racially insensitive comments are commonplace. Neetu reported that stereotypes abound among peers and faculty: "You hear jokes about Desis. Our teacher likes to joke around about bindis (a mark of Hinduism, worn on a woman's forehead), turbans, and camel riders—he's an idiot." Some Desi parents also reported feeling discrimination from faculty when they visited the school. Mrs. Malik recalled a parent-teacher conference: "The teacher started talking to me, like really slow, like she's almost spelling out each word, because she thinks I won't get what she is saying . . . until I answer her and she's taken aback because she just assumes, by my color, that I'm literally jahil [illiterate], that I don't know what she is saying. I am sure they have run into people who are not as educated, or maybe they have not run into anybody. . . . They have a stereotype in their head, but they have not interacted with anybody from that side of the world."

Desi teens' remarks indicate that a White hegemony still prevails at their predominantly non-White schools. Although their schools are diverse, unless events are explicitly labeled multicultural, school events are by and large classified as "White." Rekha, an upper-middle-class Desi girl, makes an effort to go to events that her friends deem "too White" for their enjoyment. Although her friend Shabana critiqued the Aloha Dance, which kicks off the school year—"It's mainly a White dance and there wouldn't be people for us to kick it with"—Rekha maintained her position: "I'm going. I'm going to kick it with my White friends there. I'm a senior this year, and I don't want to feel like I missed out on everything because I have that attitude about it."

Desi teens who do not have exclusively Desi friends gravitate toward White peers if they are upper middle class and Latino peers if they are middle class. Devan, a middle-class Indo-Fijian boy, remarks about this dynamic at Waverley, "A lot of Desi kids come here for the magnet program. I come because I live a mile away. When a person looks at me for the first time, they're not gonna go, 'oh, he's Indian.' And I've been told many times I don't look Indian because my friends are not Indian. I don't know if you thought I was Indian or Mexican the first time you saw me. I don't go for stereotypes. Because I associated with Mexicans, people thought I was Mexican." For Devan, there is far more confluence with middle-class Mexicans than there is with upper-middle-class Desi teens who attend the school for the medical magnet program. Numerous other students expressed a similar sentiment. Such dynamics draw attention not only to racial meaning but to the ways youth spend time together.

DESI TEEN SOCIAL FORMATIONS

Desi teens belong to multiple, overlapping groupings across school and community. Along with their families, they belong to ethnic communities; with friends they belong to cliques in high school; through other activities, they can seek membership in a number of other groups. The ways youth spend time together and the commonalities around which they organize themselves socially have been referred to in numerous ways. Studies of youth culture emphasize that youth form subcultures with an articulated set of concerns in response to particular social conditions (Clarke et al. 1976; P. Cohen 1997; Gelder and Thornton 1997; Hebdige 1979; McRobbie 1991; Thornton 1997; Willis 1977). Like subcultures, Desi teens who spend time together create, share, and reflect upon semiotic systems of meaning. Yet, unlike the "double articulation" of subcultures as oppositional to both a parental culture generationally and a dominant culture socially (Clarke et al. 1976), Desi teen culture does not share such clear-cut orientations. At times, teens are more closely bonded through a particular cultural or linguistic practice than some other type of affiliation. Such "communities of practice" (J. Lave and Wenger 1991; Wenger 1999) are not about membership in some abstract sense, but the actual endeavors, practices, and relationships that create a group (Eckert and Mc-Connell-Genet 1992).[3] Drawing on insights from the literature of subcultures and communities of practice, I use the teen term "kickin' it," a popular term for spending time together or "hanging out."

Kickin' It • Kickin' it provides a time and place for Desi teens to understand themselves as individuals, apart from their parents and communities, as they seek new and generationally distinct ways of being Desi. Kickin' it connotes regular and habitual activity, and while it does not encompass a fixed set of activities, where it happens and with whom it happens form a routine part of the school day. Kickin' it can seem insignificant but actually has longer term consequences. As Paul Willis (1977) illustrates in his classic study Learning to Labor, time that "the lads" spend together in school shapes who they become after high school. Similarly, Desi teens together

67

create shared modes of interpretation, test the boundaries of the self, and reformulate and reinstate ideas about who they are and who they seek to become. The ways Desi teens kick it are influenced by a number of factors, including their community background, their cultural and linguistic practices, and their ideas about friendship, trust, loyalty, and kinship. From the more momentous activities of school performances and attending the prom together, to the everyday sharing of stories and jokes, kickin' it provides a space for teens to explore themselves and maintain social ties.

An intricate cultural logic governs how teens kick it and represent themselves. This dynamic is expressed through teens' fluid use of the terms "FOBby" and "tight." While the term FOB is not unique to Asian Americans, it has received a great deal of usage in Asian diasporas, especially in the context of post-1965 Asian migration. A prototypical usage can be found in Henry David Hwang's (1979) play about Chinese Americans, entitled *FOB*. Here, Hwang's "preppie" orator lists all of the undesirable attributes that FOBs embody, which include being clumsy, ugly, greasy, loud, stupid, four-eyed, big footed, horny, and "like Lenny in 'Of Mice and Men.'" He goes on to note that "girl FOBs aren't really as FOBish. Boy FOBs are the worst, the . . . pits" (Hwang 1979: prologue 1). Such a description offers judgments about later post-1965 Chinese American arrivals by those who have already adopted desirable American styles such as "preppie," and sets apart new arrivals from those who have learned requisite cultural codes (see also Chiang-Hom 2004; Labrador 2004; Reyes 2007). FOB can also refer to refugees, stowaways, and those attempting to enter or leave a nation illegally (Kumsa 2006). In a different turn, Terrence Loomis's (1990) study of migrant labor and race in New Zealand illustrates the flexibility in this term to index social characteristics rather than migration status alone. Loomis (1990) argues that FOB is used both as a label that socially divides by nationality, age, and ethnicity, and as an insult toward those who are not new immigrants but nonetheless lack a desired social knowledge. He elaborates, "Whatever the context, 'FOB' contrasts clumsy, backward behaviour with an urbane sophisticated style" (Loomis 1990: xii).

Recent work on second-generation Asian American youth reports a more complex set of judgments about how they might identify and align themselves with some aspects of their heritage culture in ways that compliment local ways of being hip. For the most part, second-generation

Asian American youth deflect FOB onto first- or 1.5-generation youth to distance themselves from the negative connotations of the term (Jeon 2001; Loomis 1990; Talmy 2004). They also contrast the term FOB with what they consider to be identifiers of American life. Karen Pyke and Tran Dang (2003) report that second-generation Asian Americans use the term FOB in contrast to "whitewashed." FOB has also been noted to differ from "Twinkie" among Korean American youth in college who are either oriented toward their heritage culture or American culture (Kim 2004). Other edible comparisons, such as bananas, coconuts, and similar products with centers lighter than their shells, are common descriptors of a condition in which Asian American teens can become White on the inside while remaining brown or yellow on the outside.

Silicon Valley Desi teens rarely assessed one another in terms of foodstuffs; rather, the term FOB was contrasted with "tight," or California slang for "cool." These terms were current during 1999–2001 when I conducted my fieldwork. Desi teens use "FOBby"—the adjectival version of FOB—and tight to critique elements of style and offer metalinguistic assessments of one another. The nuanced usage of these terms deserves closer examination. Aesthetic and linguistic stances that constitute FOBbiness are based on locally created Desi teen culture that draws on a globalized youth culture (see Maira and Seop 2005). While it may seem that FOBby should refer to all things South Asian and tight to anything American, a far more complicated system of judgment is at work. In light of India's recent neoliberal globalization and the emergence of Indian youth culture and consumer culture, not everyone who migrates from the Subcontinent is a FOB. The media, commodities, urban lifestyles, and consumerism available in urban South Asia can be far more cosmopolitan than that of San Jose, California, neighborhoods. Desi teen quickness to admire certain styles generated in South Asia and displayed in Bollywood movies or Desi clothes in their local store as tight or even as "hella," or very tight, suggests that FOBby does not simply index anything South Asian. Likewise, tight does not blindly praise all things American.

While being FOBby is undesirable, being FOBulous is tight, as evidenced by the terms' usage among popular Desi teens. Consider, for example, Mercer High School's popular six-member Desi girl clique, who call themselves "the FOBulous Six." For their senior class picture, the girls bought matching shirts in rainbow colors and decorated them in glitter pen with their nickname on the front and their pager code number and "FOBulous Six" on the back. Amahl, a Muslim girl, confirms that "FOBulous" is a play on "FOB," the subject of much of their inside humor. In taking the otherwise derogatory term and combining it with "fabulous," these girls have reappropriated the term "FOB" to signal their group's unique and diverse style. The FOBulous Six includes Muslim girls from Pakistan and Afghanistan as well as Hindu girls from India, and being FOBulous means different things in each of their lives. Amahl's Pakistani Muslim family is far stricter than her friend Shabana's, and she is seldom allowed to go out at night without her older brothers or parents. She does not plan to attend her prom or other school social functions. Her family is close friends with the families of several other Muslim teens at Mercer High School; because of this, she and Shabana are close. Her friends' parents allow them to move about more freely with these other girls. Although they are each allowed to express themselves differently, they are nonetheless invested in the group representations they create for their clique. In this way, terms like "FOBulous" indicate the sophisticated cultural position of teens who are aware of how immigrants have been mocked but have reclaimed the term in a positive light.

In the uses of the term I observed, FOB operates as a shifter (Silverstein 1996b). In other words, it is defined contextually and relationally. For each group of teens, being FOBby is always relative; that is, most teens construct what it means to be tight against those they can identify as FOBby. Talmy reports a similar process, whereby ESL students create a "newly articulated subject position" by unwittingly naming another student to refer to iconically as FOB (2004: 169). For Desis, being FOBby can include not adequately following fashion trends, having oily hair, or speaking a heritage language at school. It has been widely documented that youth use numerous registers or varieties of language to communicate in the distinctive manner of their social group. Mary Bucholtz (2002), for instance, shows how racial identity, especially whiteness for nerds, is constructed through code choice of "extreme whiteness." Ana Celia Zentella (1997) documents the complex ways in which youth group themselves according to values linked to language practices, and Adrienne Lo (1999) notes that speakers take moral stances about certain types of registers and language use in code-switching (see also Chun 2001).

While Asian American identities are formed relationally with other identities and not simply through language use (see Lo and Reyes 2004), Desi teens place language use at the center of this system of judgment through which they define themselves against their peers and shape the meaning of their group. Asif Agha (1998, 2003) has elaborated on the ways in which stereotypes of speakers enable the production of social realities through the predictability of their behavior. In this way, Desi teens define their usage of FOB with relation to language, among other markers of style. Desi teens use the term FOB to refer to teens who are actually not Fresh Off the Boat at all—in fact, many were born in California or elsewhere in the United States or Canada. This is so because Desi teens are invested in promoting their particular brand of Desi and can be deeply critical of other Desi teens who, in their estimation, present themselves in inappropriate or embarrassing ways. For each group of teens, being FOBby is always relative; that is, most kids construct what it means to be tight against those they can identify as FOBby. Through this self-reflexive and group-reflexive process of assessment, teens continually redefine what it means to be Desi in ways that articulate with as well as depart from parental and peer expectations. These locally defined terms are central to how youth organize themselves into social cliques and claim space on their school's campus.

Claiming School Space • Cliques are an inevitable part of high school life in the United States, and Silicon Valley high schools are no different. By and large, cliques form along ethnic lines. Most of the cliques I describe here are predominantly, if not exclusively, Desi, and fit right in to a school full of teens also clustered around ethnic and racial lines. Although these cliques are sometimes perceived to occur naturally, like the Desi communities I described in the previous chapter, they take a lot of work. Indeed, a considerable amount of effort goes into forming and maintaining ethnically exclusive groups of friends, not the least of which involves finding a place to kick it. The spatial politics of high schools are governed by complicated yet unspoken social dynamics. Scholars have noted the significance of space and place in organizing social meaning (Basso 1996; Feld and Basso 1996), and teenagers are acutely aware of the unwritten rules of their school campuses. Just as members of a clique are territorial about membership, so too are they of their place in the school.

All teens have a regular place where they kick it with their friends during the short morning break or lunch. The sprawling layout of their schools necessitates this in order to maximize time together. The layout of each school consists of blocks of classrooms arranged on a campus alongside a library, gym, auditorium, and offices. In the grassy or concrete areas between buildings are picnic tables, benches, and courtyards in which students eat and congregate. With lockers attached to the outside of buildings and food sold at kiosks, the school campus is occupied with bodies whenever class is not in session. The "quad" is the physical center of school, where lunchtime performances, general announcements, and other social activities occur.

Where kids feel comfortable kicking it is not arbitrary; rather, it can be directly reflective of how they develop a sense of ownership over school resources through the physical spaces they seek to occupy. This is not unusual, as marginalized groups usually do not occupy central spaces in high school. The farther away from the quad kids locate themselves, the less able they are to hear and participate in the happenings of that day. This choice often signals discomfort or disinterest in school activities (see Gibson 1988; Perry 2002). Notably, this spatial order also facilitates faculty monitoring of youth activity. Cliques are easy to find and watch, and a group's absence from its usual spot can arouse suspicion about potential fights, illicit activities, or cutting school.

The importance of finding a social place at school is underscored by the careful social logic by which cliques are formed. The three high schools— Waverly, Greene, and Mercer—each shape the character of the cliques they host. Sometimes there is crossover between community life and cliques, where teens who know one another through their communities become friends at school. Upper-middle-class cliques tend to be single sex while middle-class cliques were occasionally coed. A possible reason for this difference is that an upper-middle-class clique of girls usually socializes with a clique of boys, both at school and at peer-exclusive social events outside of school. In contrast, middle-class youth socialize less with friends outside of school, and when they do, they have less freedom to engage in coed interaction. School, then, is the only space for coed interaction and socializing in general for some teens. While most teens accept cliques as a way of high school life, a small minority choose to have just one close friend whom they trust implicitly rather than relying on a group.

Cliques of Populars, Geeks, and FOBs • In Silicon Valley high schools, social hierarchies are an ingrained part of everyday life and interaction. Here, like high schools elsewhere, youth are organized into categories such as lads and earoles (Willis 1977), jocks and burnouts (Eckert 1989), nerd girls (Bucholtz 2002), and myriad other groupings.[4] Three predominant Desi teen social categories are populars, geeks, and FOBs. Populars are renowned for their style, attractive looks, intelligence, and, well, their popularity, while studious geeks are generally the underdog in every aspect of school life but academics. The FOBs, often so labeled for their less than trendy cultural and linguistic displays, are an altogether marginalized group in the social order. The precise composition of these categories varies across schools and, presumably, across time. Being popular could look different at each school, as well as different from what it may have looked like in the past. In these Silicon Valley high schools, these categories are shaped by class. Moreover, all categories do not appear at all three schools. For example, FOBs are practically nonexistent at Mercer, where upper-middle-class populars and geeks abound, but they are a strong presence at Greene. Similarly, Greene has some populars but fewer geeks, and Waverly has mostly FOBs and geeks but very few populars.

The mere fact that these Desi teen categories are so specific to each school and this particular time period underscores their partial nature and limited ability to capture the complexity of high school social life. While I avoid relying entirely on these categories and emphasize numerous other aspects of youth lives that transcend them, to bypass them altogether would be telling only part of the story. Social positioning vis-à-vis cliques is important not only because it affects Desi teens' everyday engagements with school activities, but also because it shapes their overall orientation to their time at school. It is worth noting that youth alone do not self-segregate; school faculty and administration foster and help maintain these distinctions through their interactions with students by privileging some over others. The tension between how Desi teens are defined by their peers and the school versus how they think about themselves informs identity formation and social positioning of these three categories.

Being stylish, participating in school activities, and having a reasonably likeable personality makes some Desi teens popular. Their extensive cultural knowledge—both Desi and American—means that they always have their finger on the pulse of the latest trend. Popular teens easily navigate

73

school spaces and activities and move fluidly from pep rallies to school dances to elected positions. They unquestioningly call the quad and any other centralized school spaces their own. Many Desi populars are lauded for their academic and social skills alike and grace honor rolls and dean's lists. Popular teens are far more likely to be girls, but some boys are popular as well. They largely come from upper-middle-class families that support their clothing and apparel purchases and buy them cars for their sixteenth birthday.

Predictably, the very traits that make Desi teens popular also mark them as targets of jealously and contempt. Managing "haters," or those who wish ill and negativity upon them, can become a serious preoccupation, as can keeping up appearances in general. Any missteps are noted and celebrated by those snubbed by or just plain jealous of populars, who appear to have everything working in their favor. Desi populars prevail at Mercer, and cliques of popular girls and boys are well known and admired within each grade. By contrast, populars at Greene and Waverly are fewer in number. Greene has fewer upper-middle-class students and proportionally a smaller set of Desi populars. At Waverley, where middle-class Latino students dominate and the Desi population is small, the handful of Desi populars are middle class and have Latino friends.

Geeks are usually left to fend for themselves, which they do very well academically but with little success socially, though it is understood that they will ultimately excel.[5] As I hope this broader discussion of social categories conveys, not all Desis are geeks. Although the model minority stereotype would have it that Desis as Asian Americans are studious and antisocial, only some are.[6] Desi geeks resemble those of any other ethnicity. Crowding the rosters of physics club, math league, and, for the especially articulate, the debate team, geeks shy away from the noisy excitement of life in the quad. Unlike their FOBby counterparts, their self-segregation is sanctioned and encouraged by the school. Rewarded by faculty for their responsible and respectful attitude toward their studies and school equipment, they are often allowed to kick it in unused science classrooms during lunch. Their space in the school campus, then, is nearly invisible, as they are almost always inside unused classrooms or the library.

Desi geeks tend not to socialize much with non-geek Desis, though they are happy to fraternize with geeks of other backgrounds. Boys outnumber girls in this category, but geek girls are also prevalent, especially if they are upper middle class. Girl geeks tend to be more socially adept than boy geeks, primarily because they mind their appearance and have better developed social skills. They are less marginalized and sometimes even run for student body offices, but they never quite have that unmistakable charisma of a popular. Like their popular peers, geeks are especially interested in excelling at high school to secure a place at a competitive four-year college. While several of Mercer's twenty valedictorians in the class of 2000 were Desi, Greene has fewer Desi geeks. Desi geeks at Waverley are especially different from the school at large. All of Waverley's Desi geeks are in the medical magnet program and know each other through their school's Indian Student Association.

The defining characteristic of the group here called FOBs is that the vast majority of them are not actually fresh off the boat. The term is used by populars and geeks to refer to masses of middle-class Desi youth who cluster in the back corners of the school campus, code-switch between English and either Hindi or Punjabi, and express little interest in school clubs and activities. Sometimes they are called "SOB," for "still on the boat" (they do not seem to associate this with this acronym's other meaning). The ability of FOBs to code-switch fluently and actively use their heritage language closely bonds them as a group while it also separates them from the majority of students, who follow the dictates of this English-only environment. Unlike geeks and populars, who are familiar and comfortable with their group name, FOBs are usually not aware that they are being referred to by this moniker. FOBs themselves have a very different idea of which Desi kids are *actually* FOBby. Although Renu, who was born and raised in San Jose, is considered FOBby by populars and geeks, she defines her place in the social order of the school by comparison with another group of girls, whom she described as "really FOBby! Those girls hold hands, they're always on the [pay]phone. No one likes them and they make *us* look bad."

Cliques of FOBs are predominantly middle class and consist of second- or third-generation teens but occasionally include "1.5-generation" youth, who immigrated during childhood. They cluster at the margins of the school grounds, behind buildings far from the quad. What FOBs seek to get out of school, and how the school regards them, can be very different from the experience of geeks and populars. While these latter groups enjoy social or academic success, FOBs are most likely to get overlooked and left behind. Even the most well-intentioned teachers usually do not try to unmake the feelings of alienation felt by FOBs, and instead foster popular youth who already excel at school. FOBs shy away from mainstream school activities, and some admit they have little interest in attending school at all. Like other high school social outcasts, they proclaim indifference about what the rest of the school thinks of them but often admit in private that they wish they were not so excluded. For the most part, however, they express and exude a contentedness about who they are. They enjoy each other's company, keep each other laughing, and support one another through challenging times.

There are no FOBs at Mercer; it is not a relevant Desi category. At Waverley, FOBby cliques are a minority. Geek girls such as Azra made sure to differentiate themselves from Waverly's FOBby boys, who are the object of ridicule by several Desi cliques. Azra explained that she and her three Muslim friends who know each other from musjid used to kick it near the parking lot but had to find a new spot away from FOBby boys who slowly encroached on the area. Azra noted the importance of distancing herself from these FOBs: "There are some Indian guys, FOBs, they hang together. I try to get away from them. Not me, I don't like their acting. They bust out [in] Punjabi. I don't think it's bad, only once in a way for fun is okay, but [not] all the time! It's like, why are you doing this? It's awkward to me. We have CDs that we put on in the van, but at school I don't feel comfortable putting them on. I tell Mom to turn it down. They stare at you, people. It's not rap! When we get out of school we [turn] it up again." Azra's comment addresses why FOBs are at the lowest part of the social order. Her remark "Once in a way [it's] okay" is the key here, as she and the other Desi cliques who avoid FOBs think they are more adept at code-switching between various cultural and linguistic genres.

Yet FOBs themselves do not see it this way. Joseph, who attends the school because he lives close to it, kicks it with Chandra and a crew of other Desi boys whom the other Desi kids call FOBby. These boys kicked it in a classroom, code-switch between Hindi and English, and listen to Bollywood and bhangra music. When I asked Joseph why they do not socialize with the larger group of Desis by the science building, he shrugged and said, "They don't hang out with us." Joseph and his friends were acutely aware of the disdain other Desi students direct toward them: "I go to the

Indian club meetings sometimes, once in a blue moon. I don't think they want to know what I am thinking. They probably care about themselves and their friends a lot more than me and my friends." Joseph and his friends were bothered about being ignored at ISA meetings. Although they were secretly referred to as FOBS and sometimes even SOBS and rarely tried to participate in performances, they continued to attend events and represent themselves at meetings.

Cliques of FOBS abound at Greene High School. Several cliques kick it near a picnic table in the back corner behind the "C" building next to the library. At lunch and break, these teens drop off their purses and backpacks at the table and head out to the nearest vending machines and food kiosks. Populars and geeks have dubbed this area "Little India," a term FOBS themselves now jokingly use. They are far less self-conscious about monitoring themselves or caring what others think about them because other Desi teens already avoid them. In most of these groups, kids actively code-switch and code-mix primarily between English and Punjabi. They expressed little interest in school activities and are often excluded from them when they try to participate. Many FOBS complete four years of high school without ever taking part in school activities or sports. When I asked FOB boy Ranvir why he and his clique did not care for student activities, he did not hide his annoyance with my question. From his slouched position against the C building, he gazed over at the quad area and mumbled, "Desis don't really get involved in school stuff. I don't really *care* about jumping up and down and singing on the stage. Mostly leadership people just participate, no one else volunteers to do it." Populars and geeks are aware that FOBS are marginalized, which is all the more reason for these groups to maintain their distance. School administrators are cognizant of this group when they want to "keep an eye on them" for suspicious activity or breaches in school codes.

Some teens have a harder time finding a clique to kick it with. Like Rafiq from the start of this chapter, Dilip and his friends are not typical geeks, in that they are studious but have a sense of popular culture and style and sometimes socialize outside their clique. Somewhere between popular and geek, this group of friends is neither the center of activity nor the object of ridicule. Dilip, who was one of Mercer High School's twenty valedictorians, learned to play the *tabla* (a Hindustani percussion instrument) when he was ten years old from a cousin of the renowned musician

Zakir Hussein and as a child was often asked to play at community get-togethers. Although he enjoyed it, he complained that it kept him from playing with other kids and subsequently did not have a lot of friends when he was growing up. Toward the end of elementary school he formed a close group of Desi male friends who have remained together through high school. Dilip's Hindu parents moved from Chicago in the 1980s and bought their spacious Fremont home a few years ago. He commented that after he graduates, he hopes that he does not have only Indian friends in college. Trying to distance himself from what he sees as the drama and gossip of circles of Desi friends, he keeps focused on his academics.

There are students at all three schools who struggle to defy classification. Unlike many Desi teens at Mercer, Feroze is neither wealthy nor upper middle class like his Desi peers. His parents moved from Bangladesh to Los Angeles in the 1970s and to the Bay Area in the 1980s. They struggled to find a place in the area surrounding this school so that he and his siblings could attend. They rent a small older house, and both of his parents work at computer companies. Unlike his friends, who dream of becoming multimillionaires, Feroze wants to become a teacher. He is an active member of the Muslim Student Association, to which FOBulous Six members Amahl, Shabana, and their Muslim friends also belong. Here he met many of his close friends, but he is reluctant to limit his friendships to this group and makes a concerted effort to have a diverse circle of friends. Explaining his frustration about cliques, he stated, "Everybody goes to the same things. They do the same things. They speak the same way. They interact with all these same people. It's pretty narrow-minded." Feroze and his diverse circle of friends wander around or kick it near the gym. He is careful not to limit himself to one group in one place and instead tries to meet as many students as possible.

For girls, avoiding cliques can be more difficult, yet some boldly do so. Lata is a studious and assertive girl who resents the cliquish nature of her school and prides herself on having no part in it. She explained that she doesn't limit herself to having friends of any one ethnicity. She is involved in a number of school activities, especially those related to leadership. Lata's Tamil Hindu family moved to Silicon Valley from Madras when she was six years old. Her family is upper middle class, and she has two older sisters. Her father works as a chemical engineer and her mother is a guidance counselor. Lata is academically motivated and explained, "I think my high school is pretty fun. I am involved with my school, I enjoy being here, I like learning, so obviously if you like learning, you have a good time also." She looks forward to college, where she can better explore academic and career options. Lata finds her place at school in leadership and other school activities. Although she does not kick it in the quad like popular Desis and has a varied group of friends, like Rafiq she finds her own way at school. While numerous other teens expressed their discontent with the insularity of their social world, Feroze, Lata, and Rafiq are among the few to actively challenge this social order.

CONCLUSION

Desi teen culture signals a generational consciousness and an effort to further define the category of Desi. As it forms and diversifies, variation in this group will give rise to new ethnic and racial meanings. While most teens have an active notion of what it means to be Desi, these meanings differ across class and other statuses. How Desi teens form social cliques draws attention to how and why some Desi teens are able to parlay their ethnicity into popularity while others are relegated to FOB status. These social groupings and the meanings that underlie them lay the foundation for how Desi teens are positioned in the race- and class-based hierarchies of their schools. The way they socialize with one another and the relationships they form with the school shapes how they think about school, opportunity, and their future.

How Desi teens form cliques is a reflection of their family life. Kickin' it with their cliques is similar to how they kick it with their extended families and friends: as a closely knit, supportive group that must manage gossip and reputation. For middle-class Desi teens, being marginalized at school makes community life all the more appealing. Their definitions of style, their aesthetic choices, and their values regarding material culture are definitively shaped by their families. In the next chapter, I examine how style shapes Desi teen culture, especially for middle-class teens who are on the margins at school.

LIVING AND DESIRING THE DESI BLING LIFE

Meru, a popular girl at Waverly, kicks it with her Latino friends in the quad at school, as well as with Desi geeks. She reflected, "High school was really routine for the first three years. I kicked it with mostly Mexicans. My friend Angie had a baby. There was a lot of us, about twelve to fifteen of us. Junior year I got more involved in the Indian club. I didn't kick it with any Indian people at all before that. Even though I was part of the Indian club [before that], we never really did things. It looked good for college, but then I got more involved." Meru's time with her Latino friends shows in the way she wears her hair, in her makeup, and in her sense of style, which her geek friends cannot begin to emulate. Meru and her family live in a small two-story home in East San Jose, the first home that her father and uncles bought and shared when they moved to San Jose from Yuba City. Her father is now a truck driver and her mother is a quality control inspector on an assembly line. Compared to the numerous orthodox Sikh families that live in her neighborhood, hers is far less religious, as they cut their hair and do not follow Sikh dietary guidelines of vegetarianism. When she and her siblings clamor about buying a fully loaded new car or all the things they want at the mall, their parents are quick to remind them how hard they worked picking peaches for paltry wages to pool their savings and buy homes in San Jose in the early 1980s. All Meru remembers from this time is how much fun it was growing up with her cousins and the sibling-like way in which they still interact. Meru is fiercely protective of her family and takes great pride in her extended family, but she sometimes wishes they would trust her more. She explained that she and her sister "want to get out sometimes and spend time away from parents, but they don't understand. They are so paranoid. We just want to get out and relieve some stress sometimes. They are afraid I am going to become my own individual."

Growing up in the 1990s in Silicon Valley meant admiring and desiring lifestyles of local dot-com millionaires alongside hip-hop artists, teen idols, and athletes whose homes, cars, and shopping trips were ubiquitously available for public consumption and envy on television and in glossy magazines. As I discussed in the previous chapter, Desi culture is informed by a variety of influences and the ways teens are able to position themselves at school. This chapter takes a closer look at how Desi teens and their families define and desire aesthetic tastes through their engagements with consumption and material culture. Material culture defines Desi style and success on a number of levels. Desi teens engage with commodities and create distinctive styles that inform their identities and shape the character of their cliques. Using an amalgam of youth terminology, I call this style "Desi bling" and explore its construction and significance for Desi teens. Desi bling is reflected not only in objects but also in the types of lifestyle choices teens and their families make. Access to Desi bling predictably varies according to social class. Middle-class and upper-middle-class youth have access to different types of commodities and lifestyles, and such variation manifests itself in peer-based aspects of shopping and self-presentation. Both peer- and community-based consumption practices inform as well as define Desi bling.

Language use mediates the relationships that teens and adults form with objects. Consumption is inherently social, and language use imparts additional layers of complexity and meaning to this practice. Although middle-class teens have far more limited access to Desi bling, they nonetheless create relationships with objects they value. Desi bling is constructed with words and objects together, and verbal practices of narrative and gossip help to circulate particular meanings. While teens enjoy shopping for designer clothing and families set their sights on owning the latest Mercedes Benz, social relationships and community values are always prioritized. Indeed, consumption practices are primarily undertaken to impress one's own clique or community rather than a broader, anonymous public.

Material culture and language use together enable particular types of teenage style as well as community connections. Desi bling can be shared across generations, with teens and their families together participating in styles and lifestyles that they value. Desi teens and their families articulate, pursue, and desire a Desi bling lifestyle in peer-exclusive spaces as well as community contexts. Middle-class teens in particular, along with their families, form material, verbal, as well as visual relationships with objects, especially cars and electronics. Desi bling shapes the aspirations of upper-middle-class youth and defines the priorities of middle-class youth as they look toward adulthood and consider the future of their communities.

CONSUMPTION AND DESI BLING

Consumption has been described as a language of communication, in which objects communicate meaning within shared symbolic systems (Barthes 1972; Baudrillard 1988; Hebdige 1979). Objects that confer status in one's clique or community are highly valued and shape meanings of identity, community, and success. While Desi teens are deeply invested in maintaining relationships with their cliques, extended family, and community members, they are nonetheless engaged in contests of status with them. Thorstein Veblen (1953) and Pierre Bourdieu (1984) argue that objects are used as social markers to signify social class, especially in larger societies where people judge by appearances in the absence of personal relationships (see also O'Dougherty 2002; Patico 2005). Alongside status, consumption is also central to shaping identity as well as kinship, emotional expression, and relationships (Miller 1995). Countering Veblen, Mary Douglas and Baron Isherwood (1996) argue that although some social environments are individualistic and competitive, others are governed with social codes operating under different logics (see also McCracken 1991; Miller 1987; Patico 2002; Rutz and Orlove 1989). Consumption, then, can be about deepening connections that already exist between people.

Whether maintaining the closeness of their clique or showing their community they have succeeded, Desis rarely use consumption and display to gain social mobility outside of their group. Rather, these practices are integral to defining a distinctive style in one's own clique or community, and testing and reinforcing those social bonds in the process. Studies of Desi consumption practices tend to highlight ethnically marked elements, including the use of henna, bindis, bhangra music, and other Desi cultural forms (Maira 2000; Purkayastha 2005; Sandhu 2004), or to examine consumption in conjunction with ritualistic functions such as dowry (Bhachu 1994). Desi teens in Silicon Valley engage with a wide range of commodities and cultural forms, some of which are ethnically distinct and some that are generic but nonetheless significant.

Suburbs, one would suspect, should bring about the certain death of style and all that is original, countercultural, and just plain interesting about youth culture. Unlike Dick Hebdige's (1979) seminal study of subcultures, where clothing is used to index countercultural movements such as punk rock, style in the suburbs has a less overt political message. In the absence of such distinctive markers as the Mohawks of the punks that Hebdige describes, suburban teens turn to other avenues to distinguish themselves as a group. Penelope Eckert (1989: 49) explains that "clothing and other forms of adornment, ways of speaking, territory, and even substance use and school performance all have symbolic value in the adolescent context." Likewise, Norma Mendoza-Denton (1996) discusses how small-scale bodily adornments, such as applying eyeliner in a distinctive fashion, can signal group affiliation. Although Desi teen style is at times unremarkable and may not appear to signal a group affiliation, it is nonetheless a distinct style that is recognizable among peers.

Most Desi teens, not unlike the vast majority of their high school peers, are not interested in offering a social critique about anything through their clothing. While the body remains a youth-controlled domain of decoration and display, Desi teens face numerous limitations in this realm. For teenage girls especially, wearing revealing outfits, dying their hair, getting tattoos, and other visible markers are especially taboo. Even if their own parents do not object overtly, their community members would likely comment in ways that reflect poorly on their family. If anything, Desi teen styles signify their desire for certain types of lifestyles. Such a turn, where style is more about the objects themselves than the signification of a broader ideology, is especially prevalent in the suburbs. Whereas in subcultures past, brands were used to represent a larger ideology or practice that held a group together, the commodity has now become the ideology.[1] Indeed, while objects have been markers of success for decades, an age where brands themselves provide the ground on which youth bind together speaks to a broader shift in the significance of teenage material culture.

Such an emphasis on brands is epitomized by the prevalent aesthetic termed "bling." I use an amalgam of youth terminology in my term "Desi bling," which refers to a depoliticized emulation of hip-hop aesthetic infused with distinctively South Asian elements. "Bling," a term from hip-hop lexicon, refers to showy diamonds and jewelry that are often part of a broader lifestyle replete with luxury automobiles, branded apparel, high-end electronics, and mansions outfitted with every imaginable amenity. In the late 1990s bling became an aesthetic prevalent in many social environments in the United States and worldwide. Indeed, the term has become so widely used in the entertainment industry and by cultural critics that the *Oxford English Dictionary* added it to its online update in 2003. Although the term originated from hip-hop, its ubiquitous usage among northern Californians and popular media in general is usually devoid of the complex race-, class-, and gender-based politics of hip-hop music.[2]

Desi teens use the word "bling" or its original form, "bling bling," to refer not only to diamond and gold jewelry, but also to other signifiers of a particular flashy style. These include high-end cars and large SUVs "tricked out" with top-of-the-line audio systems, upholstery, and other embellishments, as well as home theater and sound systems and branded clothing, sneakers, and other accessories. While referring to them generally as bling, youth additionally describe these objects as "mad tight" (very stylish) and respect people who are able to own them because they make "hella bank" (lots of money). Some youth report taking aesthetic cues about bling from hip-hop videos filled with luxury cars, mansions, and fine clothing and jewels, while others credit their hip friends and family as their motivation to acquire bling.

Rather than wholly emulating hip-hop bling, Desi teens selectively choose aspects of this aesthetic and combine them with other elements that make them uniquely Desi. Like the finely calibrated dynamic of FOBby and tight I introduced in chapter 2, Desi bling is not simply a rejection of all things South Asian and a championing of all things American. Indeed, influences from South Asia and elsewhere are prominent factors in defining this style. Anyone who has witnessed a South Asian wedding may recall the dazzling displays of jewelry, gold-embroidered silks, and gilded decorations applied to any surface that can support their weight. Examples of what I call Desi bling push these meanings of style even further. Recent Bollywood films further this aesthetic by featuring lavish weddings and lifestyles replete with branded items. The young, attractive characters in these films jet-set about clad in clothes emblazoned with Polo, Gap, Adidas, and other logos. That youth would look to Bollywood films featuring American commodities to signal what is desirable in their own local shopping mall is indeed evidence of the global, intertextual character of modern media and consumption. In a South Asian context, where jewelry, fine clothing, and other material markers of status have long been valued, Desi bling is a newer incarnation of familiar styles of consumption, and now includes the massive suvs and high-end home electronics that abound in northern California.

Shopping for Style • Desi teens aspire to and often achieve Desi bling lifestyles by shopping. Desi teens shop to define their individual and clique identity to their school peers and communities. Everyday shopping trips as well as more focused missions, such as shopping for a prom dress, illustrate different aspects of sociality, membership, and belonging that are accomplished through these activities. Daniel Miller (1998a: 190) describes shopping in Trinidad as a social spectacle, in which young West Indian women dress up to see and be seen and shopping is about "imagining the possession and use of goods." For Desi teens, the act of shopping creates a social space and communal activity (Shields 1992: 15). This speaks not only to the dearth of social activity in their suburban communities, but also to the centrality of the mall and clusters of stores in providing a social space for teens to congregate. Especially in the suburbs, the mall can be central to creating and eliciting desire (Bocock 1993: 93) and solidifying the role of consumption in shaping identity and lifestyles (Langman 1992: 58). For many Desi teens, going to the mall is an eventful social activity where they can meet up with friends, eat, and look at other teens. Even when teens have no agenda and no cash, each of Silicon Valley's malls remains a desirable destination.[3] Despite the relative safety of these malls, some parents do not allow their kids to go for fear they will appear unmonitored and become the object of gossip.

Middle-class as well as upper-middle-class Desi teens embark on unending quests for Desi bling. Style varies according to class, clique, and high school. Popular teens are most invested in style, as are many FOBs and a few geeks. Upper-middle-class teens spend far more time than middle-class teens shopping at high-end stores and closely following fashion trends. Middle-class teens also enjoy shopping, and middle-class populars are especially creative with their limited resources. FOBs shop with greater constraints and challenges. Though each clique has its own style, some styles are universal, such as active wear by Adidas, Nike, Puma, Fila, and the like. Kids of all class backgrounds frequent some chain stores, such as The Gap and Old Navy. For some FOBs, as well as upper-middle-class teens, style is strictly limited by cultural and religious dictates. For girls, this means no skirts or shorts, tank tops, cleavage-bearing tops, or anything too tight.

Style remains important even to teens who are limited in their ability to participate in such practices. Sikh youth, for example, are forbidden by religious code to cut their hair. Some orthodox Sikh and Muslim girls wear headscarves to school, but turbans make hairstyling impossible for boys. Some Sikh girls are nonetheless adamant about styling their long hair and wake up hours early on schooldays to create elaborate hairstyles with clips, ornaments, and styling products. For those who are limited by religious, economic, or other reasons, many a lunch period is spent poring over teen magazines such as *Seventeen* and *Teen People* and critiquing styles. Despite their inability to fully partake, they participate vicariously through their friends and engage in extensive discussions about style.

Middle-class popular girls like Meru at Waverly gravitate toward a Latina-inspired "gangsta" look for their Desi bling styles. They emulate their Latina friends and tweeze their eyebrows into sharp arches, wear dark lipstick or dark lip liner paired with a clear gloss, and slick their hair into tight ponytails with carefully placed loose strands to frame their face. The male version of this look borrows from hip-hop icons as well as local gang-inspired gear and includes puffy jackets, sweatshirts, baggy pants, logo-covered track suits, shell-top Adidas sneakers with fat laces, and fade haircuts. I saw all these accoutrements and more for sale when Avinash, a FOBby boy from Greene, kept his plan to go to Eastridge Mall with me after school even when his friend canceled at the last minute. The usually reticent Avinash upheld his reputation for being so until we passed Foot Locker, when the verbal flood gates opened. Pointing at specific brands of shoes, clothing, and other branded gear, he began to talk about how various brands are affiliated with particular gangs and narrated his knowledge of and participation in gang-related activity in the San Jose area. Like other FOBs, Avinash prefers clothing with the name brand featured prominently; spending money on name-brand clothes is only truly worthwhile when the label is on display. Middle-class teens follow this aesthetic when they wear Desi clothes as well; boys choose baggier Desi clothes and heavy gold jewelry, and girls choose dark, bold colors for their *lehengas* and saris.[4]

Popular girls are especially invested in high-end cosmetics. When Shabana pulls her wand of Armani lip gloss out of her Louis Vuitton bag during English class, girls in the class are fixated as she applies a viscous layer of glittery sludge. Whether they stare in admiration, envy, or sheer boredom, Shabana's work of maintaining her status as a trendsetter is done. Popular girls like Shabana dabble in mid- and upper-range chain stores. While populars sometimes display brand names or wear branded sports apparel, they also opt for logo-free designer clothing that signals a sense of style without flashing a brand name. Coveted styles in magazines that are far out of reach for middle-class teens make them all the more appealing for upper-middle-class teens. Populars, and to a lesser extent geeks, shop in San Francisco as well as the high-end malls of Silicon Valley.

On a trip I took to Valley Fair Mall with popular girls from Mercer, anything in the realm of retail seemed possible. In this gleaming bastion of consumption we glided along the polished marble and faced tough decisions of where to begin shopping. Although they had nothing specific to purchase, Shabana, Tara, and their two friends were armed with their parents' credit cards and ready to buy at a moment's notice. We wandered in and out of high-end clothing and shoe stores as they pointed out items that friends of theirs had, or how certain styles were imitations of apparel worn on television shows and music videos. After nearly two hours of surveying material, we adjourned to the food court, where the girls panned the room for boys to rate and fashion transgressions to critique. When upper-middle-class teens dress in Desi outfits, they emulate the looks of Bollywood stars they consider stylish, especially Rani Mukherjee and Preity Zinta. They choose gossamer, resplendent silks in light colors, wear subtle but visible makeup, and straighten their hair or wear it in a neat up-do.

Shopping reaches frenzied proportions around prom, especially for girls.[5] Talk about this formal dance starts soon after New Year's and continues ceaselessly until well after the event. Girls study dresses and hairstyles, shop devotedly, have their hair done, and accessorize to the last detail. Some Desi girls eschew prom dress madness in favor of wearing Desi clothes. Whereas several years ago this may have seemed FOBby, recent trends set by Bollywood stars as well as eastward-looking American celebrities have recoded it as tight. Indeed, this generation of Desi teenagers grew up watching Madonna chant "Om Shanti" and present Grammy awards in a sari-like garment with her forehead adorned with bindis and hands decorated with *mehendi* (henna).[6] Seizing on the cachet of a look emulated by the pop star Gwen Stefani and others, Desi girls value saris, lehengas, and other Desi outfits as potential fashion statements. Not only can blouses and hemlines be altered to fit current trends, but apparel can also be accessorized in distinctive ways. For special events such as prom and other school dances, wearing Desi clothes is growing in popularity as an alternative to the traditional prom dress.

Attending and accessorizing for prom is a topic of ongoing discussion and obsession. While many FOBby girls are forbidden from attending because their parents are uncomfortable with its coed, nocturnal character, others manage to convince their parents by bringing along a chaperone (which I ended up being for several teens). Once teens are permitted to attend, the unending quest for a dress begins. Unlike upper-middle-class popular girls who shop for couture dresses in San Francisco boutiques, middle-class FOB and geek girls face a far more challenging set of circumstances: they have to find a dress that fits not only their small budget, but also their body in a way that covers them sufficiently to please their parents.

On a prom dress shopping trip to Eastridge Mall, middle-class geek girls Aaliya and Sunita tried to remain motivated. With prom less that two months away, they were unsuccessful at other malls and were worried that they had waited too long to sift through racks of JCPenney and the smaller boutiques. Although their parents suggested that they should wear Indian clothes, they did not want to. When their friend Veena had decided to go this route, Sunita warily remarked, "Even my little sister said no, everyone will laugh at me!" Moreover, they had to worry about coordinating with their clique, as there could be no duplicate colors within their circle of friends. After deciding which color they would each wear, they began the process of trying on numerous dresses that were either too big or unflattering. To worsen their anxiety, they ran into a couple of friends from school who were already picking up dresses they had left for alteration.

When prom day finally arrived, they had found satisfactory dresses but were unable to take their eyes off their friend Veena. She had decided to create her own Desi bling outfit out of a resplendent pink and gold lehenga. She had collaborated with her mother, who was able to alter the skirt to be less voluminous than a regular lehenga and the blouse by switching the cap sleeves to gold spaghetti straps. With a matching bindi and fresh flowers in her up-do, Veena stood out and was admired by others at her prom. This lesson was not lost on Aaliya or Sunita, who also noted the cluster of admirers around geek girl Ananya, who arrived in a bright red sari with copious zari (gold embroidery) and bling jewelry dangling from her ears, wrists, and fingers. Like most Desi girls and boys who confidently arrive at school events in Desi clothes, these prom-goers were objects of envy, not ridicule.

For upper-middle-class girls, the main challenge is finding a distinctive dress. One girl at Mercer explained to me, "Because junior prom is a month earlier than our prom, all the juniors get their dresses at Macy's and it gets really picked over because they don't restock with new dresses and you don't want to have the same dress as someone else. A lot of people go to San Francisco for their dresses." Several girls related their competitive shopping experiences in downtown San Francisco on their quest for a unique prom dress. Uninterested in this rat race, Shabana proudly explained that she is wearing a $30 chiffon sari and is making her own jewelry. She gushed, "It's so tight! I'm making this peacock feather on a leather band for a necklace. Last year I spent so much money on this dress—$250 for a dress that I can't ever wear again for a school function. It was such a waste, and I didn't even have a good time. This year I am wearing a sari." Although Shabana's parents could have easily afforded a $250 dress, she opted for a more distinctive style of her own.

While prom shopping and shopping in general are major teenage preoccupations, elements of Desi bling that interest them as much, if not more, are cars, electronics, and other markers of a tricked-out lifestyle.

MATERIAL CULTURE AND LANGUAGE USE

As the discussion of consumption and Desi bling illustrates, objects in cultural context communicate social meanings. Indeed, objects are described as having social lives (Appadurai 1986), biographies (Kopytoff 1986), and even agency (Gell 1998; Latour 1993). The social power of objects can endure beyond the owner to others who are connected to it (Weiner 1992). While upper-middle-class Desis can easily acquire cars, electronics, and other types of Desi bling, middle-class Desis may need to form other types of relationships with the objects they desire. Language practices are instrumental to this process, as they mediate people's relationships with objects and with one another in the context of consumption. Linkages between the material and linguistic dimensions of the sign speak to this complex relationship (Voloshinov 1973), and connections between language and material culture are explored through metaphor (Tilley 1999), semiotic ideologies (Keane 2003), accent (Cavanaugh 2005), and even the inadequacy of words to describe relationships with objects effectively (Miller 1998b). Yet, how can language use aid in forming relationships with prestigious objects that one does not own?

Consider the following case. One sunny day, Meru and Jasbir were about to visit their relatives who lived across the street in their middle-class San Jose neighborhood when I arrived at their house. Pulling me out of my car, Meru squealed, "Come on! You have to come with us see the new baby and CLK!" and led me to her aunt's house. After congratulating her aunt and uncle on their baby, I quietly admitted to Meru and Jasbir that I could not remember who CLK could be from the many Kapoor family events I had attended. Highly amused, Jasbir exclaimed, "Who? What are you talking about?" Meru laughed, "The CLK! The Mercedes Benz CLK convertible. Don't you remember our cousin Sim's graduation party? Sim's dad grabbed the mike and yelled, 'Your real present isn't here yet! CLK, baby, CLK!'" The Mercedes Benz CLK convertible, affectionately referred to by Meru, Jasbir, and now me simply as "CLK," received nearly as much adoration and attention as the new baby who joined the family around the same time.

CLK does not garner notoriety by simply sitting in a driveway next to the Lincoln Navigator Sim's father bought himself or by cruising the congested roadways of Silicon Valley. Rather, its most widespread fame comes from talk about it. Four types of language use are instrumental in understanding the connection between CLK and extended members of the Kapoor family: referentiality, indexicality, objectification, and metaconsumption. These types of language use are important because although Meru and Jasbir do not own CLK, they nonetheless develop a relationship to it through words and images. Such types of language use are crucial for middle-class Desis such as the Kapoors, who are invested in achieving a Desi bling lifestyle even when they do not have the means to do so. Referentiality is a type of language use that directly refers to that which it describes. When Meru and Jasbir talk about the CLK that is sitting in their cousin's driveway across the street, they are speaking referentially about this car. They create narratives to describe the CLK in a variety of ways, including telling its biography or specific character (Kopytoff 1986) and what is meaningful about it to them.

By contrast, indexical language use allows Meru and Jasbir to allude to the broader sense of style CLK connotes. Indexicality is a linguistic function that enables speakers to subtly point to complex notions and signal entire social systems of meaning without having to explain them directly (Silverstein 2003).[7] Indexical references are always contextual. In this case, even a massed-produced automobile like CLK has a unique significance in this social circle in comparison to identical CLKs elsewhere. CLK indexes a bling lifestyle that members of the Kapoor family might have only dreamed of when they worked in peach orchards in Yuba City. In contrast to an upper-middle-class Desi who might own the same car, the biography of this CLK is particular tò the Kapoors' family history and standing in their community.

Through indexicality, the objectification of CLK becomes socially significant. Objectifications are externalized meanings and values subjects create about objects in social context (Myers 2001; see also Irvine 1989; Latour 1993). Drawing on Daniel Miller (1987), Fred Myers (2001: 20) writes, "In objectification, cultural objects externalize values and meanings embedded in social processes, making them available, visible, or negotiable for further action by subjects." Objectification can be understood as a process in which an object becomes or is recognized as socially meaningful. It can also be regarded as a noun, as the socially and verbally produced meaning of an object in a certain setting. Although objectifications are not generally thought to perdure apart from the object itself and beyond the social context in which they are generated, I argue that through talk, certain objectifications can be created and circulated in lieu of the object itself.

Objectifications can potentially confer status to those who are able to affiliate with them by speaking about them directly or indexing them through talk. Highly valued objects such as CLK are instrumental in connoting prestige. If CLK itself can connote status, can the objectification of it do so as well when it circulates? It may seem paradoxical that people affiliate with objects without actually possessing them, and that such claims would be recognized as socially meaningful. This appropriation of objectifications is characterized by a degree of reflexivity often associated with speech practices. Michael Silverstein (1996b: 193) notes that pragmatics refers to "the meanings of linguistic signs relative to their communicative function" and identifies types of language that enable speakers to reflect on their utterances. "Metasemantic" speech events, for example, are moments when speakers reflect on the meaning of their own speech, while "metapragmatics" allow for an analogous conceptualization of the pragmatic structure of language (Silverstein 1996b: 216; see also Silverstein 1993).

Such a logic of reflexivity—where speakers analyze how language is used to produce a particular utterance—draws attention to additional dimensions of meaning that can be extracted from a speech act, as well as the potential power of these "meta" processes in shaping future language use. While consumption practices refer to meanings created by the circulation of objects through display in particular social contexts, I call the creation and circulation of objectifications, rather than the objects themselves, through talk "metaconsumption" (Shankar 2006). Through metaconsumption, objects, as well as objectifications, can confer prestige.

In metaconsumption, the objectification, rather than the object itself, is shared, circulated, and consumed. This objectification can impart status to and shape identity for those who are able to lay claim to it through language. CLK and other tight cars, as well as large-screen televisions, massive stereo systems, and similar objects with large personalities, are highly valued in middle-class Desi communities. Although that afternoon I had the opportunity of meeting CLK in person, many family and community members' most frequent interactions with the car is through its appearance in videos and photographs.

For events big and small, photos and videos capture everything from the first passengers who emerge from their cars to the last dance of the event. Youth and families carefully document family events and repeatedly review them with family and friends. In this way, owners as well as nonowners of commodities can form relationships with these objects by relying on borrowed, rented, or even imagined encounters with them. Desi families watch VHS and DVD productions of weddings and birthday and graduation parties with the remote control close at hand to pause and rewind for extended commentary on particular guests and events. The remote holder is also in charge of forwarding through parts not worthy of commentary—usually speeches, religious ceremonies, and dining.

This careful manipulation of visuals enables the most effective commentary: distilled talk about elements worthy of metaconsumption. At one such video viewing, I was able to revisit an event I had initially forgotten: the verbal gifting of CLK to Sim by his father. The professionally produced videotape captured every aspect of Sim's graduation party at a restaurant with about two hundred guests. Seven hours of dancing, eating, gifting, and gossiping had been edited into a slick production with music and special effects. This product was so polished that I could barely recognize it as the event I had attended, until I unfortunately spotted myself on the dance floor. During the screening, viewers narrated myriad details about the clothing, cars, and other objects pictured within. Producing and narrating visual documentation enables people to identify particular objects as Desi bling and verbally link themselves to these items vis-à-vis relationships with their owner.

Community Contexts of Consumption • As indexes of Desi bling, cars are a consistent point of focus and commentary. Talk about certain types of objects, such as new cars or televisions, is far more common than talk about jewelry or other items they may have inherited—ostensibly heirlooms. People who own these latter items usually display them during weddings and other special events, but the items are seldom discussed in everyday conversation as objects of prestige. While their value is acknowledged, they do not seem to have the same cachet. This is due in part to the fact that their value is not as easy to ascertain as a new Mercedes, which is unequivocally agreed to be a marker of status in a way family jewelry or a sari may not be.[8] Indeed, the centrality of automobiles in social life is not to be underestimated in California (Miller 2001). Like many Californians, Desis are entranced by automobiles and note their importance in the construction of style. Upper-middle-class teens routinely receive cars of their choosing for their sixteenth birthdays and as graduation presents. The student parking lot at Mercer High School is crammed with new Audis, Acuras, vw Beetles, and custom cars with high-end sound systems. While most middle-class teens at Waverly and Greene do not have new cars, or cars of any age for that matter, they talk about new cars they hope to own as well as vintage automobiles that they want to lower and detail.[9]

Not only do youth and their families discuss the cars themselves, but they associate people in their community with specific automobiles. The Kapoors, like others in their community, routinely display visual media for friends and family who visit and accompany these viewings with verbal narrations and extensive commentary on the documented event. Associations with particular objectifications affect social status for families within their community. During the viewing, Meru and her younger brother were especially taken with their older cousin's new red Audi convertible, whose arrival at the start of Sim's party they replayed several times. Their close relationship to this cousin is included in the narration. This verbal link, which relates the noteworthy Audi and the Kapoors' closeness to its owner, enabled the Kapoors to establish a relationship to the Audi as well. Verbally referencing their cousin's Audi, either while viewing its image or in other social contexts by referring to it as "our cousin's Audi" or "our family's Audi," indexes Desi bling that Meru and her brother cannot afford but have some access to through their close relationship to their cousin. As the objectification of the Audi as a Kapoor family car circulates through narratives and video, the aim and expectation of this verbal strategy is for Meru and her brother to become associated with the Audi and the prestige it communicates in their community.

Indexing status through these types of verbal and visual objectifications is usually quite deliberate. The Audi and its owner managed to arrive during window of time when they were likely be captured on video. They pulled up to the front of the venue where the videographer was stationed rather than simply parking and walking to the entrance. Indeed, the potential status of being captured on video is important to many middle-class Desis who feel they have an object worth their community's attention. Mrs. Kalra, the mother of Simran, Preeti, and two younger girls, confided in me her long-standing desire to own a Lexus. The Kalras are a middle-class observant Sikh family who follow the rules of Sikhism and do not cut their hair. Despite these restrictions, the two sisters wear their hair up in fashionable styles with numerous accessories and care a great deal about Desi bling. The family moved from Yuba City to Sunnyvale, but ultimately found a home they could afford in San Jose in 1986. Mrs. Kalra recounted that the United States has been a good place to live but a hard place for her and her husband to make ends meet. She explained, "When I came [from India] my husband didn't have that much money. It was really hard for us when we had a kid and had to pay off the house money. I called my mom to take care of the kids, and that was better, I started working." Looking up at the numerous pictures of Sikh saints on her living room walls, she sighed, "It was hard before, but with God's grace it's better now." Not being able to afford a Lexus has never stopped Mrs. Kalra from wanting one. She conceded that with modest incomes and four daughters to care for, a new Lexus was out of their price range.

One Sunday afternoon I waited in the strip mall parking lot of the restaurant where I was to meet Mrs. Kalra and two of her daughters for her niece's *sangeet* (a prewedding event). As I was on the lookout for their preowned Toyota Camry, I watched the videographer pan across the parking lot to focus on a gleaming gold Lexus sedan. Mrs. Kalra rolled down her window to wave at the camera while her daughters slowly emerged from the car. Like others in her community, Mrs. Kalra was interested in having her arrival in the Lexus documented in order to display her Desi bling to extended family and friends who would later watch this video. Her daughters were equally invested in being taped emerging from the Lexus dressed in their Desi finery. After pulling into a parking spot, she proudly exclaimed, "We got a Lexus!" Although the event inside the restaurant was starting, we lingered in the parking lot to appreciate the car's myriad features. When I asked how she was able to finally get her dream car, Mrs. Kalra explained, "We bought a preowned one from 1995. It has eighty thousand miles but it looks new, doesn't it?" Mrs. Kalra's dream of owning Desi bling had finally become a reality. Objectifications of the Lexus, which perhaps only other Californians could recognize as being preowned, circulate as members of the Kalra family discuss details of the event at school with their peers and with friends and family who come to their house to watch the video. Other relatives can also potentially affiliate themselves with the Lexus through its appearance in the video and their relationship with the Kalras.

As people talk about cars, stereos, and televisions in association with certain families, questions of ownership can even fade out of the conversation. Indeed, as objectifications circulate, ownership becomes less important and other types of associations become more central. Rented automobiles are especially popular during special events. Arriving at a wedding or prom in a tight car is a marker of prestige. While we were watching a video of Meru's uncle's wedding, she excitedly described how she and her cousins designed the *barat* (the groom's horseback procession), and explained, "These American horses get scared by the firecrackers and noise, so we decided to do it different. We rented these hella nice cars and drove in them instead." As we watched the video, one of numerous copies that had been freshly dubbed and distributed to friends and families in the region and beyond, Meru quickly forwarded through the religious prayers in the beginning to the automobile procession traveling one mile to the gurdwara. "We all had our bling on that day," she recalled, pointing to the attractive motorcade and occupants of each car dressed in their finery while her brother and mother chimed in with comments. Although only a few members of the Kapoor family can afford to own such cars, it is a source of great status that they were able to perform this barat in this style. In this metaconsumptive practice, objectifications of the rented cars embellished by talk during viewing enable the Kapoor family to become known for staging a far more prestigious wedding procession than would otherwise have been possible.

Home electronics are also coveted markers of status, especially for those who want to bolster their reputation in their community. For Janvi Chawla's family, having the image of their family's Desi bling circulate to their daughter's future in-laws was very important. The Chawlas, unlike the Kalras and Kapoors, have accrued relatively little wealth in Silicon Valley. Being a single-income family in a small San Jose home, luxury automobiles were beyond their reach. They did, however, decide to purchase a giant projection-screen TV as a gift for their son's twenty-eighth birthday. Janvi told her friends at school that she and her family had recently gone shopping and bought a TV for her brother, as well as furniture intended to impress her older sister's future in-laws during her upcoming engagement ceremonies. When she invited her friends and me to come over and see these new acquisitions, she admitted that her brother had rejected the television on the basis of its gargantuan size, and that it still resided at her house.

As we entered her home and removed our shoes, Janvi gave us a mere moment to glance at the new sofa set before she herded us toward the new television. In the corner of the small kitchen that once housed a dining table and chairs sat a giant projection-screen television. The entire kitchen had been rearranged to accommodate it; the dining table was pushed into a corner and the chairs exiled to various bedrooms. Facing the TV was the old sofa from the living room, as well as a mat and cushions on the floor, together serving as a makeshift eating and viewing area. Now a focal point of their small home, the television had transformed the Chawla kitchen into the central video and Bollywood film viewing location for their family.

For the Chawlas, the projection television became a marker that potentially elevated their status to their daughter's future in-laws. A few months later, Mrs. Chawla told Janvi to invite me to watch a video of events of her daughter's wedding, which I had attended. "Baito, baito [Sit down]," Mrs. Chawla said to me, motioning at the kitchen sofa as Janvi inserted the videotape and turned on the large TV. Although I attended the wedding, I now saw it from a very different perspective. While I recognized several extended family members whom I had met, as a viewer my eye was continually drawn back to the television, which served as the backdrop of nearly every shot. While we watched, Mrs. Chawla instructed Janvi to pause at particular moments as she talked about new members of her family and things they had said about the Chawla home. She especially remarked on compliments the television had received from her daughter's new in-laws, and recalled that she had announced to her guests that it was a gift for the groom and his new bride.

The television appeared to be a central personality in various videos of events held in their home, and talk about it circulated along with the videotapes. Even though most viewers of the wedding video do not have the opportunity to see the image of the television on the machine itself, they likely hear of its biography, which Mrs. Chawla takes great trouble to circulate widely. In this metaconsumptive practice, objectifications of the TV circulate through the video as well as talk about how and why it was acquired. The social life of this objectification, like that of the Audi, the Lexus, and CLK, circulates well beyond those who see these objects in person or speak to their owners directly.

While owning Desi bling or affiliating with objects owned by extended family is the preferred option for displaying status, there is a third possibility: renting. Rented sound systems and automobiles, often newer and more powerful than those people own, are a readily available way to create a specific style and aesthetic for an event. Though people readily admit that these objects are rented, they are nonetheless considered to add value to an event. Like the cars rented for the Kapoor wedding that accompanied their own cars, other objects are also desired in this way. Stereo systems rented for house parties are reminders that small homes can still sound and appear large for an evening. During a joint birthday party for Meru and her cousin, who were both turning eighteen, their other cousins decided to rent a sound system that they described as "off da' hook" (amazing). The party was held at her cousin's family's modest, one-story home in a congested neighborhood. Family and friends packed into the small living room; overflow was accommodated in the garage and front yard. Guests spent the early part of the evening admiring and compliment-ing each other's outfits, jewelry, and up-do hairstyles while one of Meru's cousins walked around with a camcorder. As people ate and mingled, the male cousins began to cart in sound equipment and set it up. The sound system occupied a significant portion of the room and displaced several guests into the garage and outdoors. The speakers—powerful enough for a nightclub—nearly scraped the ceilings after they were placed on their stands.

Remixed bhangra music soon began to pump through the room, caus-ing balloons to burst and young children to cry. Sound reverberated up and down their street as the room quickly filled up with any and all ambulatory guests, who danced well into the night. As with numerous other videotaped events, this one grew in stature as the video and narra-tives of the party circulated through their community. Although I attended the party, on my next visit to the Kapoor house I was treated to a full photo and video show about the party, including a running commentary on noteworthy material aspects, of which the sound system was lauded as a key feature. When family friends who were unable to attend the party stop by the Kapoor house, they are invited to view the video and are debriefed on aspects of the party that make it memorable. Remarks about the stereo index a broader set of stylistic concerns for the Kapoors. For this extended family interested in being known in their community for conducting themselves and hosting events that epitomize Desi bling, the rented stereo accomplished this goal.

CONCLUSION

For Desi teens and their families, material culture is one of the most tangible and immediate ways of signifying success and style to one's clique and community.[10] Material culture enables both adults and teens to create alliances and differentiate themselves from others. A wide range of material and linguistic preoccupations and practices defines Desi bling. Owning Desi bling or indexing it through metaconsumptive practices constitutes style and connotes prestige in this context. Desi bling offers insight into why people value certain items enough to not only own them, but to link themselves to their objectifications. Laying claim to objectifications of Desi bling through family or rented objects is not as prestigious as ownership but is nonetheless highly valued. Metaconsumptive practices index family-based, rather than individual, identities. The type of prestige garnered by an objectification is seldom sought for an individual; more often such attempts affect an entire nuclear, if not extended, family. Instead of creating an exclusionary relationship through consumption, metaconsumption enables those who do not possess certain objects to have some connection to these objects in the eyes of their community.

Desi bling works because it is intergenerational rather than youth-exclusive. Youth and their families care deeply about Desi bling, for it shapes their goals and aspirations and defines who they want to be to peers and community. Especially in Silicon Valley, where narratives of prosperity and progress abound while middle-class Desis contend with rising home prices and costs of living, the pressure to appear successful to one's community is especially strong. This pressure to succeed is impressed upon Desi teens and shapes visions of their future. People acquire and display objects or affiliate themselves with objectifications primarily to gain respect and elevate their social standing *within* their own community rather than to seek entry into a different group altogether. Even middle-class Desi families who have the means to move into an upper-middle-class community opt not to do so because other values prevail. Indeed, ties of family, caste, religion, and language trump consumption as a basis for social affiliation. Although contests of status occur within these communities, Desis rarely leave them altogether. In these ways, Desi teens use material culture and language to shape the sensibilities of the communities they stand to inherit. In the upcoming chapter, I focus on language use as another marker of style that is premised in intergenerational as well as peer-exclusive connections.

4

DESI FASHIONS OF SPEAKING

Abhijeet is a popular boy at Waverly who has lots of Desi friends but prides himself on not belonging exclusively to one clique. "Drama!" Abhijeet exclaimed. "That's what you get with Indian people. I have no idea why, that's why I try to stay away from them. High school immaturity maybe? I kick it [with] whoever I think is cool." Abhijeet and his friend Gurdas kick it with football players, Desis, Latinos, and anyone else they find good company. Abhijeet jokes that this means everyone except his younger sister, Geetu, who just started as a freshman. For Abhijeet, being cool means kicking it with family, speaking in Punjabi, and participating in bhangra competitions. He asserted, "I feel comfortable speaking in Punjabi with friends. If you want to say something behind someone's back, it's good for that or for joking around. Some guys tease you about being a FOB or something like that, but with those [people], I make them feel stupid for not knowing Punjabi. But for the ones who are cool with it, you just speak. It's a language, just like English. The guys are not uncomfortable with it—it's the smart ones who speak for themselves. Having a second language is cool!" An avid dancer, he choreographs and competes in local competitions with his friends and cousins. Abhijeet's parents were born in Punjab and came to Yuba City after they were married. They moved to San Jose because they are well educated and wanted more challenging work, or, as Abhijeet puts it, "Both of them have BAS, they can do a lot better than going out and picking peaches." In Silicon Valley, his father is an engineer and his mother is a technician. Abhijeet explains that his upper-middle-class Sikh family is not very religious, although they tried to send him to Sunday religion classes at the gurdwara. He soon quit, jokingly explaining, "Sunday is basketball day and football day. If God is so smart, why would he schedule all that on the same day?"

Language use, whether considered FOBby, tight, or somewhere in be-tween, is an integral part of Desi teen culture and is linked to different types of style and success. Desi teens use language to share humor and insider knowledge and reaffirm bonds of friendship and family. Language use helps define whether youth are FOBby or tight, the types of choices they make in schools, and how they relate to their families and commu-nities intergenerationally. Desi teens use language in ways that vary ac-cording to religion, social class, social clique, and gender, and ideologies of monolingualism affect Desis of different class backgrounds. How youth decide to speak a heritage language, with whom, and how this positions them at school is linked to cultural capital (Bourdieu 1985).

Desi teen "fashions of speaking" (Whorf 1956) serve as expressions of identity and solidarity while also acting as markers of racial otherness in school contexts. Speaking a heritage language in an increasingly mono-lingual America draws attention to the contradictions between the way language is valorized by discourses of multiculturalism as a marker of culture with a capital "C" and the ways it is received in day-to-day contexts outside of performances. America has long been hostile toward languages other than English, and immigrants are expected to relinquish their heritage language in favor of English in the public sphere. Early Desis were especially subject to this constraint, as theirs was a far less tolerant age than the post–civil rights era that later Desi immigrants enjoy. Indeed, in recent decades the prevailing sentiment about heritage languages has shifted somewhat, enabling Desi teenagers of today a more open and encouraging relationship with their heritage language. Yet despite rhet-oric about multiculturalism and multilingualism, the choices speakers make and the consequences of these decisions are far from straightfor-ward. The peer-exclusive as well as intergenerational ways Desi teens use language shape their cliques and communities while also affecting their positioning at school.

LANGUAGE USE IN DIASPORAS

Desi teen language use shapes identity, cliques, and diasporic commu-nities in a number of ways. Language use, rather than simply language, is a central aspect of shaping social life for Desi teens in Silicon Valley. Saus-sure (2000) and numerous others have noted the stark difference between language in its pristine, complete form and language as used by speakers in contexts governed by power dynamics. This difference is especially acute in diasporic contexts. While language is a routine topic of inquiry in migration and diaspora studies, approaches to its study vary widely. Whether or not a generational cohort speaks a language has been statistically quantified (Rumbaut 2002; Zhou 2004; Zhou and Bankston 1996), but *how* and *in what contexts* it is spoken has rarely been examined.[1] Studying how people use language, rather than treating language as a static entity to be retained or lost, shifts the focus to how youth speak it, their ways of speaking, and the consequences of their speech practices (Harris 2006; Heller 1999; Rymes 2001; Urchiuoli 1999; Zentella 1997). Along these lines, emergent work on language use in the South Asian diaspora (Eisenlohr 2006; K. Hall 2002; Rampton 1995; Shankar 2004b) and Asian Pacific American communities (Chun 2001; Lo and Reyes 2004; Reyes 2006) investigates these issues.

Language Ideologies • Language use is guided by language ideologies, which are cultural representations of language in the social world (Gal and Woolard 2001; Kroskrity 2000; Schieffelin, Woolard, and Kroskrity 1998). Mediating between social structures and linguistic forms, such ideologies are not just about language; they link language to identity, community formation, and social meaning. Language ideologies illustrate diasporic speakers' predispositions toward language that travel with them. A long-standing tradition of multilingualism prevails in South Asia, one that stands in stark contrast to the American ideological norm of English monolingualism (Crawford 1992, 2000; Silverstein 1996a). Over the millennia, the Indian Subcontinent has absorbed waves of invaders and settlers, along with their languages. During the colonial period, the British introduced English without seeking to eliminate local languages.[2] Unlike French colonizers who instituted educational instruction primarily in French, the British offered English-language schools alongside local-language schools, a dichotomous system that still exists today (Cohn 1985; Khubchandani 1983).

Central to this particular multilingual ideology is that different languages are appropriate modes of communication for different interactions and domains. South Asia currently has fifteen official languages and more than fifteen hundred others that are spoken (Jacobsen and Kumar

2004: ix–xxiv). Beginning in childhood and continuing through schooling and beyond, speakers learn and use a variety of languages as well as registers defined by contexts of use. For example, a native Tamil-speaking child living in Bombay might speak in Tamil with her family in the morning, in Marathi to the rickshaw driver taking her to school, in English in class, code-switch between English and Hindi with peers during lunch time, and produce a dialogue for French class.

English deserves special mention in the Desi context, as it is used alongside other languages in South Asia but arguably has an elevated social power as a means of entry into prestigious careers and higher education (Bhatt 2001; Pennycook 2007). Chaise LaDousa (2005) notes the tension concerning whether Hindi or English should be India's national language and if a "one nation, one language" model would be suitable for India. As the language of the Empire, globalization, and of diasporic locales such as the United Kingdom, British Canada, Australia, and the United States, English is imbued with more power and status than other Desi languages (Kachru 2000), a distinction that is significant in diasporic settings. Recent work on Asian American language use has noted the salience of English as a language of investigation in diasporic contexts and advocates for deeper study of English use in favor of documenting a linear retention or loss of heritage language (Lo and Reyes 2004). In these ways, English is a valued tool in identity-making practices for Desi teens and is central to this discussion of language practices.

Despite English's elevated status, heritage language use plays a crucial, though not straightforward, role in shaping diasporic identity (Eisenlohr 2006; Farr 2006; Shankar 2004b). Language use in the South Asian diaspora is so varied that general observations tend to obscure more than they inform. For instance, Patrick Eisenlohr's (2006) study of "ethnolinguistic belonging" in Mauritius, where Hindi is highly valued, presents different norms and usages of heritage and local languages than Ben Rampton's (1995) work on Bengali youth "crossing" by speaking different languages and registers in the United Kingdom. Such examples underscore the wide range of language politics and practices in different locations of the South Asian diaspora. Language use and class are closely linked, especially in those locales where Desis of different class backgrounds are all subject to the same linguistic norms and expectations.

Bilingualism in Silicon Valley • According to the 1990 U.S. Census, over 70 percent of Desis in the United States are bilingual in their heritage language and English (Garcia 1997: 4); the 2000 Census confirms these trends. About 95 percent of youth in my study understand their heritage language; about 75 percent are conversationally fluent in it. While parents educated in South Asia learned at least three languages, their children raised in the United States usually speak only two: their heritage language and English. In addition to this bilingualism, children acquire linguistic skills that reflect a wide range of communicative competencies that are linked to different social identities, activities, and practices. For example, although many families do not speak Hindi, teens develop varying levels of competence in Hindi by watching Bollywood films. This rarely means they can converse fluently in Hindi, but they are able to incorporate dialogues, phrases, and song lyrics from these films into conversation. While most Bollywood films are in Hindi, native speakers of Gujarati, Punjabi, and Bengali as well as Tamil, Telugu, and Malayalam avidly watch them with subtitles.

Religion, class, and gender contribute to how teens relate to their heritage language and use it with family, community, and peers. Muslim families emphasize the importance of learning Arabic to read the Koran in Arabic as well as speaking their community's language. They are members of musjids whose constituencies generally speak Bengali (from Bangladesh), Urdu (from India or Pakistan), or Hindi (from Fiji). For Muslims from India and Pakistan especially, learning the proper forms of conversational etiquette and address in Urdu is extremely important and relevant to everyday interaction. In addition to going to musjid every Friday evening, many young Muslims attend weekend religious instruction, which includes language tutoring in Urdu.

Parents teach their children cultural and religious material in Urdu and make a point of maintaining Urdu as the home language. Azra recounts that she learned Arabic when she was six and has been going to religious school for about ten years. Her family immigrated from Rawalpindi, Pakistan, and she was born in Silicon Valley. She uses Arabic to read the Koran, something her father has told her to do in her free time, but she uses other languages for speaking. She explained, "We speak Farsi, it's Urdu and Punjabi mixed. It's a whole different dialect. My friend speaks Punjabi, but if she hears me and my mom speaking she will want to know what we are saying. Its like Hindi and Urdu have different words, it's like that. We all speak in the family. My friends, if they speak Urdu to me, I'll sort of know how to speak it. Mostly at school we always use English." Like Azra, other Muslim youth learn Arabic but speak Urdu, Farsi, Bengali, or Hindi.

Similarly, Punjabi is central in Sikh households. Many Sikh youth go to gurdwara weekly or biweekly and participate in casual conversation in Punjabi as they wait in line for *langar*, the meal offered after prayer. The San Jose gurdwara additionally offers a Sikh summer camp at which youth receive two concentrated weeks of religious and language instruction. When Sikh parents and their children speak about language, they often link it to religion, stating that it is a way to stay connected to Sikhism. Mrs. Kalra, Preeti and Simran's mother, wants her children to be fluent in Punjabi: "I want them to speak my language, at least in the house, so that they can communicate with my mom, with my parents. . . . I want them to try to teach their kids; at least they will understand where we come from. Even though we're here I still want them to be part of India." All four of Mrs. Kalra's daughters speak Punjabi, but Simran and Preeti are more fluent than their two younger sisters.

Among Desis, Hindu teens are the least likely to be fluent in their native language and seldom speak it with peers. Many of their parents are fluent in English and so there is no need to use a heritage language to communicate. Moreover, no one language predominates in Hindu temples, leaving time in these spaces, and religious study more broadly, linguistically dispersed. Some temples offer classes in Sanskrit, a language no one speaks and few teens understand. English or another regional language, such as Hindi or Tamil, is used to communicate. Many Hindu families choose to visit the temple closest to them regardless of religious sect or language spoken by the priests. Christian teens find themselves in the same situation, attending services in English. With no linguistic uniformity and less formal language instruction, Hindu and Christian teens use their heritage language with those outside of their community far less frequently.[3]

Desi teens from communities whose language is not well represented have far less opportunity to use their heritage language with their peers. Without a critical mass, teens whose families are from South India, Orissa, or smaller areas with less of a presence in Silicon Valley have far fewer opportunities to speak their heritage language. As a Tamil speaker, geek girl Lata is at a disadvantage for participating in conversations in languages other than English with her peers at Greene. Although she speaks Tamil with family and community members, she lamented, "I never get to speak in Tamil to anyone else as I am the only person here. . . . I feel horrible about that. I learned Punjabi because of my best friend. Whenever she talks to friends or family, I pick up words." Likewise, Ananya, also a geek, is the only one in her clique who speaks Oria. She has had to create alternative ways of establishing shared language practices with Sunita, Aaliya, and the rest of what she calls "the Indian Clan": "We would speak in Hindi, just because it was something that we would understand and nobody else would understand, and it was kind of a good way to practice." For Ananya and others like her, speaking Hindi is the only non-English option for a group of friends who want to connect in a South Asian language.

Biracial youth usually have less language exposure and fluency in their heritage language. Anji, an upper-middle-class girl at Mercer, has an Indian father and a Catholic mother who is half-Irish and half-Italian. She was one of the few kids in my study who did not grow up in a multilingual environment. She commented: "We speak mainly in English. When I was little, I had an Indian babysitter and I only spoke Hindi, but I wasn't learning English. My parents didn't want me to fall behind; they took me to an English-speaking babysitter because I knew so much more Hindi than English. Now I don't know very much. I feel bad [that] I don't understand it." Other kids whose parentage was a mix of Sikh and Chicano also have a different relationship with their heritage languages than those raised in bilingual homes where both parents speak the same heritage language.

Desi Community Contexts of Speaking • Speaking a heritage language at home is highly valued in many Desi communities in Silicon Valley. A great deal of social value is attached to teens being able to not only understand, but also participate and perform in a home language.[4] The extent to which this occurs varies according to teens' fluency in their heritage language as well as how much English is spoken at home. In family contexts, certain types of communication—especially humor, anger, affection, and gossip—are primarily expressed through a South Asian language. English, by contrast, is spoken to convey information about work or school.

Upper-middle-class and middle-class Desi teens use language differently from one another. Such variance is rooted both in the cultural capital of their families and in critical mass and clique tastes. Upper-middle-class parents who were educated in English-language schools, whether in South Asia or elsewhere, tend to speak English far more at home. In these families, parents generally feel comfortable in English and often speak to each other in a native language but speak to their kids in both languages. Their children by and large reply in English and speak English among themselves.

Teens can usually speak their family's native language and speak it at community gatherings or with grandparents who do not speak English, but otherwise they speak in English. Some mention that as they have gotten older they do not feel as comfortable as they used to speaking their heritage language. Dilip, an upper-middle-class boy, explained, "My parents usually speak in English, but when they want to yell at me or something, they start speaking in Hindi. Sometimes I don't know what they are saying! I understand it pretty well but I can't speak that well. I used to be fluent when I was younger, but forgot it." Dilip's mother regretfully added, "We used to speak in Hindi at home, not any more. They understand but do not speak now, especially Dilip, [he] is the worst. He does not even try speaking Hindi. He knows that I know he understands. It's easier to communicate in English. You get used to it and forget lots of Hindi words." In these upper-middle-class families, English can almost entirely replace the use of a heritage language, especially for Hindu teens.

Teens whose grandparents were their primary caregivers in early childhood were at one point fluent in their heritage language, since these elder relatives often speak little or no English. Umber described how having live-in grandparents has helped her keep up her language skills: "Mostly we talk Punjabi with my grandparents. The only English they understand is 'Shut up' because me and my brother fight a lot. I talk in English with my parents, unless they get mad." Other kids, however, recall that they became less fluent once their grandparents stopped being active caregivers. Madhu, a middle-class Sikh girl, admitted, "[Now] I speak Punjabi with my grandparents, with lots of 'ums' and 'ahs.' When I was younger it was easier. You go home and your grandparents are there taking care of you. Now we struggle more with speaking. Now we hardly speak it with our parents—they'll talk to us in Punjabi and we reply in English." Although their Punjabi is not quite as good as it once was, Madhu and Neetu are still able to communicate in this language when they need to.

Middle-class Desi teens display higher levels of spoken and comprehensive fluency in their heritage language than upper-middle-class teens. This is often so because at least one parent or live-in relative of a middle-class teen does not speak English fluently. These teens speak their heritage language to parents and elder relatives, and speak English to their siblings. For example, middle-class Sikh families predominantly speak Punjabi at home. Even adults who attended high school in Yuba City or elsewhere in California keep their Punjabi in continuous use through the solidarity of their community networks and the continuous arrival of Sikhs from South Asia and elsewhere, so much so that they seldom speak English to one another at home. Youth whose parents studied in local-language schools may be able to read, write, and comprehend English to varying degrees but may feel less comfortable speaking it. This situation is further complicated by those who emigrated from major cities, where they may have had more opportunities to speak English than those from smaller towns and villages, where English is seldom spoken.

Regardless of the language teens use to speak to their parents, they speak to their siblings and cousins in English. Amahl, a popular Muslim girl, commented, "I talk to my parents in Urdu, but not my brothers. I don't really speak it with friends at school. Sometimes with cousins." Similarly, Renu, a middle-class Sikh girl, explained, "We speak Punjabi at home with parents but English with sisters. My Punjabi got sort of messed up and broken because I speak in English so much." Some teens with young siblings, however, note that they are careful to speak in their heritage language to younger siblings in hopes that they will become fluent. Kareena, a middle-class Sikh girl, reported, "My parents really want us to know our traditions, our rituals, our language. They don't want us to forget who we are. We're not just American, we're Indo-American. So they expect us to know Punjabi at home. If there are words I don't know, I ask. I [try to] talk to my other siblings in English, but the youngest ones don't know how to speak Punjabi much. My mom understands English, but speaking it is harder, especially using bigger words." In these instances, older siblings play an important role in bridging the language gap between their parents and younger siblings.

DESI TEEN FASHIONS OF SPEAKING

Desi teens use language in a variety of creative ways. Three such language practices are code-switching, code-mixing, and the use of accented English. Code-switching is the process by which speakers alternate between two or more languages in conversation (Auer 1998; Gal 1987; Heller 1988; Milroy and Muysken 1995). One of the most common occurences of code-switching is when teens want to gossip about someone who does not understand the language, or, conversely, to make fun of each other directly. Code-mixing, by contrast, involves combining words and phrases in conversation from more than one language, often in patterns of tight alternation or even combining parts of words, while mainly speaking in one language. For example, while speaking mainly in English, a speaker might include words from Punjabi or Bengali or use a word that combines both Punjabi and English elements.[5]

In my study, code-mixing occurred especially among kids who are less fluent in speaking a particular language variety. These kids create shared knowledge bases from their particular language uses. Madhu and Neetu, for example, explained that while they sometimes speak in Punjabi when they do not want people to understand them, they more often use their own version of English and Punjabi. Neetu elaborated, "We put our 'ings' and 'eds' after every action—I was '*dekhing*' [looking], I was '*sunning*' [listening]. We both have the same level of speaking, so we can use it suddenly if we need to." Such group-specific talk functions as a form of insider language in the context of a range of other practices that contribute to the construction of Desi teen culture and cliques.

Using Indian-accented English is a popular linguistic choice for nearly all kids, but especially for upper-middle-class kids, who occasionally code-mix but rarely code-switch. More often, they use accented English and ways of speaking exclusive to their social group. Indian-accented English does not refer to any one South Asian language in particular, but is more of an invented, generic accent youth fashion after the language use of their parents and older relatives. FOB accents (Reyes 2007), "Mock Asian" (Chun 2004), and "Stylized Asian English" (Rampton 1995) all ridicule the nonstandard English associated with recent Asian immigrants. The character Apu on the television series *The Simpsons* has immortalized such an accent. Accents, as well as other types of references, can convey humor and establish in-group connectedness only if others are able to detect the intended indexical references.

Though direct uses of Indian-accented English can be understood and considered humorous by anyone, more complicated expressions require certain types of insider knowledge. Bivalent homophonic puns are one such area.[6] Like all puns, they are based on wordplay, often the kind that makes people wince and laugh despite themselves. These puns, however, are bivalent, in that they have meaning in two distinct languages (Woolard 1999). I use the term here in conjunction with homophones, words that are phonetically similar, if not identical, in both languages (or Indian accents of both languages).[7] Families are adept at using bivalent homophonic puns to share humor across generations. Especially for families who tend to speak less English, English words can be modified to fit the semantics of their heritage language. Umber, a middle-class girl whose family speaks Punjabi at home, recalls that when her uncle married a Brazilian woman named Raquel, the family had to rename her. She laughs that the only way her family could pronounce the name Raquel was "Rakhel," which sounded too much like the Punjabi word for mistress or prostitute. They renamed her Raveena, but smile in amusement when they recall her original name. Following and participating in such humor facilitates communication and affinities across generations.[8]

Sometimes youth make jokes at the expense of older generations. Sheetal, popular girl extraordinaire, told her friends and me about a humorous incident as we drove back from lunch at Burger King in her new silver Honda. Barely able to contain her laughter, Sheetal giggled about how her uncle, who lives in a pastoral region of California, had spotted a deceased cow in his neighbor's backyard and called to inform her. In a thick Indian accent, she mimicked, "There is a dead *gai* in your backyard!" She then inserted in her regular voice, "Because, you know, the Indian word for cow is *gai*," and once again switched back into the accent: "There is a dead *gai* in your backyard!" Waiting for the peals of laughter to die down, she completed the anecdote by explaining that when her uncle's neighbor started to get hysterical, he realized his error and stammered, "I mean cow! There is a dead cow in your backyard." Sheetal's use of Indian-accented English indexes her uncle's FOBby misuse of language and also relies on shared knowledge with her Desi friends and their ability to relate to that situation.

Occasionally, such puns are found and admired in media. One day at lunch, Harsimran, a middle-class Sikh boy, shared one of his favorite scenes from the film *American Desi* with his friends Uday and Ranvir. In the scene, Punjabi men in turbans dance at a party with a multiracial population. As they raise their arms and shake their shoulders, they emphatically shout a Punjabi chant: "Ho! Ho!" Harsimran imitated the dance while he impersonated the various voices for his friends: "They're all like, 'Ho! Ho!' [snapping his fingers in bhangra hand gestures] 'Ho?' [in African American English] 'Who you callin' a fuckin' ho?' Some Black lady goes, 'Who you fuckin' callin' ho?' " Uday and Ranvir laughed and joined in the chanting. Harsimran's reenactment of this movie scene, like Sheetal's telling of the "dead gai" joke, relates more than a humorous anecdote shared among friends. It is a verbal performance that demands particular kinds of linguistic knowledge. In Sheetal's telling of the joke, her friends begin laughing as soon as she finishes mimicking her uncle's first line, making her next statement, in which she explains the meaning of "gai," superfluous. The joke is effective because her friends immediately recognize the comic value in the bivalent homophonic pun gai/guy. Likewise, Harsimran, Uday, and Ranvir are entertained by the way the Punjabi word "ho" is a homophone for the American slang term, a shortened version of "whore" popularized by African American hip-hop artists. The pun is especially effective because an African American woman misrecognizes the shouting as an insult directed at her.

As these two examples indicate, bivalent homophones truly become puns during these contexts of retelling. Their double entendres are only elucidated and appreciated by those outside the original context of occurrence. Desi teens engaging in such linguistic practices must possess the bilingual competence to decipher the meaning of each individual term in order to appreciate the humor generated by the pun. Such mutual recognition allows bivalent homophonic punning to be an amusing language practice among these Desi teens.

Language Use in Cliques · Language use is an integral part of forming and maintaining cliques. In school, populars and geeks rarely code-switch and only occasionally code-mix in everyday conversation. Most feel that school is not an appropriate venue for speaking their heritage language. A few popular teens think differently on this matter. Like Abhijeet at the start of this chapter, popular teens who can speak well often do so proudly. By and large, however, most other popular and geek teens consider speaking more than a few phrases of their heritage language at school to be too FOBby.

FOBs vary among themselves on what the boundaries of language use should be. In everyday life and in media FOBby teens are acute purveyors of language. They routinely code-switch and code-mix in their conversations and pride themselves on their ability to do so. Teens use language not only to affirm clique boundaries, but also to test the limits of gendered expectations (Mendoza-Denton 2007; Woolard 1995). Even among FOBs, heritage language use is marked and gendered, and certain types of language are considered to be more appropriate for boys or girls. Along these lines, FOB registers are gendered as well. FOBby girls code-switch in English and Punjabi when they discuss Bollywood and other types of Desi media, or when they are conversing with one another about private or sensitive matters. By and large, their use of heritage language is restrained and personal. By contrast, boys' use is far more flamboyant and hypermasculine when they socialize among themselves (Cameron 1998), as with Harsimran's "ho" impersonation and the widespread use of profanity in general. Preeti, who speaks in Punjabi with her parents, relatives, and younger siblings but mainly in English with her sister Simran, explained that there are certain languages for certain moments. She speaks Punjabi with Simran and her friends at school, but "not all the time. If it's a Punjabi kind of feeling . . . [like] what happened or what they did or how someone looks, then you'll just talk in Punjabi. But if it's about school, it's English."

FOBs can be quite critical of those whom they consider less linguistically adept. When discussing the film *American Desi* one day during lunch at Greene High School, Pinki and Nidhi debated the authenticity of the female lead based on her linguistic skills. Pinki asserted that Nina is a believable character because she seems to have some knowledge of Indian culture but is also savvy about her American life. In response, Nidhi offered strong criticism of the character, arguing that although Nina claims to know all about Indian culture and teach it to others, "she says one line in Hindi and she can't even speak it right!"

Even Bollywood actors and actresses whose light hair and eyes make them look more White than Desi maintain their credibility by being able to speak Hindi fluently. Characters who do not claim authoritative cultural knowledge, however, are pardoned. For example, Nidhi and Pinki accepted that the male lead, Kris, in *American Desi* knows as little about Indian culture or language as he claims, and therefore his linguistic foibles and social gaffes are excused. Such critiques underscore the importance of language use in connecting the actors and actresses to the roles they play on screen. Speaking a heritage language with peers is valued only if one can speak it well. This, among other reasons, is why many upper-middle-class teens gravitate toward English while middle-class teens are more confident in their heritage language usage.

FOBby girls especially enjoy dialogue from Bollywood films and manage to work it into their everyday conversations. One day, during a fleeting morning break, Pinki tape-recorded a conversation for me between herself and Janvi, Renu, Harbans, and Raminder as they sat at their usual picnic table behind the C building. In the transcript below, the five friends transition from discussing a tongue-twisting acronym that one of them invented while studying for a test. Taking turns to see who can recite it the fastest and bursting into laughter each time, they eventually tire of this topic. Using the classic teenage segue "anyway," the topic quickly refocused on Janvi's cough and its remarkable likeness to that of the actress Madhuri Dixit's coy, flirtatious throat-clearing in the immensely popular film *Hum Apke Hain Kaun!* (Who am I to you!). The excerpt begins with Harbans's attempt to move the group on to a new topic.

Ahmmm-ahmmm

HARBANS: Aaaanyway.

JANVI: Aaaannnyywaaayss. Ahm-ahmmmm [throat-clearing].

RAMINDER: They're like . . .

JANVI: Allll rightyyy.

RAMINDER: I was teasing my mom yesterday.

JANVI: Ahmmm-ahmmm [two distinct coughs rather than one long one].

RENU: Ahmmm-ahmmm [giggles].

PINKI: Ahmmm-ahmmm.

JANVI: What is this movie?

PINKI: Ahmmm-ahmmm.

RAMINDER: It's from *Hum Apke Hain Kaun!*, uhooo-uhoo [exactly like the movie].

PINKI: Uhooo-uhoo [in a higher pitch].

RENU: Shut up, shut-up! [mimicking the intonation of the cough; giggles].

RAMINDER: No, she goes: uhooo-uhoo [like the movie].

The conversation continued for several more rounds of coughing and giggling and finally came to an abrupt halt when Janvi shrieked, "Eeww, Raminder ate an unwrapped piece of gum from her backpack!" and everyone cringed in disgust.

During this exchange, the girls quickly pick up on an everyday cough and take it as a distinctive verbal cue from film dialogue. The reel quote, "Uhoo-uhoo," is less of an actual cough and more of a demure, flirtatious noise that Madhuri Dixit's character makes when interacting with Salman Khan's character, her love interest in the film. During their initial humorous, coincidental meeting, she deploys this coy cough in an attempt to mask that she is laughing at him. This distinctive, feminine cough enables the actress to hide her mouth, giggle, and bat her eyelashes—all of which Madhuri Dixit does exceedingly well. So well, in fact, that it soon becomes a hallmark of their romantic interaction, as Salman Khan begins to echo the "uhoo-uhoo" cough as a flirtatious response.

The utterance takes on a life of its own that extends far beyond its reel presence. In the girls' dialogue, an actual, everyday throat-clearing and cough are recontextualized as a movie quote by the subsequent moves of Renu and Pinki. Equally significant is the fact that Janvi recognizes their imitation of her as not simply teasing, but a reference to the movie. Girls teasing one another about the sounds they make is hardly unusual, as the rounds of "aaaanyway" that start this exchange indicate. Only Raminder and Pinky can correctly identify the film and accurately replicate the sound, but their friends know a reference is being made. The indexical value of this utterance creates a particularly humorous situation for those who can identify the cough as a film quote. Moreover, it allows girls who are less comfortable quoting dialogue to immediately participate in the banter, thereby creating a truly shared source of amusement.

Bad Language • Boys also share such linguistic humor, but it tends to center around more illicit topics, especially cursing. Some FOBby boys enjoy using Hindi or Punjabi swear words that are not recognizable as transgressions by school administrators but communicate solidarity, humorous insult, and rancor among friends. Moreover, boys far prefer Punjabi or Hindi for routine teenage male conversations about genitalia, scatology, bestiality, illicit relations with female relatives, and other curse-worthy subject matter. Although they are quite adept at swearing in English, many prefer Hindi or Punjabi as exceptionally rich and colorful languages that allow for shades of meaning not available in English.

For some Desi boys, cursing is more than an occasional speech act; it is a specialized register requiring considerable skill and knowledge. Their practice of crafting and trading lewd and usually crude insults in the presence of cheering friends until one is declared the winner bears close resemblance to the African American verbal practice of "playing the dozens." While the dozens generally feature "yo mama" along with other family members and need not include profane lexical elements, the version Desi boys practiced showcased what they called "hard" language—a register filled with the most vulgar lexical elements they can find. By using hard language, a term they borrow from hip-hop lexicon, boys seek to be "hard" in general, which, figuratively speaking, is pretty much what it sounds like. Through this speech practice, boys strive for a heightened sense of masculinity by using insults, curses, and other profanity that features their interlocutor's *behen* (sister) or *ma* (mother). In the Desi version of the dozens, *behen chod*, or "sister fucker," is usually preferred to *mader chod*, the familiar American favorite, "motherfucker."

Cursing is a favorite pastime for the FOBby boys who kick it behind the C building at Greene High School. They perch on the C building's wheelchair ramp railing during break and lunch and carry on loudly with their joking, profanity, and other talk in both Punjabi and English. They engage in boisterous exchanges followed by explosions of laughter and cheering that are audible from a distance, making them a conspicuous presence. For FOBby boys, speaking in Punjabi or Hindi is a source of humor and solidarity in an otherwise dull and alienating school environment. Although they know the consequences for cursing in English, they are quite certain their bad words go undetected by school administrators Mr. Lopez and Mr. Alvarez. Although they curb their activity in the presence of Desi girls, they only barely manage to contain themselves as these school administrators whiz by in golf carts on their surveillance rounds, and watch amusedly as their White and Latino peers occasionally get apprehended for linguistic violations in English or Spanish.

Unlike FOB boys, Desi girls across the board are cautious about their language practices because using good language is part of a larger code of propriety to which girls are especially subject. Although using good language does not automatically make them good girls, using bad language can very quickly earn them a bad reputation. For Desi teenage girls, using profane language is linked to improper comportment and even being sexually active in a cultural context where chastity is valued. They are subject to peer policing as well as scrutiny from school faculty. Mercer Vice Principal Tanya Hill remarked about Desi girls in particular, "These girls, if they knew the tough language they used, their parents would be absolutely floored that their kids even know these words, let alone have them come out of their mouths! In a lot of cultures, girls are supposed to be more reserved. The parents would be surprised to see how uninhibited they are with the opposite sex." As Ms. Hill's comment implies, bad language is linked to what must be bad behavior.

Desi girls are expected to display levels of chastity not demanded of girls of other ethnicities, and cursing is a potentially dangerous way of tainting one's reputation. In an effort to avoid becoming the topic of rampant gossip at their school, most Desi girls seek to distance themselves from curses and their generators. Popular girl Avneet explained about the FOBS, "The girls are nice but some of the boys are kind of weird and can act sort of rowdy." Even FOBby girls who code-switch shared this point of view. One FOBby girl, Dilpreet, who knows most of these FOBby boys from her gurdwara, glanced in their direction as we walked by the C building and commented, "At first the boys start out in proper Hindi [but] then they end up swearing and causing trouble." Although it may seem like a victory for FOBby boys to remain unpunished because they cannot be understood, not getting caught swearing is a double-edged sword here. Instead of being penalized for using what *they* consider to be bad words, Desi teens are actually subject to a different set of judgments premised on the perceived deficiencies of being bilingual in an environment that privileges monolingualism. I discuss this point further below, especially in chapter 6.

CONCLUSION

Globalization, closely knit communities, critical masses of Desis, and the multicultural atmosphere of Silicon Valley at the turn of the millennium impact Desi teen language use. Language ideologies shape language use in ways that vary according to family background and cultural capital. Choices about language use are influenced by religion, class, critical mass, and gender. Across generations, teens value being able to communicate with family and share humor, emotion, and gossip. The type of cultural capital with which kids enter high school is a key part of how they make choices about language use.

Whether youth code-switch regularly or only use accented English, these language practices and others are integral to shaping meanings of identity in schools. Most populars and geeks are quite reserved in terms of when, how, and with whom they choose to display their bilingualism. They code-switch only on limited occasions and in general reserve displays of bilingualism to performative contexts such as multicultural day celebrations, which I discuss in the next chapter. By contrast, FOBs tend to openly code-switch between their heritage language and English with friends in day-to-day school settings. Frequently switching between English and a heritage language is one of the attributes that earn them the FOB name. Even among FOBs, gender differences shape language practices. Girls and boys engage in different types of speech practices and are often subject to different standards and valuations. For FOBs especially, language use is shaped by and important to maintaining gendered notions of what it means to be Desi. Girls certainly code-switch, but do so in ways that draw far less attention than boys.

In the monoglot Californian high school, where bilingual education is quickly fading into memory, speaking languages other than English can be a major liability. Despite the dynamic and pervasive language practices present in the daily lives of many Desi teens, there is little designated space for non-English linguistic expression in their schools. For these Desi teens and others who choose not to follow the dictates of English monolingualism, the consequences for using heritage languages is becoming increasingly complicated. Although multiculturalism is still a widely accepted tenet in high schools, languages other than English seem to have little place outside of designated festivals or pedagogical contexts. FOBs are either unaware of or choose to disregard the nuanced linguistic codes that govern the public space of schools. The ways these language practices are received complicate the model minority stereotype and what it means to be Desi in California today. The intricacies of linguistic and cultural expression, especially in the context of multiculturalism, are examined in the next chapter.

BEING FOBULOUS ON MULTICULTURAL DAY

Tara has been looking forward to multicultural day since she started at Mercer. She met many of the girls in her popular clique as children in her Gujarati community. Tara lives in the maze of streets atop the Fremont hills. Her parents moved to Fremont from Gujarat via Chicago in 1981, when Silicon Valley was beginning to become world renowned for its technology work. For years, Tara and her friends have kicked it in their six-girl clique on a bench in the quad at lunch. Now that they are seniors, they meet in the parking lot to go out to lunch in the new cars they received for their sixteenth birthdays. Although some of her friends understand Gujarati and can speak it to each other, they do so only for gossip or jokes, like her friend Sheetal's "dead gai" joke, discussed in the previous chapter. Compared to the parents of the other girls in her clique, Tara's parents place the fewest restrictions on her social activities and allow her to stay out late and date boys—taboo activities for nearly all her friends. Tara knows how unique her relationship is with her parents. She explained, "Me and my parents are so close. Actually I am lucky to have them. They are so liberal, they let me do anything I want. I guess that's a good thing. I won't be doing things that they don't want me to be doing." Her father expressed his viewpoint on his daughter's social life: "I told Tara, 'Keep your eyes open, if you like someone, go for it!' If they don't find someone by that time, we will try to find them. I have no problem, Black, White, Chinese." With her friends unable to party and with no boys worth dating at her school, Tara confides that there is seldom a worthwhile outlet for her freedom. Tara has been pouring her efforts into their multicultural day dance. All six girls are Hindi film fans and love to choreograph and perform dances based on Bollywood dance sequences. They have cinched top prizes with their amateur troupes at regional Desi dance contests.

Multicultural day performances like the one Tara and her friends are planning are carefully conceived and enthusiastically received by school audiences. Their choreography and music—painstakingly selected to incorporate a wide range of cultural forms—flow seamlessly together. What such short performances obscure, however, is a broad range of enduring inequalities of race and class that dominate the everyday lives of students. As the only sanctioned space for cultural expression in high school, multiculturalism draws attention to complicated issues of equality, participation, and who is responsible for upholding its tenets. Although multiculturalism's ideologies of equal rights and representation grew out of various civil rights and postcolonial struggles, they often lose their potency during implementation. Silicon Valley high schools have created annual events that reflect the egalitarian spirit of multiculturalism, but execute them in inconsistent ways that offer little support to ensure equal access. The rhetoric of these programs suggests that they are open to all, but little is done to include interested students.

In Silicon Valley high schools, multicultural initiatives overshadow historically produced systems of advantage and disadvantage among particular racial groups and obscure socioeconomic cleavages that exist within them. In this chapter I focus on two performances, the politics of representation that precede them, and the responses that follow them. The first *discussion* examines representation across racial groups at Mercer High School, and the second highlights tensions that can emerge within a racial group at Greene.[1] Both interrogate questions of rights, meanings, and representation for students. Moreover, they draw attention from the sanctioned emphasis on Culture with a capital c—which includes food, clothing, music, and dance—to the dynamics of inequality that underpin different racial and ethnic groups.

Despite all their flaws, multicultural programs are valued spaces of representation for Desi youth. Indeed, these spaces are rare and cherished opportunities for Desi teens to define themselves to their peers. Choices of music, costume, choreography, and other stylistic elements enable them to display Desi teen culture to their schools. Such choices are far more complex and nuanced than the reductive stereotypes of Desis in the media or in their curricular lessons about "Indian Culture." Yet it is often this very essentialist notion of South Asian culture that their peers and school faculty expect to see during these programs. Indeed, the reductive character of multiculturalism often lays to waste students' efforts as audiences anticipate cultural representations they consider to be authentic or traditional. Negotiations of what it means to be Desi come to a head in these programs, as do broader questions of race, class, and gender equity.

MULTICULTURALISM IN AMERICA

Multiculturalism emerged in the United States in the late twentieth century as a response to the European cultural hegemony that prevailed in American universities from the late nineteenth century onward (Goldberg 1994; Stam and Shohat 1994). This Eurocentric perspective was in harmony with prevailing policies and attitudes toward immigrants during that period, which included the eventual cessation of Asian immigration and denial of citizenship to Asian Americans. In contrast to the attempts to acknowledge and respect diversity that mark present-day constructs of multiculturalism, the late nineteenth century and early twentieth favored a "melting pot" model of assimilation (Glazer and Moynihan 1963) that required immigrants to relinquish any cultural values or language practices that conflicted with Anglo-European monoculturalism and English monolingualism. This pressure to assimilate came under increasing attack during the second half of the twentieth century, a period marked by emerging postcolonial nations worldwide and ardent civil rights movements in the United States, as well as a relaxation of U.S. anti-Asian immigration laws.

Although multiculturalism emerged out of movements for greater civil rights and freedom, its nature has been a site of contentious debate. Conservative critics oppose the idea outright and have railed against curricular reform, affirmative action, and political correctness. Dinesh D'Souza's (1998) *Illiberal Education* typifies this perspective. Others invested in furthering the call for substantive economic, political, and social reform have noted that multiculturalism is most often recognized in a purely celebratory manner through festivals, fairs, and other "ethnic" events. This critique acknowledges that multiculturalism focuses on how immigrants, people of color, and other minorities add diversity to American society without actually addressing the power relations that contribute to inequality between and within these groups (McLaren 1994; Takaki 2001; Taylor 1994; Wallace 1994). In any case, it is essential that multicultural efforts not challenge White hegemony (Frankenburg 1993; Lipsitz 2006; Perry 2002;

Winant 1997); indeed, diversity is tolerated in these contained displays insofar as it does not disrupt the racial order. This norm of Whiteness is one on which multiculturalism is premised—a point that is evident in how teenagers discuss the meaning of this term and align themselves with their high school's multicultural initiatives.

MULTICULTURALISM IN SILICON VALLEY HIGH SCHOOLS

While the ethos of multiculturalism is about unity, equality, and cultural expression, its implementation can exacerbate and reinforce race-, class-, and gender-based divisions among students. Neither Mercer nor Greene High School offered any "formal" or politicized multicultural efforts in their curricula. While race and ethnicity are examined to some extent through class work or projects, multicultural programs stand alone as the designated space where racial difference within the student body receives public attention. Showcasing dance, music, food, and art, these carnival-like programs offer day- or weeklong displays of Culture for general consumption by students and faculty. When this type of public expression is quarantined to a single day or week of the entire school year, all "cultures" appear to exist in harmony next to one another and disparities between them are erased. Dance and song productions, along with ethnic food and music, are displayed as representative of entire countries, regions, and even continents, such as in "African Culture" or "Latin American Culture." In actuality, such monikers barely even represent the diversity of students from these groups who attend the high school. Moreover, such parsing of time and attention overshadows historically produced systems of advantage and disadvantage between racial groups and ignores cleavages of class that exist within them at schools.

At Mercer High School, "Multicultural Week" began in the mid-1990s and evolved into its present format of a weeklong festival. Each of the first four days is dedicated to a different racial group—African Americans, Asian Americans, Latinos, and European Americans—and students are encouraged to dress in corresponding ethnic clothing. Friday is Unity Day, when the week's events culminate in an hour-long assembly of performances held in the gym and performed twice to accommodate the oversized student body. During an extended lunch period on Unity Day, student clubs are invited to play music and sell ethnic foods and crafts.

"Ethnic" food at Mercer means choosing between egg rolls and samosas instead of the "normal" fare of bagels and burritos. While eating a kabob, students can get a henna tattoo bearing the name of their favorite NSync band member or purchase woven goods from Central America. Similarly, at Greene efforts focus on food and dance but are condensed into an extended lunch period on a Friday. All "International Day" activities are staged in the quad, the least diverse area of the school campus.

At both schools, students believe that multicultural programs amount to little more than entertainment. Nonetheless, students of color at both schools describe these days as the only ones over which they feel a true sense of ownership. Compared to other school productions such as homecoming and school dances, which Desi teens usually refer to as "White" events, Multicultural Day can truly be theirs. Taahir, a geek boy who likes to wear his *sherwani* suit (a long, fitted coat) for Asian Day at Mercer, commented, "I think Multicultural Week is cool because we can express ourselves in another angle that people usually don't see us through. . . . We're able to dress up, it helps show who you are." Likewise, José, a Latino boy, describes the vibrant character of the week and exclaimed, "I find it extremely interesting. Everyone is kinda representin', like, this is what I am!"

For many students, securing a place in the schoolwide program is important precisely because of this scarcity of ongoing opportunities for public expression. Although Desi teens admit that these venues are primarily about displaying dance, music, and food, they nonetheless value them as one of the few spaces they can call their own in an otherwise White high school culture. Indeed, even though White students are a numerical minority at Mercer and Greene, events such as homecoming, rallies, school dances, and prom that Desi teens regard as White dominate the public space of school and rarely take into consideration the music or aesthetic choices of non-White groups.

By contrast, multicultural programs allow a space for Desi teens to carefully craft representations that reflect aspects of their heritage as well as their lives in California. These expressions differ from the static, timeless notions of South Asia that they may learn about in their classrooms and instead mark a more time- and place-specific way of being Asian American. Desi teens can use these spaces to convey more heterogeneous and potentially radical versions of themselves than they otherwise can in high schools, and than their peers would likely learn about in class.

While Multicultural Week may not appear contentious, in a teenage world it is fraught with multiple layers of political and social significance. Indeed, if high school is considered a microcosm of society, then multicultural programs provide a staging ground for rights and representation. "Cultural citizenship" draws attention to the political underpinnings of quotidian struggles; Renato Rosaldo and William Flores (1997: 57) define this concept as "the right to be different (in terms of race, ethnicity, or native language) with respect to the norms of the dominant national community, without compromising one's right to belong, in the sense of participating in the nation-state's democratic processes" (see also Ong 1996; Siu 2001). As one of their students' only public forums, high schools necessarily serve as sites in which to examine the dynamic struggle for rights and representation (Kymlicka 1996; Werbner 1997). In this sense, organizing a dance for a multicultural performance is illustrative of broader dynamics that position as well as empower students to advocate for particular rights and viewpoints.

Although numerous teens want to participate in Multicultural Day and seek greater representation in schools, only some have the cultural capital to actualize their visions. Indeed, how students gain access to these programs and find their way onstage is reflective of the broader ways students of different racial and class backgrounds are able to use the school to meet their needs. Going backstage, so to speak, to examine the casting, creating, and rehearsing of these performances reveals how these expressions of racial and cultural identity are sites of negotiation and exclusion for many students. At Mercer this struggle occurred between various racial groups; at Greene it occurred among Desis themselves. Both cases are fraught with a similar twofold tension of students vying against one another for performance time while also attempting to challenge essentialized notions of cultural identity.

ASIAN AMERICAN DOMINANCE AT MERCER

Should students from all ethnic groups be included in Multicultural Week? The issue of whether the program should take to heart multicultural ideology about equal access and representation or instead prioritize the requests of the majority of the student body spawned debates and school newspaper editorials for months. The controversy began with the way the student committee in charge of the multiculturalism program handled auditions, which were necessary to manage the overwhelming student interest in participating in the hour-long program. The planning committee appointed an entirely White panel of teachers to judge auditions scheduled three months prior to the April performance.[2] Chosen primarily based on their willingness to stay after school for the auditions, judges were asked to evaluate each act on content, choreography, and overall "entertainment value." Although students were alerted about the audition in early November, little information was offered as to how to prepare.

From this early stage onward, differences in cultural capital among students became apparent. Hopeful participants Tara and her friends were able to draw on the experiences of friends and siblings who performed in previous assemblies as well as their own knowledge of school activities. Nonplussed by the school's lack of directives on how to ready themselves, they asked the girls in their clique, some members of the FOBulous Six, and a few other girls to join their dance. Having won several Desi community dance contests, they were no strangers to how dances are choreographed, rehearsed, and costumed. The hard part was choosing from the spate of popular Bollywood songs and dances currently en vogue. A dance popularized by beauty queen Aishwarya Rai was a must. Determined to make it into the program, the girls held regular practices at various homes after school, as well as during weekends and winter break, and ten girls slowly mastered the dance. As the audition drew closer, one of the experienced dancers in the group had her mother shop for matching tops at Ross Dress for Less specifically for the audition.

When asked how they knew to prepare so thoroughly, Tara explained that they had watched seniors in previous years go through this and that they had heard about how competitive the audition could be. She added, "We really want to get selected for the program. We have always wanted to do this during senior year. If our group gets in, we can make up the rest of the dance however we want." Serious and focused, they even appointed me as an understudy since I had watched countless practices, in case they needed a last-minute replacement for the audition (thankfully, they did not). Motivated by the prospect of representing themselves to their school, they invested significant time and effort to procure what they knew would be a highly coveted spot. By January, Tara and her friends had successfully trained and costumed their fleet of ten girls into nearly flawless audition material.

Only some groups, however, were able to draw on the knowledge of seniors and their own past performances. While some groups had the advantage of already being well versed in school events as well as having friends who schooled them about the ins and outs of this particular program, others approached it cold. On audition day, such differences were apparent in the auditions of the Asian American, African American, and Latino groups. In a lengthy affair in which ten groups vied for four places, a number of Asian American groups arrived with costumes and props alongside a smaller number of representatives from the Black Student Union (BSU) and the Latino student group MEChA (Movimiento Estudiantil Chicano de Aztlán).[3] These two groups together make up less than 7 percent of the school's population, and they sought to increase their visibility and presence in the school by representing themselves in this forum. Their audition was enthusiastic but without costumes and their full cast of performers. Unfortunately, it was passed over in favor of ten Desi girls in matching outfits, the Chinese girls who performed a traditional ribbon dance using props owned by their families, the Filipino boys and girls who did a dance with lit candles that they had performed at community shows, and a uniformed Japanese martial arts group doing a number based on karate. Additionally, two outside acts would be hired by the school to supplement student performances.

Issues of Inclusion • While generally accepting of an audition framework, some students, faculty, and parents were outraged that the school would hire outside performers and turn away interested students who were not represented in the program. This outcome evoked widespread discontent and frustration for African American and Latino students, who regarded the day as their only space for cultural expression in a school where they were vastly underrepresented. The BSU decided to take action against this decision. They called on their advisor, Monique Albert, a young African American math teacher, who spent much of her busy first year at Mercer helping them with this struggle. Quick to mention that she, along with another African American and an Asian American woman, were the only teachers of color at this school, Ms. Albert was forthcoming and articulate about the perceived inequities underlying this process.

On the day I spoke to her, she and the only other African American faculty member, who was also a young woman, were staying after school to compose a letter to the school newspaper outlining their grievances with the multicultural audition and selection process. Their main critique was the lack of detailed information about the audition. Standing behind her colleague, who typed into the classroom computer, she looked over her shoulder at me and exclaimed, "I didn't know that it was a full-on audition! I was completely unfamiliar with the whole setup. We sent representatives to the meetings, but not enough info came out of them." Despite her frustration, Ms. Albert was somewhat accepting of this outcome, and graciously added, "The [BSU] leadership is all new, all young freshmen. So how could I really prepare them? I'm new too! We weren't prepared, and we accept that fact." Her protest, however, stemmed from MEChA not being chosen, despite four acts they had prepared. They were exasperated that despite their efforts and working hard for the audition, the Latino group was still excluded.

The African American and Latino students I spoke with were magnanimously supportive of the chosen performers and instead took issue with the school administration for not advocating on their behalf over professional adult performers, and for leaving the program in the hands of four Asian American students whose priorities were not inclusion of all interested parties. Students also expressed their frustration by writing letters to the editor of the school newspaper. Juanita, president of MEChA, submitted a provocative letter to the paper that summarized the student position on this situation. She argued that audition flyers did not call for costumes and polished pieces. She especially took issue with the vague concept of "entertainment value," asking why, if it was not an important criterion in other schoolwide programs, it was important for Multicultural Week. Was Multicultural Week inherently less interesting and in need of special efforts to make it more appealing? She emphatically concluded, "If students are proud of their heritage and are willing to share it with their fellow students, they should be allowed to."

After several letters to the school newspaper, MEChA requested to take the place of the professional Latin group and represent themselves. Juanita recounted in frustration that the committee told her they favored keeping "the Brazilian or Bolivian dance group." In a state with thousands of Chicano students, having a dance from South America barely seemed like representation, about which Juanita parenthetically wrote, "We are still not sure because the committee can't distinguish the two diverse countries." The administration's hands-off stance left the program entirely under the jurisdiction of the activities coordinator and leadership students, whose priorities were different from those of the excluded students.

Despite their best efforts, the two young African American female teachers and their students were unable to overturn a decision that rested firmly in the hands of Mr. Watson, the young White male activities director who had worked at the school for several years. When I asked him about the controversy, Mr. Watson shrugged and said, "This is the first year we've ever had any complaints, and really those came from those groups that performed in the tryouts and weren't chosen. Of course they were bitter about that. And they had a different viewpoint—their viewpoint was that we do a kind of quota-type thing, that you take people regardless of how well they perform, and you just put them in because you want to get all the ethnicities that you can. Again, there is no way we can possibly do that, nor is that our point."

Mr. Watson's comments echo a familiar hue and cry against affirmative action, which is that only those who achieve on their own should progress. His stance suggests that the school is in a postracial society where such differences have been erased and efforts toward inclusion are not necessary. Not only does his position do little to further equality, but it also confirms that access is actually not a cornerstone of an event that, by its very nature, is designed to be culturally inclusive and unifying. Mr. Watson silenced groups seeking representation and turned the school into a microcosm of familiar dynamics of exclusion and resentment about affirmative action that run rampant in colleges and in the workplace. Especially in California, where the UC system did away with affirmative action in their admissions policy in 1997, attitudes like Mr. Watson's make multiculturalism's inclusive agenda seem unimportant. With the school administration showing no indication of intervening and with no other teachers who wanted to advocate, the program went on as planned and Multicultural Week finally arrived.

Showtime at Mercer • On a sunny morning in April 2000, a gymnasium packed with eleven hundred students and their teachers rose as a student sang the "Star-Spangled Banner" with electric guitar accompaniment that fell a bit short of Jimi Hendrix but was respectable nonetheless. In the adjacent locker rooms, Desi girls fidgeted with their shiny golden head jewelry and generously applied makeup while Desi boys enacted Star Wars–

style fights with their *dhandiya*, the decorated sticks they would use in their dance. The national anthem ended and students settled onto the bleachers in noisy anticipation of the hour-long multicultural program that had replaced their third- and fourth-period classes that day. Elaborately costumed groups of enthusiastic students began to perform their well-rehearsed dances and martial arts routines. When the Indian student club was introduced, six Desi girls struck a pose in a circle at the center of the gym while a multiracial group of thirty-four other performers stood poised and ready to enter on cue. The inner circle of Desi girls began to dance gracefully to "Taal," the title song from Aishwarya Rai's Bollywood hit.[4] Fourteen more girls in coordinated green and gold skirts joined in and were soon followed by their twenty male partners. The gym echoed with a reverberating bass and the howls of kids cheering for their friends while the performers enjoyed their moment in the spotlight. The music quickly segued from one lively Bollywood song to another, and the choreography toggled between bhangra and hip-hop-influenced moves and *filmi* flirting and courting rituals.[5] The dance closed with a dramatic pose that sent the audience into wild cheering.

After watching the full show of Asian students and two professional acts of Chinese acrobats and Bolivian folk dancers, students expressed appreciation for the assembly. Although they enjoyed the performances, many could not discern if the assembly had a larger purpose. Rekha, a FOBulous Six member who did not dance but liked watching her friends perform, remarked, "It's a good opportunity to learn about other cultures." My question of whether she had learned something elicited a long pause. She eventually replied, "Somewhat. We've had it every year. You don't *really* learn anything, but you get to see what other cultures do. It's fun to see that. A lot of people don't really know about other cultures, so it's a good chance to learn . . . I guess." Rekha articulated the commonly held student viewpoint, which is that multicultural programs do not adequately convey knowledge about other cultures. Feroze, an active member of the Muslim Student Association, paused from selling kabobs for his club and remarked, "It's all right. It could be better. Put more effort into it! Right now it's food, that's all we do. There isn't any entertainment until Friday, when we actually *do* something. They don't *do anything* throughout the week." Other students who felt like spectators rather than participants in this program shared his sentiment.

Students noted that the groups chosen for the assembly closely mirror the racial composition of the school. About the Asian-dominated program, Stephanie, a White student who enjoyed the assembly, commented, "That's about as multicultural as it's going to get here. Even though it's a relatively diverse school, there's only a handful of different cultures. There isn't exactly something representative from every part of the world. But for us, it's a pretty good program." Likewise, José, a Latino and a member of MEChA, asserted that there are hardly any African American and Latino students in the school, so it is not surprising that they are underrepresented in the program. Being in the minority, however, does not diminish a group's desire to be included. Shaniqua, president of the BSU, admits that their group was "prepared but unorganized" at the audition, but also added, "I don't think the rest of the students like us very much. This school is very different from other schools. We've just had a hard time. It's not diverse, we don't feel a lot of support."

Shaniqua's comment, as well as others, betray the lack of ownership African American students feel over the program. Along with Monique Albert, Alicia, a BSU member who had tried out for the program, is among the few who challenged the notion that having several Asian acts this year, as in years past, is not considered repetitive, whereas two years of African American acts would be. She generously commented, "I liked it this year, it was really good. But the only thing that kind of made me sad is that nothing was there to represent the African or African American culture, and when we proposed it and said, 'Look, we'll hire someone to come in, just like you hire people for other cultures,' they said, 'No, that would be redundant to have something from the African or African American cultures two years in a row.' So I just really did not like that, especially because that's what it's all about, you know? But other than that, I thought it was great—the students, the acrobats, they were all great." When I asked her how the problem could have been handled better, she reflected for a moment and then replied, "I think instead of having the Chinese acrobat people—because they didn't represent anything for culture, it was more just a goofy side show—that's where we could have . . . not we . . . there could have been an African or African American anything." Alicia's comment, especially her shift from "we" to "not we, there" underscores how little ownership African American and Latino students feel over school activities and functions.

Mercer High School's multicultural program served to reinforce existing race-based hierarchies in the school. Those groups historically underrepresented at the school remained so, and Asian Americans, already the
majority at the school, dominated the public display time at this program
as well. By the same token, having an hour-long assembly serve as the
year's primary public arena for cultural expression in a school with an
Asian American majority is problematic in itself. This predicament is
further complicated by the entertainment-centered character of this program, which leaves little room for deeper understanding of the very issues
that caused this unequal situation. An analogous situation emerged during International Day at Greene that also challenges the premise of unity
and understanding that underlie this day. Here, issues of class and gender
among Desis manifest as obstacles for students who want to use this
space for cultural expression.

FOB-FREE AT GREENE

Should students in the same ethnic group be assured equal access to
multicultural programs? While Desi teens at Greene did not have to compete with other groups to secure a place, they did battle among themselves
to perform on International Day. The events that unfolded received no
school press coverage or parental intervention, but were problematic all
the same. At Greene, there were no auditions. There was no policy against
having two dances from the same ethnic group. In fact, there was not even
a stipulation that groups had to be affiliated with a student club. In other
words, there were no rules. A perplexing situation resulted from this
seemingly open invitation: although there was plenty of room for all
interested students to participate, only some were able to do so.

When the International Day program was announced, there was widespread interest among FOBs. Yet popular girls Jaspreet and Amanpreet
announced their intentions to do a dance on behalf of the Indian Student
Club before any other groups had properly mobilized. For these two popular sisters, International Day is yet another program in the endless roster
of school activities they dominate. Though they are Sikh Punjabi like the
majority of Desi teens at Green High School, they are notably different.
Unlike their peers, these upper-middle-class girls live in a posh home in
the hills and are avidly involved in school leadership, pep rallies, fashion

shows, proms, and other social events. They are even the self-appointed leaders of the Indian Student Club, an organization FOBs at the school know little about. Along with their clique, they occupy prime real estate on the grassy steps of the school's quad, a space they unquestioningly call their own. Jaspreet and Amanpreet are especially concerned that they not be mistaken for FOBs, which, to their dismay, has happened on occasion. Amanpreet recalled one such incident in which she and her clique were kicking it near the library rather than in their usual spot in the quad and someone called them "the Indians." She admitted, "We just forget and just think about ourselves as whatever, but not really Indians. . . . We are of a really different crowd that are not just Desi-oriented." Drawing on the cultural capital of their upbringing along with expertise in school events, Jaspreet and Amanpreet began to effortlessly organize their dance.

Meanwhile, several cliques of FOBs solidified their interest in performing as well. Yet they were perplexed by the general lack of information on how to participate. Janvi and others were reluctant to approach popular Desi teens or to visit the leadership office for information. Although Avinash, Charanpal, and other boys spoke enthusiastically about the possibility of doing a bhangra dance, no one took the initiative. In all, four different groups of FOBs expressed their intention to dance, but none was able to mobilize. It soon became clear that International Day was no different from the other school programs toward which FOBs felt general discomfort. In its present form, the program seemed more like an obstacle than an opportunity. With little cultural capital and even less clout in school, the FOBs' ability to plan a dance was limited from the outset.

Politics of Participation • While Jaspreet and Amanpreet had no logistical trouble, they encountered a different type of dilemma: in order to achieve their artistic vision, they needed more Desi girls in their dance than their exclusive popular clique afforded. With their original four, they needed several more, and quickly realized they would have to involve at least a few FOBs. Finding the prospect of visiting the back corner more awkward than they had expected, Amanpreet decided to ask some of the FOBby girls she knew from her classes. Nidhi and her two close friends convinced one another to join. Gurinder, who kicked it with the FOBs but also enjoyed many school functions, decided to join as well. The rest of the FOBby girls and boys shied away from the prospect of joining the dance.

Although Janvi kicked it with Nidhi, she still felt out of place and commented, "I wanted to join their dance, but they're kind of snobby and live way up in the hills, so I don't really want to do it with them." Rather than forming a second group, interested FOBby youth resigned themselves to not participating because Jaspreet and Amanpreet were doing the dance. My gentle reminder that there could be more than one Desi dance was met with uneasy shrugs and mumblings about how it wouldn't be tight to have two dances from the same country.

Problems soon arose that highlighted the socioeconomic differences between popular and FOBby girls in the dance. Although most of the girls are Sikh Punjabi, middle-class FOBby girls have far more restrictions on where they can go and what they can wear, and none of them owns a car. This made attending rehearsals, which the sisters decided to hold in their home rather than the easily accessible school grounds, a major hassle. To further complicate matters, the popular sisters choreographed and outfitted a dance that offended the sensibilities of FOBby girls and even some of their popular friends from more conservative families. Gurinder expressed her objection: "You have to do all this motioning across your chest and spread your legs. It's like, some kind of seduction dance." Other girls agreed, and to make matters worse, the "slut dance," as it was quickly dubbed, was to feature what were considered excessively revealing outfits. Gurinder further remarked, "The lehengas have slits in them up to here [pointing to her midthigh], the blouses have a hole cut out of them. I told my mom about these lehengas and she asked why they don't just wear miniskirts." With moves and costumes that they regarded as too sexually suggestive, several girls, including some of the popular girls in the dance, decided to drop out. Frustrated, the popular sisters decided to compromise rather than cancel the dance altogether. They would tone down the dance and let performers wear their own lehengas, which exposed as much as each girl deemed appropriate.

Showtime at Greene • On a warm spring day in April 2000, International Day finally arrived in the quad. The stage area was adorned with decorations, including a colorful banner naming the event, surrounded by hand-painted flags from various countries and an arc of helium balloons that stretched from one end of the concrete stage to the other. As the bell rang to signal the start of a lunch period specially extended for this event, students packed onto the steps surrounding the quad and spilled over onto the grassy area facing the stage. Only a handful of FOBs came to watch the program—some to show support for the few friends who made it into the dance and the rest to keep those spectators company. "I heard the dance is gonna suck," Umber proclaimed loudly, having earlier admitted that she had badly wanted to perform as part of her secret ambition to become a Bollywood actress. Avinash remarked that he came only to see his girlfriend and loaded film in his camera while I set my video camera on a tripod. One of Avinash's friends scoffed that the Indian flag was all the way at the bottom and was not even painted accurately. Upon closer examination, we discovered that several of the flags were depicted incorrectly and others were altogether unidentifiable.

When the "Indian Club" was announced, eight Desi girls in colorful lehengas—some featuring more fabric than others—took their places with their backs facing the audience. As the bass from their remixed music reverberated through the quad, they gyrated and swayed to a popular remix of a song from the Bollywood film *Taal*. While Jaspreet and Amanpreet seemed to enjoy the appreciative cheering of the audience, especially when they spun around on the ground into a series of slithering, snake-like moves, the other girls appeared to be less at ease with these provocative undulations. When their five-minute dance ended dramatically, the girls exited the stage onto the grass and laced up their sneakers. They watched the remainder of the program while the FOBs beat a hasty retreat to their back corner.

Responses to International Day were decidedly mixed. Although friends of Jaspreet and Amanpreet were duly congratulatory, the few FOBs who saw the dance were critical and immediately offered their reviews to their friends. Several FOBs who claimed they were not interested in the performance jockeyed for position to watch it on the small LCD display of my video camera. As they huddled around the tiny screen, a barrage of critiques ensued: it was too slow; it contained slutty, hootchy moves; and it was not nearly as good as in past years. With a hint of smugness, Janvi remarked, "It would have been amazing if *we* had done bhangra." Having just danced their best, Nidhi and her friends were hurt at overhearing their friends saying "It sucked." Nidhi retorted, "What do they know, they didn't even do anything!" Had the dance been more inclusive, perhaps the FOBs would have been less critical. Unfortunately, popular Jaspreet and

Amanpreet were far out of earshot and these scathing critiques fell on the FOBs who had struggled to be in the dance.

When I attended the performance the following year, only two FOBs joined the dance that Amanpreet had organized alone while Jaspreet was at college. No other Desi dances were planned. Janvi, who had vowed to be in the program for her senior year, admitted that she was not in the dance this year either. When I asked her why, she shrugged, "I don't know. I didn't feel comfortable. I didn't know [Amanpreet] and I didn't want to go to her house." The same dynamics of class and cultural capital that marginalized Janvi and others in the previous year had once again edged them out.

That popular Desi teens continued to dominate this and other events even though they are far outnumbered by FOBs reveals that some students feel a sense of ownership and privilege over school resources while others remain excluded. Class differences between FOBs and populars are divisive at Greene but receive no public attention. While Mercer's struggles were publicized and aired, Greene's dramas took place under the radar and went widely unnoticed. Excluded students did not even consider approaching school faculty or administrators for help; such a move was thought to be intimidating or pointless. Their only recourse was to criticize their own friends who had the courage to participate.

REPRESENTING DESI TEEN CULTURE

Should multicultural programs be about performing something "traditional," or should they reflect dynamic, locally constructed identities? Desi teens avowedly went with the latter but faced numerous criticisms as a result. Both Desi performances distinguished themselves by their original choreography and choice of music and costume. Unlike their Chinese American peers at Mercer who did a ribbon dance or those at Greene who did a tinikling dance from the Philippines, Desi teens shied away from known Desi dance styles such as garba and bhangra and chose instead to choreograph their own dance moves. Their music and steps were largely influenced by Bollywood but also included interludes from hip-hop and pop music. At Mercer, negotiation centered around outfits and performers. Tara and her friends created a medley incorporating three different songs and dance styles. Rather than wear typical South Asian outfits, the girls wore a close-fitting black top of their choosing with either a green or gold piece of fabric tied to look like a lehenga. Tara explained that they wanted something pretty and cute that didn't look "FOBby" and that they could get for twenty girls. To accessorize, they crafted head jewelry from plastic bead curtains they tied together and spray-painted gold. Each girl paid $10 for her costume and outfitted her partner in kurta-pyjama sets borrowed from male family members.[6]

While these style choices were acceptable to some participants, especially non-Desis, they drew sharp criticism from other Desi girls in the dance. The FOBulous Six in particular took issue with these aesthetic selections. Shabana, who has her finger on the pulse of everything stylish, commented, "I don't know why they bought the material in the first place without asking everyone, 'Oh, is this nice?' You know? Why didn't they ask me?" Shabana's friend Rekha piped up in agreement: "They should have gotten red instead of those dull colors." Shabana added, "It was so drab," and went on to reveal that so many Desi girls in the dance criticized the outfits that Tara considered changing them the night before the performance. Notably, none of the participants from other races or ethnicities voiced any protest about their own costumes. In fact, many of them were so enamored with their outfits that they wore them for the rest of the school day. In the end, the girls kept the outfits as planned. The process of representing a group, however, was fraught with tension and debate about what would be the tightest Desi style.

Another contentious decision was whether to include students of other racial groups. While there were ample Desis at Mercer to take part in the dance, many popular Desi boys decided that dancing in school was FOBby and refused to join. Only a few popular Desi boys were willing to participate, even though many know how to dance from years of participating in community festivals. Only a select handful of Desi geeks were asked. Determined to have a coed dance despite their apathetic Desi male peers, the girls broke from the previous years' tradition and opened the dance to boys of any racial background as well as a handful of their non-Desi female friends. One of the Desi girls in the dance described the benefit of this approach: "Everybody feels connected to it. You know how, when sometimes people are dancing, it's just that group. But when they see people of their own race and ethnicity in it, they're like 'Oh wow, I can do it too!'" Her tall, stocky Latino partner with bright blue eyes and dyed red hair confirmed his excitement about being included and relayed how he overcame his initial discomfort: "Basically I'm a fat guy who doesn't know how to dance. At first when I heard the Indian song, I was like, 'What is this?' And we started doing the dance, and I was like, 'This is crazy!' But now I know all the steps and the song is actually really cool to me now."

Even teens who would have preferred to perform something from their own cultural background but had no critical mass enjoyed participating in the Desi dance. One male participant explained, "I'm from Afghanistan. We have our own cultural dance. I would like to do an Afghani dance, you know, just to show my culture and what we do, but there's hardly any Afghans in our school." Being in the Indian dance was as close as he could get. Although the group was diverse in some ways, few African American and Latino students participated in the dance.

At Greene High School, gender-based notions of propriety became the point of tension in debates about style. When Jaspreet and Amanpreet began choreographing the dance, they alone made decisions about the music and moves. Here too Bollywood films were a prominent influence, and the sisters also chose to splice together a medley of popular film songs and choreograph a dance. Several of the girls in the dance had assumed they would choose bhangra since the two sisters were Sikh Punjabi. Although some FOBby girls argued for the inclusion of a more traditional bhangra song, their love of Bollywood made filmi music an acceptable second choice. Even though the sisters were in charge of the dance, they had to engage in unexpected negotiations around gender. The sisters crafted a style of choreography and costume worthy of any Bollywood starlet but one that was too racy for the average Desi teen. Amanpreet explained, "We want to do something that represents our culture, but something tight—not something FOBby and boring." What the sisters regarded tight, however, drew sharp criticism from more conservative Desi teens who knew that Bollywood stars can gyrate in skimpy clothing in ways that mere mortals dare not consider. All these factors made the process of creating a tight dance far more challenging.

Gender is also significant here because girls undertook all of the program organizing. At Mercer, Desi boys were by and large uninterested in participating, let alone planning anything. This left interested Desi girls as well as female participants of other ethnicities on their own to search for partners for the dance. Unlike at Greene, however, rehearsals, dance moves, and other aspects of the dance were not an issue. In fact, the rehearsals were a space of fun and socializing. As they were generally held at a Desi student's house, most Desi parents felt comfortable allowing their kids to attend on weekday nights because they had met the other teens' parents at school or community functions. At Greene, popular girls did not even attempt to make their dance coed, and boys did not take any initiative on their own. Holding the rehearsals at their home when the participants did not have cars and were not allowed to visit homes outside families in their communities only worsened these matters. While it would perhaps be too broad a statement to suggest that without girls, these performances of culture would not materialize, in the programs I witnessed this certainly appeared to be the case.

Managing Critiques of Authenticity • While Desi teens use these programs as an expressive space in school, faculty and other students consider the programs a space for learning about an "Indian Culture" that is pure and untouched by anything recognizably Western. Especially during multicultural programs, essentialized, timeless notions of culture triumph as authentic; such depictions reify cultural differences and bind them into homogeneous, separate units that erase their texture and difference (Turner 1994: 407).[7] While audiences at Mercer High School certainly enjoyed the Desi dance, questions of authenticity were raised, including the decision to include non-Desi participants, using remixed music and a range of innovative dance steps, and wearing nontraditional costumes. One White boy in the dance expressed his doubt: "[The dance] seems a little whitewashed. The ending that they have now seems a little less *cultural* than I hoped. It seems like it's been dumbed-down, Whitified. I don't know if I know what I'm talking about, but that's what it seems like."

Other youth similarly remarked that they had expected something more traditional but were unable to articulate specifically what they thought the dance was lacking or what it should have been instead. Tara and her friends were somewhat disappointed by these criticisms, but on the whole pleased that they had been able to do a tight dance that represented their style. Questions of authenticity also arose at Greene, but from other Desi students who would have preferred to do a bhangra number in outfits that covered more skin. As rumors about the dance circulated through FOB cliques, a prevailing sentiment arose that one FOBby girl summarized this way: "It's, like, become an American dance. We want to do something *more Indian*, you know." By calling the dance inauthentic for an entirely different set of reasons than Mercer's students offered—that is, their own exclusion from the process of creating representations—they managed to claim some sense of ownership over how Desi teen culture should be conveyed.

FADE TO WHITE

Students' negotiations of multicultural ideology reflect their local struggles with race, class, and gender. The school-based initiatives through which they are able to do so both constrain kids' efforts as well as reveal multiculturalism's fragmented implementation. I conclude with a discussion of the finale from the Mercer multicultural assembly to underscore the power dynamics exposed in these laissez-faire school programs. The final act was a "flag parade," in which students walked around the gym holding flags from various countries while the emcee announced the corresponding country names. The parade included a random assortment of flags that students brought from home in hopes of being excused from class for both assemblies. As the finale to this procession, five White boys carried a giant U.S. flag accompanied by the song "God Bless the USA."[8] Rather than taking a customary round and standing with the other participants, they circled the gym a number of times and engaged in fist pumps and other victorious gestures. They were encouraged by wild cheering from the audience and remained oblivious to expressions of discomfort and disbelief from other participants.

Five White boys parading a supersized American flag as the last word created a hostile ending to what had already been an exclusive program. After the program, several students expressed their disapproval. The following is an excerpt of a conversation between José and Alicia:

> ALICIA: The only part I think I hated was the whole USA flag part, where they ran around the [gym] three times, with that stupid "I'm a proud American" song. Aaaahh! It just aggravated me.
>
> JOSÉ: That pissed me off too. I don't know why . . .
>
> ALICIA: I know why it pissed me off. It pissed me off because the whole point

139

is that even though we are different cultures and even though we're not all White, we're still Americans. So I think instead of having the big four White guys go up there and parade around with the damn flag . . . [laughs] Sorry! They should have had, like, maybe an Asian person . . . and José, or somebody!

JOSÉ: I ain't goin' up there!

ALICIA: [laughs] You know, someone to represent different races. I still think the whole flag parade is kind of dumb and I wish they'd cut it out.

JOSÉ: It's just supposed to represent unity, you know? Let's get everybody out there, walk around with the American flag, you know? Not just a bunch of hokey, sexist, sweaty men!

José, Alicia, and a number of other students felt that this finale undermined the other performers' efforts at cultural expression. As if to reclaim control of a space that had been temporarily surrendered to other groups, these White boys asserted what they considered rightfully theirs.

As the flag parade and other power struggles indicate, cultural citizenship remains a highly contested process. Teens engage in a wide spectrum of efforts, some more successful than others, to claim a space for themselves in the public sphere of their high schools. While the problematic nature of this finale and the program went unaddressed by the administration, the general discontent prompted a more equitable flag parade the following year. During this assembly, flags hung from the ceiling and the flag parade was more unified in response to complaints of the prior year's program, in which some students disrespected flags by clowning around with them or inattentively dragging them on the gym floor. Students carried in a limited number of flags and stood in a circle with them, and the U.S. flag was one among many. Two boys, one White and one Asian American, carried the American flag, and students cheered while "Imagine" by John Lennon played and flowers were given to performers. There were still no Latino or African American performances, but at least the program ended on the more positive note of "Imagine all the people, sharing all the world" rather than the jingoistic anthem of the previous year.

In these Silicon Valley high schools, multicultural programs do little to challenge or even draw overt attention to the socioeconomic structures that maintain inequalities between and within racial and ethnic groups. While it seems as though Asian Americans dominate in multicultural programs, it is difficult to say what one hour out of an entire school year can accomplish by way of deeper understandings about race. Coupled with the reality that only popular teens make it into the program, the question is all the more salient. Although Desi girls at Mercer have the cultural capital to perform for the audition judges, the African American and Latino students are at a distinct disadvantage in this regard. Unlike these upper-middle-class Desi girls, they do not have inside information and resources easily available to them. Likewise, middle-class Desi teens at Greene are at an apparent disadvantage compared to their popular Desi peers. With very little knowledge about school activities, FOBby girls are reliant on popular girls who already dominate school events.

Cultural celebrations of this sort rarely enable true transformations of the social order. They offer some empowerment, however, to participating youth. Desi teens are able to exercise their cultural citizenship and display a sense of ownership over public space. While their representations are subject to criticisms of being inauthentic, they are willing to fight for their versions of their culture. Indeed, to not do so would be to validate an orientalist gaze that seeks homogeneous representations of non-European cultures. That these schools rely on students to create cultural representations that will educate peers and faculty is not only wholly unreasonable, but encroaches on the one space in which Desi and other teens can freely craft their own versions of cultural expression. Indeed, such reception underscores the need for more substantive education about Desis and other diasporic populations in the United States, rather than about South Asia or other homelands alone. For these teens, being FOBulous, not FOBby, is central to shaping what it means to be Desi. In the next chapter I continue to examine how cultural capital positions teens differently as they manage cultural and linguistic expression in the face of the model minority stereotype.

REMODELING THE MODEL MINORITY STEREOTYPE

Devan was born in Suva, Fiji, and moved to San Jose when he was four. Unlike some of his Desi peers who think fondly of their ancestral homeland, he feels no nostalgia for Fiji, and remarked, "I don't know—what's there to miss? I was only four when I left." Devan attends Waverly because he lives near the school. He considers himself to be different from his peers who attend for the medical magnet program. He prefers wrestling, football, and kickin' it with his Mexican friends to spending time with other Desis. "It's kind of funny . . . I've been here for thirteen years and I'm, like, the typical jock person that you see on TV or in movies. A typical Indian person wouldn't be on the football team or captain of the wrestling team." Though he had no interest in moving away from his Mexican clique of friends, he was lured away nonetheless. He recalled, "I didn't talk to an Indian person until I was in the eleventh grade and I met Aaliya. . . . She is the only reason I kick it with [Indians]. . . . Indian people are drama-filled. I kicked it with Mexicans, they didn't have dramas. If they want to go out in the middle of the night they could, and I can, but then no one else can."

Devan prioritizes sports and his relationship with Aaliya, his Indo-Fijian girl-friend, above all else. As graduation approached, he reflected, "One thing I wish is that I did better academically. I could have done so much more and better but I didn't. Academically I got lazy . . . I always found a reason not to do my best. . . . I'm the youngest so I'm supposed to be the best. I'm not the smartest, I'm actually at the lowest end. In Fiji, you have to be the best. My sister never even got a B. My responsibility would be to take care of my mom." Feeling the weight of family duty and the desire to offer a good life to Aaliya, Devan is preparing for his future by working at the Home Depot as he finishes high school and will take out loans to start technical school at DeVry Institute. When asked what he might do differently when he *starts a family, he quickly replied, "I would be there more for my kids. My mom works sixteen hours a day and I never see her. We all hope for a house, but with the growing housing prices . . . we'll see."*

School is an integral part of Desi teen culture. Longer term paths are formed and secured through everyday practices at school: how youth are able to manage their classes and seek help as needed, the extent to which they participate in school activities, how their cliques are positioned on the school campus, and what languages they use to socialize. Until this point I have focused on what constitutes Desi teen culture and how youth signify it in their cultural and linguistic practices and performances. Their orientation toward academics is also important to defining these ideas. How teens orient themselves toward their schools and communities has been significant throughout, guiding the formation of social cliques, where teens kick it at school, and the ways they relate to the school as an institution. In this chapter I focus on schooling and examine how Desi teens manage the expectations placed upon them.[1]

The model minority stereotype shapes expectations of success for Desi youth, and youth manage these pressures in different ways. More than any other arena of youth life, high school has the most clearly defined standards of what success means. Desis are regarded as among the most accomplished and wealthy players in the high-tech industry. Desi teens in Silicon Valley are similarly held to high standards, and moreover must contend with the model minority stereotype. By casting success as an innate capability, the model minority stereotype overshadows the essential role of cultural capital in shaping how Desi teens and their parents are able to manage the school system. Choices that teens make about high school and beyond are deeply influenced by their parents' orientations and ideals. Educational background, fluency in English, class status, and occupation all contribute to the type of social knowledge about schooling that parents are able to pass on to their children. Such information is instrumental not only to academic success, but also to understanding the broader codes of conduct in this institutional setting.

While cultural capital does not predetermine outcomes, it does predispose youth toward certain paths, especially in the monolingual high school. Youth who do not have the cultural capital to acknowledge and follow the monolingual dictates of their high school are especially subject to negative judgments and disadvantageous positioning. Cultural capital also helps to explain how youth dispositions are shaped, rather than blaming them for their perceived lack of motivation, hope, aspiration, and willpower (Bourdieu and Passeron 1977/1990: 207).

How Desi teens manage the model minority stereotype in high school can affect their lives after high school. The model minority stereotype discursively creates racial meanings through faculty and student narratives, actions, and school policies, and accordingly shapes youth perceptions and goals. Racialized discourse about the stereotype operates within particular bounds of power but is not easily identifiable as such (Palumbo-Liu 1999). Michel Foucault's (1979) concept of discourse illustrates how knowledge and power interact to shape social meaning: discourses "systematically form the objects of which they speak" and illustrate subject formation, especially with regard to racial meaning (49).

The relationship between what faculty think of teens and how they regard themselves and their education is often a site of contention. Whether they are college-bound and have to manage expectations of perfection, or are not considering college and have to handle the disappointment of teachers who expect them to care about higher education simply because they are Desi, these teens must negotiate a range of expectations that school faculty place on them. This stereotype creates tremendous pressure for Desi students to excel in academic arenas. With high expectations of success, Desi teens who do not succeed are routinely subject to judgment, but are less frequently offered assistance. Moreover, the narrowly conceived ideas of success on which the model minority stereotype is premised leave little room for alternative meanings generated by youth and their communities. To address these other values, I use the term "remodeling" as a reminder that not all youth fit this model stereotype, nor do they desire to. Such pressures exacerbate an already competitive school environment for some, while making others feel even more alienated. These actions bear on teen orientations toward their community and how they envision their future after high school.

Desi communities can create alternative meanings of success and look to the high-tech industry to achieve them. In a capitalist economy, where public schools tend to produce workers for a wide range of occupational positions, not all students are college-bound. Studies of social reproduction closely examine how schools both deliberately and inadvertently con-

tribute to maintaining particular social and class hierarchies. Pierre Bourdieu (1985: 11) argues that pedagogical actions "always tend to reproduce
the structure of the distribution of cultural capital among these groups or
classes, thereby contributing to the reproduction of the social structure."
Along these lines, Paul Willis (1977) succinctly subtitles his book *How
Working Class Kids Get Working Class Jobs*. While this trend was visible in my
work as well, during the height of the high-tech industry in the late 1990s
this was not the only possibility. Youth whose parents worked on assembly
lines, in food and transportation service, or in similar positions considered new opportunities in the high-tech field as a way of potentially break-
ing this cycle of social reproduction. "The promise of technology" that I
discussed in chapter 1 suggests that higher education is not a prerequisite
for wealth and fame, and middle-class youth who have a tenuous relationship with schooling use this possibility to envision other paths to success.

MANAGING THE MODEL MINORITY STEREOTYPE

For Asian American students, the model minority stereotype implies that
high academic achievement and excellent conduct are foregone conclu-
sions (S. Lee 1996). This stereotype not only keeps some Asian American
students from being considered "normal" (Zhou and Lee 2004), but also
leaves others to struggle to accomplish the high standards associated with
the term (S. Lee 2004: 123; see also Ernst 1994; Ima 1995; Lew 2004).
Moreover, some Asian Pacific American youth—especially refugees from
Vietnam and Cambodia or lower socioeconomic groups such as Hmong
and Pacific Islanders—are not poised to perform educationally like many
of their higher achieving peers from East and South Asia (Inkelas 2006).

While the model minority stereotype has been extensively challenged in
academic literature, its strength has only increased in Silicon Valley. On the
one hand, it is difficult to argue against the widely heralded accomplishments of Desis in Silicon Valley. As a competitive and lucrative industry,
high tech has drawn the lion's share of highly educated, technologically
trained individuals who are well poised to succeed. Many Desis in Silicon
Valley have the cultural capital to succeed in this process and inculcate in
their children the need to develop similar skills. Such a disposition, however, speaks more to the type of professional immigration the United States
sought rather than an innate aptitude in Desis. As I discussed in earlier

chapters, the idea of success has become so naturalized for Desis in Silicon Valley that high performance in schools and in the high-tech industry appears to be a natural quality that people from the Indian Subcontinent possess, rather than skills cultivated through schooling and privilege.

To say that Asian American students are successful merely because they are racially categorized as Asian suggests a biological underpinning to success—a sentiment that I repeatedly heard from Silicon Valley school faculty. Reminiscent of other debates about race purporting that certain characteristics are biologically determined rather than culturally acquired, a similarly reductive logic underpins this stereotype. This is not to discount the significance of race, however. If anything, such debates invite closer examination of the pervasive racial discourse that shapes everyday meanings for Desi teens in school. Being Asian American means being held to higher standards than students of other races and having to manage a rigorous set of expectations. Remarks such as those of former NYU president John Brademas lauding Asian American students for their "Confucian work ethic" or Waverly High School's tenth-grade science teacher Gita Biswas expressing shock that Desi students could actually fail her in courses convey a similar message: that Asian American students are uniformly poised to excel and to not do so is an individual shortcoming.[2] What these comments fail to acknowledge, however, is that Desi teens who perform well can quickly become the object of envy and frustration at their school, while those who perform poorly contend more often with faculty disappointment than support.

Working the System • Desi teens predictably have different ideas of what it means to be successful in high school. It can mean anything from not failing and avoiding becoming the subject of vicious gossip to being valedictorian or prom queen. For some teens who watch their peers drop out of high school to join gangs or end up in "juvi" (juvenile hall), graduation alone confers success. For others, nothing short of being ranked at the top of their class and attending the competitive college of their choice will do. Cultural capital shapes student ideas of success, including their positioning in schools and orientation toward their studies. In the previous chapter, I discussed how popular students are able to leverage their more sophisticated understanding of the school to achieve their goals in multicultural programs and, more broadly, in school activities. Geeks are also able to orient themselves to the culture of the school and find ways to manage the system. Both geeks and populars are predominantly upper middle class and their parents are actively involved in their studies. Most of these parents immigrated to the United States after 1965 with professional qualifications. Their fathers have at least a bachelor's degree and the mothers are well educated and literate in English. While many of these adults arrived in the United States unfamiliar with the school system, their comfort with educational institutions and their excellent English-speaking skills facilitated their learning about their child's schooling. They share information with their extended family and friends to build a community knowledge base about school policies and programs.

At home, upper-middle-class parents emphasize the importance of earning high grades and test scores from elementary school onward. They prioritize schoolwork and draw on their own educational background to help their children with homework and school assignments.[3] It is not unusual for Desi parents of this class background to push their children to perform academically and emphasize education over leisure.[4] These parents also have the financial means to ply their children with spending money and urge them to focus on school assignments and pursue internships that will embellish their résumés. Many upper-middle-class Desi parents want their children not only to perform well academically but to outperform their Desi peers and others at the top.[5] Mr. Shah, father of Tara, a popular girl, prioritizes his children's education over all else. While he enjoys watching Bollywood films with Tara and supports her dancing, he emphasized, "Academically, we have expectations. It was drilled into them that they have to go to college. In some White families, this topic does not even come up, but for Indian kids, they are told there is no other way. After high school, you go to college." Although Mr. Shah's comments encompass Desi youth in general, this outlook is far more common to his class than to middle-class parents.

Along with their parents, upper-middle-class teens expend considerable effort to create and maintain an advantageous position for themselves at their schools. Parents are likely to become routinely involved and assertive in school on behalf of their kids and do not hesitate to approach the school about their child's performance. Tanya Hill, an assistant principal at Mercer, remarked, "Indian parents are concerned and they are here all the time, [especially] if they feel that their kids are not excelling as

147

much as they should be. Parents come all the time and request teachers to change [grades], saying it must be the teacher, not their son or daughter. There must be an error, must be a mistake!" Ms. Hill's comment indicates that upper-middle-class parents not only place high expectations on their children to succeed academically, but intervene as needed to facilitate such outcomes.

Following their parents' example, upper-middle-class teens tend to be extremely proactive in redressing wrongs and taking advantage of school enrichment activities. Through the cultural capital instilled by their parents, they are experts at following school procedures and advocating for themselves. At Waverly, upper-middle-class geek girls Ananya and her friend are pushed by their parents but are rewarded by being the best in their school. They work hard, but they also know how to make the school work for them. They make use of all the enrichment opportunities that their medical magnet school has to offer, even if it means having their mothers shuttle them around to various enrichment activities—a luxury most middle-class teens do not have.

Handling Expectations • Upper-middle-class Desi students have earned a reputation for being relatively easy to manage and discipline. As I discussed in chapter 3, these teens understand and carefully observe the dictates of school as an English-only space and reserve ethnic and linguistic expression for designated school events or in the privacy of their cars when they are off-campus. When they use their heritage language, it is mostly for inside jokes or to gossip about people within earshot. Aside from minor infractions such as cutting classes to go shopping, they tend to stay out of trouble. Exceptions to this trend, though infrequent, are especially glaring. In one such incident that occurred at Mercer at the end of the school year before I began fieldwork, a group of Desi boys were involved in an ongoing feud with White boys at a neighboring high school that culminated in one Desi boy beating a White student unconscious with a golf club. Already eighteen, the Desi student was tried and incarcerated as an adult. Momentarily shattering the image of Desis as model minorities at Mercer, the incident sent shock waves throughout the school and community and served as a cautionary tale to Desi students with whom I spoke. School faculty and community members regarded the event as anomalous, and many blamed the boy's family for not preventing the incident.

Such rare instances notwithstanding, school faculty are dazzled by the performance of some Desi students, so much so that high performance is considered a forgone conclusion. Teachers and administrators routinely offered me unsolicited lists of their top Desi students who were also involved in leadership, sports, and clubs, and often had finished at least one year of college coursework at the nearby community college. Teachers recognize and laud what they identify as family-inculcated study habits, tenacity, and leadership skills. In class, they openly praise these Desi teens and other Asian American students, hold them up as a standard of comparison for other students, and nominate them for various awards and honors. During my conversation with Greene Vice Principal Harriet Sherwin, she directed my attention to a wall in the main office that features photos of leadership students and elected student body officers. The wall is, in fact, covered with the familiar faces of Desi teens who are active in various school activities and programs, including popular girls Jaspreet and Amanpreet, several of their friends, and elected officers Rafiq and Lata. Ms. Sherwin added that she has frequent interactions with their parents about class placement, grades, and college planning. She commented, "There's a lot of pressure here on the kids. The pressure comes from home, and it comes from within themselves. There is lot of peer pressure . . . and a certain amount of pressure from the staff too, but I think the bulk of it comes from the home." Other school faculty note the pressure students face but suggest that much of it is self-inflicted. Waverly Principal Akimoto expressed this sentiment:

> I sense that the students do perform at a very high level because their parents expect it. Not only that, they expect that the students expect themselves to function at a very high level. It's not only this external pressure, it's *internal* pressure. That's a very interesting thing because in some of the cultures, it's purely external, but this particular culture instills in their students that they ought to not necessarily respond externally to their parents but they need to listen to the internal voice that says Bs are not good enough, they only get As. There is peer pressure too. There are also cultural expectations. Not that pressure is a bad thing; it is what makes people move forward in many respects. From India, most of my personal experiences have been with those who have been very successful academically. Most of the parents I have met of Indian students are professional people and they are very well educated.

Although Principal Akimoto is Japanese American and he acknowledges the role of well-educated parents in Desi success, he nonetheless suggests that Desi teens find the drive to succeed within themselves—a cornerstone of the model minority stereotype.

At Mercer, success is not only a foregone conclusion but also a widespread expectation for Asian American students. One reason high accomplishment seems commonplace at this high school is because droves of Asian American families pay hugely inflated sums for homes in this school district and push their children to perform at the highest levels. Especially compared to the White families who have lived in this area for generations, these newer arrivals have raised the bar to unprecedented heights. These latter students are held in such high esteem that they are expected not only to succeed, but to make up for the school's shortcomings as well. Activities director Mr. Watson confirmed this trend: "Kids are focused on doing well, doing leadership and other events, getting into college. It's a good student body, particularly at a school where everything else is falling apart. If you had a bad student body, I would have been out of here, as would a lot of other teachers." Mr. Watson's comment underscores what many kids at this school already know: that the onus of success and the responsibility for claiming resources rest on the students.

Desi teens handle these expectations in different ways. For some, high school is a breezy prelude to the more rigorous academic challenge of college. Abhishek, one of twenty valedictorians in his class and geek extraordinaire, considers his performance in high school to be nothing remarkable. "High school is high school. . . . Here in the Valley, everyone who is here knows what they are doing, all are motivated, so they all do their work. . . . It's ordinary, nothing unusual." Most teens do not have as easy a time as Abhishek. Desi teens at all three schools feel pressure to succeed, but especially at Mercer. Students cram in as many Advanced Placement and community college classes as possible to make their applications to competitive four-year universities distinctive. As a result, they are stressed, overextended, and often exhausted. In spite of this toll, not achieving is not an option. Feroze remarks that his father rented a small home for his family in this district so that his children could attend Mercer. Feroze imitated his father: " 'Be a straight 4.0 student.' He wants me to be an engineer or a doctor. Stereotypical!" Likewise, geek girl Anji explained that her good grades at Mercer have not come easily, and that it is easy to get left behind. She commented, "There is a lot of pressure to perform well if you are a high achiever. I think the high achievers will do well, but the low achievers, I don't know if the Mercer atmosphere is good for them." In addition to this pressure, Desi and other Asian American students sense resentment from their White peers. Renee, a popular White girl at Mercer, summed up a common sentiment expressed toward Asian American students: "They're always studying, and we can't compete. Why should I work hard when I know some Chinese kid is going to do better than me?" School faculty remark that they frequently hear this same complaint from non–Asian American parents but are baffled as to what these parents expect them to do.

Despite all this, Desi teens attempt and usually manage to have a balanced life. Popular Desi teens participate in school activities, plan multicultural performances, and run for elected offices while remembering the importance of securing admission to the college of their choice. Geeks rarely think of anything but college, but they too manage to fit in academic clubs and other activities to their liking. FOBs have the most difficult time with the model minority stereotype and school in general.

STRUGGLING WITH THE MODEL MINORITY STEREOTYPE

Middle-class Desi teens are held to the same stringent model minority standards but are rarely equipped or positioned to perform like their upper-middle-class peers. Lacking the requisite cultural capital to take advantage of their overcrowded high schools, they consistently confound and disappoint school faculty. Middle-class parents rarely have the same professional qualifications as upper-middle-class parents. Many were sponsored by relatives already living in the United States, and their educational backgrounds vary; some have postsecondary degrees, but most have completed only some amount of high school and have experience doing agricultural or unskilled labor in Punjab, Bangladesh, and Fiji. Few of these adults were educated in English-medium schools. While they learned to read, write, and speak English as a subject, they rarely had the opportunity to become fluent in this language. Fathers of middle-class Desi teens can communicate in English, but far fewer of their mothers can converse comfortably. Most mothers either stopped their education early or never became confident speaking English; they accordingly hold jobs that require minimal

English, such as assembly line, custodial, or food service work. Other mothers do not work outside of the home or know how to drive a car. Many middle-class teens hold afterschool and weekend jobs to contribute to family income or earn spending money for clothes, music, and other things their parents cannot afford to finance.

Few middle-class parents develop the type of sophisticated knowledge about their children's schools that upper-middle-class parents do. Although they discuss many things at their community gatherings, they rarely talk about the inner workings of schools. Little information on this topic circulates in middle-class communities, and parents learn about school policies and procedures far more haphazardly. These parents rarely join school organizations such as the PTA or question the schools' decisions regarding their children's educational placement.[6] Faculty sometimes perceive this as disinterest. Ricardo Lopez, an administrator who manages Greene's ESL (English as a second language) and ELD (English language development) programs, scanned a list of Desi students he considers problematic and remarked, "See these absences? It's high. I'm kind of wondering if the parents know that. [In] reading she got an F." When I asked if parents know when their child is failing, he replied, "No. It's sad that the parents don't know the system. Probably don't know report cards, grades. I'm sure if we got the parents to school or somebody else to go over there and educate them as far as what we expect of kids, then I think they would have a bigger interest in the kid's education."

Despite their concern for their children's education, middle-class parents primarily visit the school only when summoned, which usually happens when their child is in academic or disciplinary trouble. During meetings where their child is present as a translator, a particular version of reality is communicated to the parents. In these instances, the parents remain on the outside and their children must form their own knowledge base about the school and find a way to advocate for themselves. Homework and grades are certainly important to these parents, but in most cases they are unable to offer academic help.

Managing Negative Perceptions • These dynamics affect both how faculty characterize middle-class Desi students as well as how these students regard their schooling. Teachers and administrators note what they call "an academic chasm" between Desi teens who are excelling and those left behind. Waverly Vice Principal George Miller suggested that "the middle is thinning out" and that Desi kids are either packing their schedules with Advanced Placement courses or struggling to pass basic courses such as algebra. Greene Vice Principal Harriet Sherwin added this cautionary postscript to her praise of Desi students in leadership: "You don't want to put those labels on them because that's what happened with the Vietnamese too. There are a lot of Vietnamese that are in a lot of trouble now, and they are not all your perfect students. And, that's the way people look at Indians too." Ms. Sherwin's remark suggests a fall from grace, that something "happened" to change the character of some Desi students who cannot perform like others. She did, however, reassure me that she and the faculty are equally invested in Desi students whose photos do not appear on the wall of fame: "There are a number of [Desis] who are average students. We try to accommodate them as best we can. We try not to allow them to fall through the cracks, even some of the lower ability students." Ms. Sherwin is interested in helping all students, but it is difficult to miss her disappointment when she labels some Desi students average.

Implicit in these characterizations is that as model minorities, Desis, Vietnamese, and other Asian Americans are expected to excel on their own. Faculty direct their efforts toward students they perceive to be in more dire need of assistance. In Silicon Valley, these measures are primarily aimed at Latino students. At Greene, Latino faculty members advocate on behalf of these students, but the same does not occur for Asian American students who are also in need. Student body president Rafiq is acutely aware of this dynamic, and commented:

> At this school, the administration does not make an effort to reach out to different groups. It reaches out toward the Latino group to help them out more. There is a class that I tutor . . . that helps the mediocre kids who want to go to college. The mediocre kid can either decide to go or not go to college. This class helps them decide to go. The class is full of the Latino group. The areas that we live in are populated by Latinos. Other low achievers like the Vietnamese or Punjabi kids, the way I see it, I don't think we are given that extra hand I see given to the other groups of people, probably because two of the administrators are Latino, Mr. Lopez and Mr. Alvarez, and they try to help out. It's not a schoolwide issue.

Rafiq's comment underscores why the model minority characterization is so deeply flawed. In this case, Desi FOBs as well as Vietnamese students do not have the cultural capital to perform in the ways that upper-middle-class Desi populars and geeks and other wealthy Asian American students do. While the school recognizes that Latino students may benefit from additional assistance and Latino administrators assist Latino students, an analogous system is not in place for model minorities.

Even the few Desi faculty who could look out for Desi students in need are instead preoccupied with their disappointment over low-performing Desi students. Gita Biswas, a Waverly science teacher, is surprised at the unevenness among Desi students:

> I had A students and then the others were Ds and Fs. With no in between—not a B or a C Indian student. That surprised me a lot because of my own background. All the kids in my generation are college-educated. Everyone has gone to college and has a BA, master's, or a PhD. And that really surprised me that some of these kids that were in my class were getting Ds and Fs. And being stereotypical, I thought, well, you're Indian but apparently that doesn't count for anything anymore. Some of the kids don't have that, I don't know if it's their background, but they just don't have it.

Although Ms. Biswas is aware that she is stereotyping Desi students as high performers, she nonetheless concludes that some inherently lack what is needed to succeed. Others hold Desis to such standards as well, and faculty tend to compare Desi students without taking class differences into account. Naturally such contests favor upper-middle-class students and send struggling Desi students the message that they are beyond help.

FOB Points of View • FOBS are well aware of how faculty regard them, and these ideas shape their view of the school and their studies. Among FOBS, grades are seldom, if ever, discussed. Schoolwork is mentioned as an aside or a complaint. During the summer, some repeat courses they failed during the prior year, and a few take courses scheduled for the upcoming year that they anticipate will be difficult. Preeti, a FOBby girl at Greene, remarked that she thinks many teachers regard her and her friends as a burden: "I think some teachers are not racist, but they just don't like Indians in general. I guess because they see us as outsiders, foreigners. The guys that don't get good grades. If they don't get good grades, they don't think of them as that important. They think of them as a weight on their shoulders. I hear that from other kids, too." When they have academic difficulty the FOBs rarely seek help. Renu, also a FOBby girl at Greene who has had ongoing trouble in her classes, admitted, "I don't really like my school. [My friends] are cool, but I don't like the classes. If I don't understand things, I get left behind. They just go on with the people who understand." Renu does not talk to anyone at school about her difficulty, and her teachers do not approach her either. She does whatever she can to pass: "I try to figure it out on my own or copy, get the work from someone."

FOBs are concerned about their grades, but getting all As like geeks and many populars is not always their priority. Avinash, who has a difficult time remaining interested in school, needs to keep his GPA up so he can continue playing sports. One day his coach walked by after school when Avinash, Janvi, and I were kickin' it on a bench in the back corner of the school campus. The following is an excerpt from our taped conversation:

AVINASH: [shouting to his coach] What's up, Coach?

COACH: [shouting back] Make your grades?

AVINASH: No.

COACH: Did you try to?

AVINASH: I tried!

SHALINI: What grades do you need?

AVINASH: Huh?

SHALINI: You need good grades to do what?

AVINASH: I got three Fs and . . . and 2 Bs.

JANVI: Hey, I passed all my classes! I got 4 Ds and 2 As . . . not bad for my parents. Well, it's baaaad, but I did better than last year.

SHALINI: Are you having a hard time or just not doing your work, or both?

AVINASH: I cut a lot, and once I started, it was really hard to catch up afterwards. That's what I tried to do.

JANVI: I don't think I cut.

Avinash's predicament is not unusual. He knows he needs better grades to continue to play sports, but the temptation of cutting class and kickin' it with friends is more appealing. His parents are not entirely unaware of what is happening at the school, but do not get involved themselves. Avinash has gotten himself into a place that is difficult to get out of. Janvi is passing her classes and has to answer to her parents more regularly. Although they do not pressure her, the mere knowledge of having to check in with them is enough to keep her from failing. Their friend Harminder, who also kicks it with them behind the C building, has figured out this pattern and has tried to become more invested in school. He explained, "My friends don't think about this stuff. I'm probably at a different level. I finally know that without an education you're nothing. They probably haven't figured that out. . . . Everyone has a brain, they gotta go in the right direction. I guess it's the influence you have from your friends." Harminder related that he almost got derailed himself because of friends; he has started to kick it with Avinash, who cuts and smokes marijuana but at least tries to come to school.

Such dynamics contradict the prevalent belief that Desis simply do not need assistance when it comes to performing in school or planning for their future. Desi youth who are able to keep up with but not excel at their school work are rarely encouraged to aim high. Simran, a FOBby girl who contemplates becoming a nurse, has become ambivalent about pursuing a postsecondary degree. Although she used to think about college often, discussions with teachers and guidance counselors have eroded her enthusiasm: "My teachers tell me don't apply to Stanford or Harvard, just apply to Chico State and UC Davis. You don't have the grades for it." While Simran and other FOBs most likely do not have the grades for Stanford or Harvard, they receive virtually no assistance with this process and must fend for themselves or give up. Already marked as mediocre in the eyes of the school, they become conspicuous in other ways as well. They tend to cut class frequently and are cited for insubordinate behavior, fighting, and other transgressions. They also do not recognize or follow the monolingual dictates of high school—an oversight that can have longer term consequences.

SPEAKING IN THE MONOGLOT HIGH SCHOOL

Although many areas of high school life openly cultivate the model minority stereotype, one that quietly underpins it is the English monoglot standard. Language practices, among other cultural factors, can complicate how students of color relate to their education (Cammarota 2004). How youth use language can vary according to class and is differentially problematic for boys and girls. For some Desi students, being bilingual and steeped in practices of code-switching in school can lead to incorrect assessments of student ability. The symbolic capital of language is not to be underestimated. Pierre Bourdieu and Jean-Claude Passeron (1977/1990: 73) note, "The influence of linguistic capital, particularly manifest in the first years of schooling when the understanding and use of language are the major points of leverage in teachers' assessments, never ceases to be felt: style is always taken into account, implicitly or explicitly, at every level of the educational system."

Faculty keep a close watch on FOBs and listen to them during their day-to-day activities at school. Indeed, Desi youth at Greene who do not catch the busy eye of faculty by procuring a spot on the wall of fame in the main office are instead located by surveillance. FOBs are most subject to this type of attention from faculty because they kick it in the back of the school and code-switch loudly. Though neither of these activities is forbidden, they nonetheless draw the attention of Mr. Lopez and other administrators who patrol the school campus in their golf carts. While FOBs mind their behavior when they see an administrator or teacher approaching, they generally do not stop code-switching. As I discussed in chapter 3, FOBby boys openly curse in Punjabi or Hindi not only because it is enjoyable, but because it is undetectable as profanity. Though it is not punished as profanity, faculty nonetheless mark it as different and take note.

Loud displays of profanity are how Mr. Lopez initially noticed several cliques of FOBs. He recalled his surprise when he realized they are not Latino: "Where did they come from? Our population is so brown. And you were color-blind, let's say. East Indians look like Hispanics. Some of them are real dark, they may look like Afro-Americans. They come here, and it's not like they have a big flag saying 'I'm East Indian.' " In a veritable sea of brown faces at school, Mr. Lopez explains that it took a while to realize that these students are not Latino. This racial ambiguity, which is rarely an issue for East Asian or Southeast Asian students, is quickly cleared up by language use. Mr. Lopez notes that he hears them speaking in "Indian" (that is, Punjabi or Hindi/Urdu) when he patrols the school campus. As we sit in his office, he scans his list of Desi students in remedial English classes. The associations between his list, ESL students, and youth who code-switch but speak English fluently are quite loose. When he sees groups of Desi teens not speaking English, they potentially become Desi teens who may not be able to speak English well.

Surveilling the School Campus · On a typically sunny California morning, Mr. Lopez offered to show me how he makes such assessments and invited me to accompany him on his golf cart for surveillance rounds during the morning break. I was eager to take this guided tour but did not want to be seen riding in the dreaded conveyance that is synonymous with discipline. After offering my most compelling pitch for walking, he reluctantly agreed. We covered less ground, but a pattern nonetheless emerged about how he and other school administrators make judgments that link language use with other types of school-related dispositions. Gesturing toward the FOBs, Mr. Lopez remarked, "Of the kids I talk to, a lot don't speak English really well yet, the ones who are making that transition. . . . To participate in school events, you need to communicate, and they haven't got to that level yet where they can communicate adequately with the rest of the population. Because of their English, they pretty much stay by themselves, which hurts, because they speak their own language and they don't speak in English and they don't get any better." This association between having limited proficiency in English and being bilingual can be very detrimental to FOBs. While a handful of youth actually need ESL classes, the vast majority of FOBs speak English fluently and with an American accent; many actually speak it better than their heritage language. Yet faculty who see FOBby cliques kickin' it together and speaking loudly in Punjabi or Hindi assume that these Desi teens are not comfortable speaking English. This, along with their infrequent and reticent interactions with school faculty, exacerbate the situation.

Several remarks Mr. Lopez made on our tour led me to initiate a lengthier conversation with him about the school's stance on languages other than English. The Home Language Survey, which Mr. Lopez and I discuss below, is part of the 1995 California Education Code (Article 313), which attempts to determine which language(s) are spoken in a student's home. Mr. Lopez paraphrases the questions and offers his perspectives on how this survey identifies students as needing remedial help with English.[7]

> SHALINI: I've noticed that kids who are native English speakers are in ESL or ELD classes. Why is that?
>
> MR. LOPEZ: One of the biggest problems we have with our assessment process—what triggers off assessment is what is called a "home language survey," where four questions are asked: what language you learned first;

what language is spoken to you at home; what language do you speak mostly at home; and is there another language spoken at home? Obviously if you're not White, there was another language spoken at home, by somebody—I'm sure a grandmother, et cetera. Minorities haven't been here that long that somebody in our family doesn't speak another language. So obviously they're going to say yes to that question, and that triggers off a test. I mean, the kid can speak nothing but English, the parents can speak nothing but English, but if Grandma comes over and speaks to them in Spanish, then we have to test them. A lot of the kids we're getting here, regardless of their background, don't have grade-level skills. And that has nothing to do with language, but the Office of Civil Rights and all the higher-ups figure that if there's another language at home, that it's going to interfere with your school work. So we test, and if you test low, you're ESL. It makes no sense, but that's what it is.

SHALINI: Even if English is their only language?

MR. LOPEZ: Yes.

SHALINI: But they don't test kids who need English help but speak no other languages at home?

MR. LOPEZ: No.

SHALINI: That's a bit troubling, isn't it?

MR. LOPEZ: Yeah, and I've been fighting that for a long time. Hopefully they'll come up with another instrument. I have always fought that fourth question, and I think next year they are going to take that off. So if there is English, English, English answered to those questions, then the fourth one doesn't count anymore. If they take that fourth question off, it would save us a lot of heartache, because those kids—the parents come in and say he or she has never been in ESL classes and I don't want them in ESL classes. If they ask me that, I gotta grant them that, and put them in mainstream classes.

Mr. Lopez affirms that the school's policy on languages other than English is deeply problematic. The test privileges an ideology of English monolingualism and singles out immigrant and bilingual youth, both of whom are predominantly students of color. Students of European descent are tested only when their family immigrated recently, which in this case means a small group of Russian and eastern European students. By and large the test is administered to Latino and Asian immigrant children, children of immigrants, or even grandchildren of immigrants.

Mr. Lopez readily admits the discriminatory nature of this test and is frustrated with the system he is in charge of enforcing. Although he would like to closely monitor the progress of all ESL students and place them in mainstream English classes as soon as possible, other priorities usually take precedence. In light of the massive population growth this area has experienced, he is barely able to find desks and classrooms for every student and manage fights that break out on the school campus. Properly understanding and addressing the needs of every ethnic group of students on campus seldom happens. He and the other faculty do the best they can and expect students and their parents to be proactive in taking advantage of school activities and resources and bringing problems to their attention.

Until the test changes, parents are welcome to request that their children be mainstreamed or moved out of the ESL track and into regular classes. The problem, however, is that most middle-class parents rarely approach the school about anything. Most are not even aware that their children are being tested and placed in these classes, and their children are reluctant to urge them to contact the school on their behalf. This decision is not surprising, as few FOBs believe that the school faculty will actually help them, especially when extra testing caused this predicament. Avinash and Charanpal are among the FOBs who are misplaced in ELD classes. Avinash was born in San Jose; he understands his heritage language, Punjabi, and some Hindi from watching Bollywood films, but he is fluent only in English. Although Charanpal speaks Punjabi, he moved to San Jose when he was six and has been educated almost entirely in the American school system. Avinash expresses frustration about getting tracked into ELD and exclaimed, "I don't even speak Punjabi! The only language I speak is English!" While Charanpal does not make quite the same claim, he too is fluent in English. They are most likely in ELD because of their low grades in English, among other subjects, and because they responded on the survey that they live with Punjabi speakers.

While students are technically supposed to move out of ELD after a year or two, they can become stuck in this track. Even when ELD teachers recommend that kids be mainstreamed into regular English classes, the school is often unable to accommodate them in these overenrolled classes. This makes school even more discouraging for students like Raminder, a FOBby girl who was born in Hong Kong and moved to San Jose when she was eight years old. Although she speaks English fluently, she was placed directly into ELD classes. Despite her pleas to the administration to mainstream her, her parents have not approached the school because neither of them can take time off from their assembly line jobs during the day. Even if they did, Raminder would have to translate for them, and she has decided that the entire event would be futile. Her ELD teacher, Kim Parker, noted that her attendance has become increasingly sporadic. "She's bored with this class, which is why she cuts. It's totally understandable, it's not challenging for her." For many FOBs, their lack of involvement in school activities and unreflective use of a heritage language in school settings place them at a serious disadvantage and draw them toward other options.

THE PROMISE OF TECHNOLOGY

Despite their school's assessment of them as average, most middle-class youth do not glamorize blue-collar life as a means of rebelling against this judgment. Instead, they say they want a chance to make something of their lives—a process that depends on achieving financial security. Even middle-class teens who hold afterschool jobs hardly glorify the work they do. Raminder regaled her friends with war stories from working at the fast-food restaurant Wendy's. As we sat around the school picnic table, she complained that she gets yelled at when her register total comes out wrong and that cranky customers scream at her from the drive-through window. Her friends are sympathetic; none envy her. Raminder is herself concerned about how to find her way into more satisfying work options. For middle-class families, achieving at school and attending a competitive four-year college is certainly prestigious but is not the only means by which one can attain status and financial security. Another viable and respected option is taking the necessary steps to find a well-paying job.

Many middle-class teens aspire to transcend their parents' class position and occupation. The potential for such a shift lies in a plethora of midlevel technology positions, such as systems operators and network administrators. These low-tech niches in the high-tech industry connote professional managerial status; moreover, they are accessible, well paying, usually offer better hours, and confer a prestige that is out of reach for their parents. Neetu, a middle-class Sikh girl, recounted, "My mom is living out her dreams through us, me and my brother. She wants us to become something, so we don't have to work long hours. They have been working a long time, long hours. They don't want us to do that." Teens who have a harder time finding their way in school look to the high-tech industry as a way of making a better life for themselves than the life their parents have.

Desi teens who have had trouble staying in school emphasize the importance of parental supervision during these formative years. Uday, whose uncle saved him from dropping out of school, considers himself lucky compared to his friend Charanpal, who has dabbled in drugs and gang-related activity; both of Charanpal's parents work on the same assembly line shift. He commented, "If you have [both] your parents working at the same time, you have all the free time to do what you want. His parents work together from 3:30 p.m. to 12 midnight, and he has nine hours of free time. My parents can watch us." He added about his own future, "I don't want to work as hard. With my kids, it's going to be up to me to get my education and get a good job." This desire to break out of this pattern contrasts with the type of social reproduction Paul Willis documents in *Learning to Labor*. Willis's lads resent their schools' mediocre assessment of them but make it a self-fulfilling prophesy by dropping out and eventually taking up their parents' working-class jobs. In contrast, these Desi teens want neither their parents' jobs nor the mediocrity of their parents' working-class lives and are turning to their communities for alternatives that their schools do not provide.

High-Tech Dreams • Desi teens who have difficulty in school take stock in the idea that the high-tech industry is not reliant on traditional academic achievement for success. Indeed, some of Silicon Valley's most renowned personalities have only a high school diploma or became millionaires during high school and make this path seem more tenable than ever. Teens such as Avinash are confident that the high-tech industry will come through for them when the time comes; he looks to this idea for reassurance when he cuts class or has a hard time focusing on school. He is not worried about his future, however: "Job-wise, Silicon Valley is really good. It will help me out later. Right now I really don't think [doing well academically] matters." Avinash and other teens struggling in high school keep in mind the countless well-paying technology jobs that require only a short stint of training at a local technology institute. After a short certification course, he can have the last laugh on high school as he performs a limited but lucrative range of technical tasks as a systems operator, network professional, or expert in an operating system such as Windows or Unix.

Technology is especially significant for middle-class teens who have little exposure to professional environments and corporate offices. Devan is the middle-class boy whose mother is a nurse's aid and whose father is a cafeteria worker at a microchip company whom you met at the start of this chapter. An episode he shared with me emphasizes the importance of cultural capital in career aspirations. Devan's English teacher arranged an interview for him for a flexible, well-paying filing job at his friend's law office to defray the costs of technical school. During the interview, Devan felt uncomfortable and intimidated about not being smart enough to work at a law office, even though he thought he could handle the work. His teacher conveyed to me that during Devan's interview as well as follow-up phone conversation, his interviewer thought he sounded arrogant. Devan told his teacher that he thought he was being respectful and was nervous.

The job was given to someone else, and Devan remains at his position at Home Depot. The wages are competitive, but his hours are long, and he has no other means of paying for his costly tuition at DeVry. Devan explained the toll it is taking on him: "Every D or F I get costs me $42,000, and it's hard because I don't have time to study." Although he exaggerates the cost of each grade, his broader point that he must find a way to pass tech school to make it out of Home Depot is well made. When I asked him whether it is worth it, he looked at me incredulously and replied, "Ever been to Home Depot? Do you see how stressful that job can be? There are, like, a hundred of you looking for me!" Although Devan cannot envision himself in a law office, he considers training for and holding a low-tech, gray-collar job both appealing and within reach.

In this sense, technology is as much about modernity and the future as it is about familiarity for teens who consider the white-collar world to be too alien for their comfort. The class mobility promised by gray-collar jobs appears to challenge the established pattern of social reproduction between generations. Although the long-term promise of these positions is unknown, their connotation of success is highly valued. For children of assembly line and other unskilled workers, the opportunity to attain prestigious jobs without postsecondary education is indeed rare, but the social significance of succeeding in this way is paramount.

In the late 1990s, middle-class youth relied heavily on their family and community networks to aid their entrance into new niches in the high-tech industry. Many Desi communities were well situated to take advantage of such opportunities collaboratively. Younger Desi adults—usually men in their twenties and early thirties—saw the benefit of addressing the need for midlevel workers and tapped into their community networks. These Desi entrepreneurs set up institutes that offered computer certification courses. Such centers were advertised on local-access television, in diasporic newspapers, and, most effectively, by word of mouth. They offered to train enrollees within six months and assist with job placement as well.

Community gatherings are an ideal place to network about such opportunities. Preeti, a middle-class Sikh girl, recounted that her parents cannot afford the $40,000 a year it would cost for a four-year college, and added, "I can't get into a university because of my grades, and I don't think of myself as the kind to go to college for four years. I have to have something quick so I can do it, get a job, and start thinking about life." Her mother added, "It's hard to raise a kid here; it's very, very expensive. We want Preeti to go to a really good school to get her degree but it's very hard for us to afford [that] because we have four kids. If it was just one then we could have it, but in our culture when they get married you have to spend a lot of money too. So we want to be even with all four of them. If one goes to an expensive school I don't want the others to be left out." Shortly after graduation, at her uncle's wedding reception, Preeti found out that the twenty-two-year-old DJ also ran a Microsoft certification school. She got his business card and an invitation to enroll. She explained, "It costs twenty-five hundred dollars and takes about twelve weeks, and then you make hella money, and you're a certified network professional. My dad really wants me to do that."

While this event may seem incidental, it is one of many such instances in which Desi teens who do not achieve through traditional academic means are able to find alternative routes to success through their community networks. Community events like these are an arena for teens to network with successful members of their community, whom they sometimes consider their role models. Indeed, teenagers hear talk about the success of their older cousins and family friends and see the signs of their newfound success in their clothes and cars. By attending short training courses, often run by Desi entrepreneurs, youth can acquire their training and find employment in a matter of months and earn salaries several times higher than their parents'.

CONCLUSION

The model minority stereotype is problematic for upper-middle-class as well as middle-class Desi teens. For the former, this stereotype creates intense pressure to succeed and elicits resentment from other students. The widespread belief that all Desi youth should excel in high school labels those who do not deficient in some way. This can become a self-fulfilling prophesy for middle-class teens. As Desis who stray far from the model minority stereotype, FOBs are marginalized socially and academically at school. Rosina Lippi-Green (1997) illustrates how "standard" ways of speaking are unmarked, normalizing, and powerful in their ability to relegate other varieties as unpreferred. In these schools, the term "mainstreaming" is widely used to refer to English language students who required reabsorbtion into a presumed linguistic homogeneity of the rest of the school. In this way, schools present themselves as multicultural and open to linguistic expression, but in actuality favor monolingualism.

Desi language practices are especially problematic from the school's perspective, following a long, contentious history of language use in California. Indeed, Proposition 227 did away with bilingual education in 1998, and Proposition 187 curtailed social services for undocumented families in 1994. Desi teens who speak a heritage language freely in high schools are not only marginalized, but can be altogether overlooked. The "brownness" of Indians, as Mr. Lopez calls it, suggests that when Desi teens are not differentiating themselves, they are either problematic or forgettable. Especially when there are few mechanisms in place to help struggling Desi students the way there are for Latinos, they are left searching for other options to make the type of life they desire.

While education is certainly valued in middle-class communities, it is not the only marker of success. Participating in one's community, engaging in consumption-based practices, and following certain social and linguistic codes that further the reproduction of these communities, all inform success in significant ways. Other aspects of social life—such as becoming financially independent, contributing to the overall household income, and acquiring material dimensions of success—are considered equally important. During the high-tech boom, these goals seemed to be within reach. In the concluding chapter, I return to the promise of technology and examine its potential in Silicon Valley after the tech bubble. Before doing so, I examine a last, but absolutely critical area of Desi teen culture and success: social life. The values that underpin social interaction, dating, and marriage are integral to maintaining Desi Land as these teens know it.

DATING ON THE DL AND ARRANGED MARRIAGES

When Aaliya first moved to San Jose from a small town in Fiji to start ninth grade, she had a difficult time adjusting. Like other Indo-Fijian families, hers moved primarily for Aaliya's education and for a more financially stable life. Her father, a night watchman at a technology company, explained that the $15 per hour he makes here is a blessing compared to the backbreaking, poorly paid labor he used to do in Fiji. Unable to afford their own place when they arrived in San Jose, Aaliya and her parents moved into Aaliya's older sister's home. Along with her husband and their four-year-old son, they enjoy living in this posh part of San Jose at the base of the hills. Outside of school, Aaliya and her mother and sister love to watch Hindi films. The family is firmly rooted in the wide circle of Muslim Indo-Fijian family friends and relatives whom they know from Fiji or have since met at their musjid. Although Aaliya and her parents plan to eventually move to Stockton, where they can afford to buy their own home, good schools and plentiful jobs have made Silicon Valley a convenient stopover for all, especially since Aaliya's mother cares for her grandson while his parents work.

Aaliya's life changed during her junior year, when she began dating Devan. Unlike Aaliya, Devan moved from Fiji when he was very young and grew up in San Jose. Devan is Hindu and outspoken in his dislike for the social rules they must follow, including keeping their relationship secret from Aaliya's parents and the world at large. When the couple goes out, Aaliya insists that her close friends come along so that it does not look like she is on a date. During weeks when they cannot meet outside of school, their only contact is through their pagers. Despite all their precautions, Aaliya's mother found out about the couple during her senior year when an anonymous informer phoned her mother. While she was at school that day, her mother searched Aaliya's room to find two years' worth of cards, love letters, photos, and gifts. Aaliya and especially Devan were furious but also shocked to learn that it was their close friend Veena, also an Indo-Fijian Hindu, who had outed them. Veena confessed that she did not find their Hindu-Muslim union appropriate, but the couple suspects that it is because she has long had feelings for Devan. Aaliya continues to date Devan without her parents' consent but is far more cautious about sharing her relationship with anyone, especially her friends.

One of the hallmarks of being a teenager is having a social life. Whether this involves pursuing a love interest or kickin' it with friends outside of school, having exclusive, unmonitored peer time is a must in mainstream American teenage life. For Desi teens in Silicon Valley, however, social life can look quite different. Desi teens face numerous social rules and systems of control that enforce them. During their children's teen years, families go on high alert, so to speak, to ensure that teens avoid developing an unfavorable reputation in their community. Although codes of conduct governing coed interaction, dating, and marriage vary somewhat according to religious community and class, some standards are widely understood to be the norm. These parameters organize teenage social time in as well as outside of school, shape how they regard the actions of their Desi peers, and influence how they manage their reputation. Maintaining face in front of their community is especially important for girls. Gossip is a powerful social force in Desi communities, and teenagers engage in peer policing inside and outside of their schools.

All these proscriptions, coupled with standards of dress and comportment, can severely limit Desi teen social life. Yet teens by and large follow or quietly work around this system. Fear of gossip makes them think carefully about what they do in school as well as whom they can trust. This makes cliques, friendships, and loyalty even more important. Youth have different opinions about these social values and believe in them to different extents. Some develop strategies to circumvent this system. Keeping their social life on the "DL" or "down low" is one such tactic that teens use to avoid gossip and still date or just stay out late.[1]

Desi teens have strong opinions about arranged marriage and how they would like to affiliate with their communities as adults. It may seem unusual that marriage is an active topic in the minds of Desi teens, but those familiar with the South Asian context have likely witnessed the deep-seated obsession with this topic. Marrying within one's caste, community, and religion, or simply marrying another Desi is an agenda that has been inculcated into these teens since childhood. Arranged marriage is not only an issue about which most teens have a strong opinion; some have personal experiences as well. Desi teen narratives about these topics illuminate the tense meeting between their community's values and the contemporary California context. Pierre Bourdieu's "habitus" is a useful tool for examining the connections between ideologies and practices around social life and marriage because it draws attention to the embodied practices that govern these areas of Desi teen lives. In habitus, tradition is silent and naturalized, and "what is essential *goes without saying because it comes without saying*" (Bourdieu 1977: 167). Habitus is especially strong because Desi teens live in closely knit communities that share defined value systems about these topics.

Being a successful community member is premised on particular gendered performances in social life, dating, and marriage. Although Bourdieu argues that habitus operates in ways that obscure its mechanisms so thoroughly as to not be visible to those within it, in diasporic contexts habitus can only ever be partial because what is thought to be natural to the diasporic community is always contrasted to a mainstream ideal. In other words, what goes without saying comes without saying until teens go to school and see how their non-Desi peers live. Community ideals about social life and marriage can stand in stark contrast to mainstream American values, leaving Desi social rules exposed and open to contestation. How teens manage these ideals and look to their future shapes the communities they aspire to belong to as adults.

DESI TEEN SOCIAL RULES

For Desi teenagers, dating is seldom encouraged as an end in itself. As an activity that is far from routine for most Desi parents and still largely absent from South Asian social life, coed interaction outside of the context of a potential marriage is not encouraged. As I noted in chapter 2, most parents who grew up in South Asia did so during an era quite different from the current, cosmopolitan age, with its new types of social activities and spaces. Youth culture had yet to take hold, and ideologies of teenage freedom and rebellion were virtually nonexistent. Offering such opportunities to their children now is a conflicted process, so much so that Desi communities can be far more socially and religiously conservative than communities in South Asia. The parents of middle-class Sikh girl Umber remarked, "Life here is harder than in India, especially raising kids. But it's not their fault! They want to go out with friends, and we want to let them, but we don't feel safe. We're still typical Indians, it's hard to change one hundred percent. We can't let them wear whatever they want. We want them to dress in full clothes, no boyfriends." Like Umber, most Desi teens are subject to constraints that are not widespread in America, especially around dating, sex, and marriage.

The underlying logic of limiting youth social activity is to ensure that children marry within their caste, religion, and ethnicity. Much of this burden rests on controlling girls' sexuality, as Desi girls are thought to be especially capable of marring their family's reputation (Gibson 1988; Gillespie 1995; K. Hall 2002). Studies of gender in the Desi diaspora note the position of women as the keepers of purity, chastity, and virginity (Bhattacharjee 1992; Maira 2002). Some Desi teens share this perspective. One middle-class Muslim girl commented, "I believe not all Desi kids know to do the right thing at my age. I have friends at other schools who have boyfriends and they are not virgins and that is not good in our culture." Her remark underscores that controlling girls' sexuality is the primary concern. For girls especially, chastity is a prized virtue, and delaying sex until after marriage is important not only for individual teenagers, but for the reputation of the entire family.[2]

While girls' reputations are integral to maintaining and furthering Desi communities in Silicon Valley, girls are not simply passive followers of all social rules placed on them. Recent work critiques the characterization of Desi women as submissive keepers of tradition and instead acknowledges their dynamic role in household and international economies, cultural change, and political action (Ahmad 2003; Bhachu 1996; Rayaprol 1997). Highlighting this agency, I discuss how girls as well as boys negotiate and contest these values, as well as why they make particular choices.

Negotiating Rules • Desi teens follow social rules not simply because they are told to do so, but because they are invested in becoming adult members of the communities in which they currently live. The trade-offs and sacrifices of following what many teens consider to be a far too restrictive social system test their loyalty to these social groups and force them to consider their present desires in relation to their longer term social aspirations. Desi youth are held to the standards of their communities, but these can vary and take different forms. In Silicon Valley, middle-class Sikh teens, especially girls, are very limited in their movements outside of school. Recall, for example, the FOBby girls at Greene who were unable to attend practice at Jaspreet and Amanpreet's home. Similarly, Muslim teenagers of all class backgrounds—be they from Pakistan, India, Bangladesh, or Fiji—are also forbidden to engage in any way with the opposite sex. At Sikh and Muslim community events and religious spaces, coed socializing is frowned upon. Harminder, a middle-class Sikh boy, explains, "Sometimes, there's a wedding at the gurdwara, and my friends and I have this anxiety about Indian parents not wanting their daughters to get with guys." Even with parents present, many teens find that they cannot speak to friends of the opposite sex in these spaces, and adults immediately note transgressions.[3]

Girls from Muslim and Sikh families are especially leery of the threat of being "sent back" to live in South Asia. Azra, a middle-class Muslim girl born and raised in San Jose, values her California life and did not enjoy wearing a burka during a visit to her family's small Pakistani village. She recalled an incident that helped her realize that she has to be very cautious so that her family does not send her to live there permanently:

> I don't try to stay out late. I don't sneak out either. During Ramadan, we have to go away from worldly things and focus on religion and stuff like that, but it was hard for me, hard for most people. My friends wanted to go to the movies to see *Titanic*, way back when it was in the theaters. They told me, 'Go tell your mom we have a project to do.' But I couldn't . . . you want to but you can't, you would feel guilty all the time. I sort of had the urge to do it, but forget it; I would get in big trouble. If an incident happens, you are finished. Your education, being a doctor, it's all gone. We would go to Pakistan. I went, 'Oh my God, no!' As a daughter I understand that I can't go outside the limit.

Azra's sense of guilt keeps her from transgressing, as does the imminent threat that all her future dreams could disappear overnight if she is forced to return to Pakistan. Going back with one's family or even being sent back to live with extended family in their homeland is strong motivation to follow the rules for girls who fear losing all they dream about, including pursuing a career, marrying someone of their liking, and staying in California.

For teens with strict parents, going out with male relatives can be a socially acceptable alternative. In many Muslim communities, male relatives are responsible for protecting the honor of family women. Amahl, whose conservative Muslim parents rarely let her go out unaccompanied, has a slightly easier time when her older brothers come home from college. Taking over for her parents, they monitor her friends and whereabouts. She remarked, "My brothers are cool, they take me out. They're protective, but they let me have male friends. They take me out with their friends [and their friends'] younger brothers and sisters." These codes of interaction are generally accepted by Desi teens, who rarely speak out against or defy these standards in everyday talk and interactions.

Upper-middle-class Sikh and Hindu youth have slightly more freedom but are still subject to many of the same codes of conduct. Tara, whose parents are far less strict than the parents of her peers, commented, "They let me stay out as long as I want . . . not *really* as late but 'til twelve or one, and that's a reasonable time for a girl." Not all community members appreciate such a lack of control over teens. Kavita, also an upper-middle-class Hindu girl at Mercer, sighed that her parents think her friends' parents are too lax about their kids: "It's a little harder for me, and also because I'm the first girl in my family so, they are overprotective. I know a lot of people don't agree if I say that—they'll say that it doesn't make a difference, but I think it does make a difference." Compared to her rowdy, disobedient male cousins who live nearby, Kavita's parents make it known that she should behave more appropriately.

Managing Constraints • Desi teens make sense of these rules in different ways. One place Desi teens look for support and inspiration is Bollywood films. Unlike depictions of American romance, which feature premarital sex and do not foreground family loyalty, romantic interaction portrayed in these films appeals to Desi teen sensibilities because it follows similar cultural codes as their upbringing. Especially in romantic comedies, a favorite genre among Desi teens, film heroes and heroines are often able to achieve the impossible balancing act of fulfilling familial duty and obligation while participating in the attractive world of consumption, leisure, and young romance. Forbidden love, love triangles, and unrequited love are the biggest obstacles for reel Desis, and they allay the anxieties that real Desis have about parental rules and community codes.

Bollywood characters face versions of these problems but ultimately resolve them in a way that many teens find reassuring. Harminder said that the terrorist love story Dil Se "related to my life, because I had a thing going on when I saw that movie, and after the movie I was like shaking. You know, it literally related to my life and what was going on with me." When I jokingly asked if he was dating a terrorist, he laughed and replied, "No, I was not dating a terrorist! I was going after this girl I couldn't get— my first actual real love. I couldn't get over her for a year." Other Desi teens do not consider crossing the line, even the way Bollywood characters do. Kareena, a middle-class Sikh girl, crooned, "I love Hindi movies, my mom got me addicted to it. I watch with my dad and mom. I like the story lines, I can relate to them . . . except the love part. . . . I think the love part can happen but I don't think I will let it happen. I'm not denying it can, but I won't let it. I know people do sometimes fall in love like that, but it is just a movie." As Kareena's and Harminder's comments about these filmi narratives indicate, many teens find the concept of romance alluring but nonetheless comply with what is expected of them.

All the same, they wish the system was not quite so restrictive. Kareena, who seldom goes out without her family, explains that she has a hard time communicating to her parents why she wants to see her friends outside of school, but, she added, "I know they are just trying to watch out for me." Sometimes restrictions can be hard for teens to follow because they believe in these values but nonetheless crave social time away from their families. Even though Preeti and her sister Simran are very respectful of their parents' rules, Preeti lamented not being able to spend adult-free time with her friends: "Sometimes we just want to kick it with friends, for some support. So we tell our mom we're tutoring and stay after at school. Sometimes things just get to me, and I want to talk to somebody else." While she knows she is not being truthful to her parents in these moments, Preeti is also certain that she is not doing anything wrong by her family's standards, such as meeting boys, drinking, or participating in other illicit activity.

Other teens, however, openly object to what they consider to be an overly controlling system. A lone voice in the crowd, Devan stands out as someone who cannot fathom the disposition of his Desi friends. He emphatically declared, "Indian people, they *never* argue [with their parents], they just listen. That got me mad! It's like, you're in America now, why don't you, like, fight for your rights? But yet they don't, guys and girls don't fight for them. They couldn't go out, date girls, and they didn't want to. *Guys that grew up here!* I fight it. I'm the youngest and if I can't win, my siblings fight it for me. If you're a teenager, you do what you want, when you want." Devan has been unable to stir any of his friends into action. While he fights for his own freedom, only his Latino friends have the freedom to kick it with him.

Desi teens lament what they consider a double standard that applies in families where boys have far more flexibility and freedom than girls do. One upper-middle-class Hindu girl who is frustrated about these conditions notes the different rules that apply for her and her brothers: "[My parents] really, really don't like me to do anything. I don't go out. I don't date. I couldn't ever disobey my parents. My [younger] brother and his friends are out all the time, they don't care." Meru, a middle-class Sikh girl, is similarly aware that while her male cousins can drink and smoke at family events, such things would be unacceptable for her and the other women in her family. This limitation seems acceptable to her, but others do not. She exclaimed, "I'm covered and all I'm showing is my arms and legs, and [my parents] think there should be some secrecy, and I'm like, '*I'm covered!*' " She takes issue with not being able to wear tank tops, skirts, and shorts in public, even though it is a restriction that most girls from Sikh, Muslim, and some Hindu families have to follow in some way.

Although boys are subject to far fewer restrictions than girls are, they are still subject to many of the same rules. For many families, the idea of their son being seen in public with "inappropriate" female company or, worse still, impregnating a girl, is a serious enough offense to keep a close watch on them. Although boys can go out later and unsupervised, they are not free to date whomever they please. Uday explained his situation: "I can't tell my mom, 'Hey, I'm going out with some girls to party!' The girls don't tell *their* parents. If my parents found out they'd be trippin'. It's not like they're telling me who to marry [but] they are, like, 'Finish high school, go to college, and *then* do what you want.' " In case this message was not clear enough to Uday, his mother offered a contingency plan if he is caught dating. She only half-jokingly told him, "If you see any girl now,

I'm going to call that girl's house, and then I'm going to break your legs!" Despite this strong message, Uday did not feel entirely without choices in this situation: "They're not telling me to have an arranged marriage, and I don't want to have one. They're not forcing me. I would *want* to marry a Punjabi. They want a Punjabi *cudi* [girl] who speaks with us in Punjabi and takes care of us." Despite his restrictions on dating, he still believes he will marry someone of his choosing.

Ranvir, a middle-class Sikh boy, says his parents subject him to far fewer rules than the girls in his family, and his punishments are less stark. They nonetheless watch his movements closely. He explained:

> Whenever my mom's cleaning my room . . . she might think I am doing drugs. Couple of times I came late and my mom came into my room and started sniffing me. I said, 'Oh my God,' and I did not say nothing. My dad did that a couple of times. My mom would go, 'Your mouth smells like you have been doing cigarettes outside.' Whatever, dude, give me a drug test! They think I do drugs, but I'm not in trouble. I never do that stuff. If I did, I wouldn't come back home the next day. I wouldn't do it here. I have friends who do it, but I would not do it here. Sometimes when I go to Fresno where my cousins are. The only time I get really, really high is with my cousins. I don't do cocaine. Just did it once.

Being a boy has made Ranvir's parents relatively lax about following through on disciplining him. Going out unmonitored, staying with older cousins to do drugs and the like is a luxury most Desi girls do not have.

While some teens follow the limits set by their parents and others openly challenge them, still others neither speak out against them nor follow them. Kavita, an upper-middle-class Hindu girl, related an incident in which she went out to dinner with her friends. Her parents assumed there were other parents present but became furious when they learned the teens were unchaperoned. She reflected, "I think they are sometimes going overboard, just going out for dinner and stuff like that. My mom was like, 'Okay, well then, don't go out next time.' And I was like, 'Okay,' but I mean, I'm not going to *not* go out next time. I'm still going to go." By agreeing with her parents but not following their rules, Kavita manages to evade punishment until they learn about her next transgression.

For Kavita, as for some other girls in upper-middle-class Hindu families, there is rarely a threat of being sent back to India or being prevented from attending college. At worst, consistent disregard for parental authority could lead to their not being allowed to move away from home for school. With greater parental leeway and less dire threats, some teens are able to push the boundaries of what they are allowed to do without the repercussions their peers from more conservative families must face. In general, however, youth who try to go behind their parents' back about these things usually get caught. Meru has learned that in her community, if she changes her clothes or makeup outside of the house, it is only a matter of time until her parents come to know about it: "People will tell my mom, 'Oh, did you see her daughter, she's wearing dark lipstick?' Or 'Did you see your daughter's clothes?' if my stomach shows a little bit." The idea that someone somewhere is always watching may sound paranoid, but given their tightly knit communities and the limited amount of public space in Silicon Valley, there is a good chance that teens will be noticed in most places they go.

SYSTEMS OF SOCIAL CONTROL

Numerous mechanisms in these communities keep transgressions to a minimum. The most direct is parental monitoring, in which parents maintain firm control over their children's movements, keep track of all incoming and outgoing phone calls, and communicate with other parents to find out about any suspicious activity. The parents of Dilip, an upper-middle-class Hindu boy, are fairly relaxed about his comings and goings but still keep a watchful eye on him. If his mother sees him with a girl, she never fails to ask whether she is a girlfriend. Other teens talked about their parents regularly going through their rooms and belongings. Ranvir relates an incident in which his mother found cards that a girl had sent him and suspected his involvement. He recounted how she responded to his potential girlfriend: "One time I was talking to a girl when my mom picked up the phone, it was 11 o'clock at night. My mom came to my room and said, 'Who was that?' I just said it was a friend from school. She asked me a lot of questions. . . . Whatever. I just tried laughing." Other teens who have little to hide nonetheless eliminate anything that might arouse suspicion. Janvi, a middle-class Sikh girl, is careful not to leave a paper trail of notes she passes in school. She explained, "One thing I do is never save any letters or notes. If someone gives me a letter or note, I just read it and throw it away. Same if I write something to someone and I can't give it to them, I just tear it up. I know my mom goes through my stuff, my bag, notebooks, and other things. I don't want to confront her because I don't want her to think I am hiding anything." Both Janvi and Ranvir believe in their family's value system. Although they do not appreciate their parents' not trusting them, they put up with it, as they believe it is their parents' way of caring about them. They accept this as part of growing up in a conservative Sikh family and do not ask their parents to conduct themselves differently. To do so, as Janvi remarked, would only arouse unwanted suspicion.

Desi teens are certainly concerned about not disappointing their parents or incurring their wrath, but this is not enough to convince them to follow this rigid value system to the letter. Rather, the fear of becoming the subject of gossip that would ostracize them and their families from their communities is what keeps them on this path. Teens are concerned about what people will say about them, but they are even more leery of the bad reputation that may befall their parents due to some misbehavior on their part. Several youth who have learned this lesson firsthand reflected on what a painful process this can be and how they are constantly reminded of these incidents at the numerous social gatherings and events they are still obligated to attend. Desis cite this system as a primary reason why they maintain exclusively Desi cliques. As most Desi teens are subject to these rules, they bond over not being able to participate fully or at all in many coed or evening events.

Having a large Desi population at school makes these rules seem less stark for Desi teens. Yet this very support can also act as system of social control. Rather than school being a relatively free, unmonitored social space, it is a site of intense peer policing and surveillance. How teens, especially girls, dress, interact with the opposite sex, follow school rules, and manage their relationships is anything but private. Desi kids often do the work of monitoring one another, extending the surveillance of home into school and other public spaces. In these tightly knit communities, where teens attend school with siblings and family friends, news travels extremely quickly. Even those teens who say they do not like to gossip find themselves circulating it.

At these schools, once gossip circulates, fact and fiction become impossible to differentiate. Angela Shen, a teacher Mercer, elaborated:

This is a school that feeds on rumors. Reputations are based entirely on the rumors: who went out with whom and did what type of thing. A lot of times they seem to involve boys that don't go to this school. It's impossible to verify. . . . An Asian girl, if she is seen kissing a boy or doing mild stuff as far as teenage sexuality is concerned, she can still get a reputation and become shamed. It seems like any girl who has anything remotely resembling an acknowledgment of her sexuality would be stigmatized, would be branded as a hussy or a ho. This is not based on the way they look or the clothes they wear or anything like that, because there are some very prissy girls who wear outrageously skimpy clothes and they don't develop a reputation.

Desi teens take precautions to quell potential rumors about themselves. This can include slowly distancing oneself from a clique. Nidhi and Harpreet used to kick it with the other FOBs behind the C building, but gradually they began to distance themselves after they witnessed how people gossiped about their close friend Inderpreet. Her relationship with Avinash was difficult to keep on the DL because school was their only chance to interact. After a few confrontations to defend their friend, they began to spend less time with the other FOBs. Although they admit to gossiping as well, they distinguish themselves from the others because they say things "straight out" to people. Challenging others to be direct as well, Nidhi remarked, "They're all hardcore behind my back. I want to see what they can say about me when I'm right in front of them." Confrontation is generally considered futile because one can rarely pinpoint the source of rumors.

Most teens are part of the problem themselves, and they accept this. Simran, a middle-class Sikh girl, is concerned about what her friends would say about her if she broke from them. She explained, "If you say you're not going to be friends anymore, there are already so many things that they know about you, that you don't want anybody else to know." By the same token, she admitted that she is part of the problem: "I know a lot of shit about other people, that's why a lot of people don't talk to me." Unable to resist divulging her latest piece of news, she gushed, "You know those FOBby Indian girls at our school? Did you know one of them got pregnant by some thirty-year-old? And she left her house to live with this man, and she doesn't go to school, she's having a kid. I was telling my mom, and she was like, 'You don't hang around with them.' " Simran's lack of proof about these happenings is not cause for hesitation in relaying them to her mother or to me. By relaying these events to her mother, however, Simran confirms her belief in this value system and differentiates herself from those who violate it. Although she resents the rules when they apply to her, relating the transgressions of others is one of the only ways she can gain her parents' trust. Other teens periodically admit to incidents in which they gossip about and "hate on" their peers, while they resent being on the receiving end of such actions. In a system in which youth have little power and recourse, hating on one's nemeses is an effective way to exact revenge for being wronged by them or the world at large.

Desi teens fear being the object of the very gossip they produce, especially when they see their extended family suffering from rumors. Neetu, a middle-class Sikh girl, recounted, "I have this cousin in Yuba City and her cousin married a Black guy, which in our society is an extreme, right? And my mom came to me while I was doing my homework, saying her mom was really upset. Usually [my mom] tries to work her way around these things but this time she just came out with it: 'You'd better not do anything like this! I expect you to marry a Jatt [a Punjabi caste] Sikh Indian boy.' I thought it was funny, she was really scared I was going to go do something like this." Her friend Madhu chimed in with a similar tale: "My mom is loud and runs the scene. I know my mom would want me to marry a Punjabi in the caste. My aunt married an Iranian guy and my grandparents were hurt." Although they cannot wholeheartedly embrace the requirement to marry within one's caste, the idea of being the object of gossip that hurts their parents makes them consider their choices very carefully.

In some cases, gossip is more than a cautionary tale; it completely ruins the lives of immediate family members. This is so much the case that I have not included numerous stories about girls and boys getting arrested, going to juvi, running away from home, or getting pregnant or eloping with Mexicans and other non-Desis because even a pseudonym may not protect these teens. One such incident has haunted a family and overshadowed all the other success they have been able to accomplish. The collateral damage from this incident has changed this family's life. Social life stopped abruptly after an incident considered scandalous occurred, and it has taken them over half a decade to return to the routine social events that went on in their absence. One girl in the family finds this predicament utterly frustrating and is extremely careful to avoid incurring more un-wanted talk about her family through her actions. Although she, her mother, and her sister have spoken to me about this situation at length on numerous occasions, she decided that memorializing the details in print was far too risky.

That this Desi teen would be so concerned that readers could recognize her family through a single event despite pseudonyms underscores the power of gossip in these communities. Her apprehension stems from years of needling from community members who continually raise this topic in inappropriate contexts. In this powerful system of social control, their community blamed the parents for their child's actions, and the remaining children are subject to more stringent restrictions as a result. Maintaining a solid family reputation is crucial as teens look ahead to their own marriages and becoming active community members, and for these reasons they try to be as secretive as possible about their social lives when they violate social codes.

SOCIAL LIFE ON THE DL

When Desi teens decide to break the rules, they keep any forbidden activity on the DL. Using a common hip-hop term that means "secret," teens who date on the DL attempt to keep their business discreet. Boys and girls take great care to conceal their activities. Charanpal, a middle-class Sikh boy, is not about to let the girl he likes slip through his fingers because his parents are opposed. "Dating?" he exclaimed. "My parents don't let me date!" Although he dates nonetheless, he knows better than to flaunt it. "I don't talk openly about this with my parents, [but] I have a girlfriend. Please don't tell them!" Charanpal revealed that they met at a mela, where they managed to discretely exchange phone numbers. He is easily able to keep the affair hidden because he can call her when his parents are at work, on the same assembly line shift, from 3:30 P.M. to 12 A.M. He explained, "Her parents have been here longer, so it's okay for me to call at her house and everything, they think I am a friend." His girlfriend's parents are more permissive about coed interaction than his own. Teens who date on the DL have a much easier time doing so if at least one person's parents let them communicate freely.

For Desi teenagers in Silicon Valley, technological innovations such as

pagers and instant messaging are integral not only to maintaining friendships and relationships, but also to handling rules set by their parents and
community. For teens who want to date on the DL but are under tight
parental surveillance, electronic communication can facilitate their relationship. These means enable teens to stay connected and stay out of sight
of their gossipy communities. Madhu explained how she hooks up with
her friends and even managed to have a boyfriend despite parental constraints: "My parents get home at six [P.M.], I usually have some activity
after school so [my friends and I] don't even talk until maybe, like, eleven-
thirty at night. Usually it's contact online. [Otherwise], I have to call
because my phone can't ring at night. Plus, my phone has caller ID so I'd
have to go back and delete everything. It's not like they suspect, but I had
to do it." About her boyfriend, with whom she has since broken up, she
remarked, "After [my parents] went to sleep, he would be outside on his
phone, and I'd be, like, 'Hold on, I'm coming!' . . . Plus, my brothers
helped me out a lot with sneaking out." As Madhu giggled, Neetu added,
"Now if we do something we tell them first, so it doesn't kill us on the
inside. Indian parents get to you, and there's lots of guilt. They might
think we are keeping things, they might suspect it, but they let us." While
Madhu and Neetu conceded they are somewhat reformed, they still attest
to the value of instant messaging, email, paging, and the telephone for
keeping their social lives on the DL.

When face-to-face contact is restricted and phone conversations are
carefully monitored, pagers are an especially feasible communication option. Pagers remain popular because living in the suburbs with strict
parents makes staying connected difficult, especially when teens are trying
to date. Ever since Devan bought his girlfriend Aaliya a pager that matched
his, they have been able to communicate outside of school. "It's especially
nice over weekends, or vacations, when we hardly ever see each other,"
Aaliya explained. "Usually he pages me 'Good morning,' 'Thinking of
you,' 'I love you,' and 'Good night.'" In this way, pagers provide the
option of discreet contact and communication without attracting un-
wanted attention. They are especially useful for youth who are not allowed
to get calls from the opposite sex at home. "Anytime a girl calls our house
asking for me, even if it is for school or something, my mom trips!"
exclaimed sixteen-year-old Uday. "She don't even have to be a girlfriend,
but my parents ask me all these questions. That's why I have people page

me." All this freedom has its downside for teens with tech-savvy parents who are aware of their kids' pagers and know how to page them. Abhijeet exclaimed about his pager, "I hate that thing, it's like a leash. My mom pages me all the time and starts to trip when I don't call her back. I never want to own a cell phone." His friend Gurdas related a similar predicament: "If I tell my mom I'm going someplace and she pages me, I gotta think fast if I'm not where I said, because we have caller ID and she can see exactly where I'm calling from. So if I call from someone else's house, she'll be like, 'Let me talk to their mother,' and then I'm screwed!" In such a situation, even the DL becomes a difficult state to maintain.

Peer Policing · While teens can see some value in parental surveillance, they thoroughly resent peer policing. Most youth consider snitching about what other teens are doing, or allegedly doing, to be egregious. Motivation for being a "hater" or "hating on" someone usually stems from spite over a disagreement or retribution for being ostracized. Haters tell their parents what other teens are doing, knowing that, more likely than not, the information will travel to other adults in their community and back to the infractor's parents. Sometimes parents directly call another teen's parents without even verifying the allegation. In cases of extreme hating, teens go so far as to anonymously call other teens' parents with information on their son's or daughter's whereabouts, social life, or potential love interest. Recall that Veena phoned Aaliya's mother to report her illicit relationship with Devan. When Aaliya's mother received the phone midday, she immediately searched her daughter's room. Aaliya recounted, "When I came home from school that day, my mom said someone called, and I knew exactly what was going down. I was like, 'Oh boy, here we go.' She didn't seem really mad, and she didn't ask too many questions. She just told me that she went through my albums and took out all the pictures of us. She didn't really do much else." Aaliya continues to date Devan on the DL and admits she is quite lucky about her mom's moderate reaction to this potentially disastrous event. Although she has forgiven her friend Veena for snitching on her, she is careful not to share any information with her.

Aaliya is not alone in her experience of being snitched on. Avinash, a middle-class Sikh boy, told me that a boy called his parents to tell them he does drugs (which he does) and that a girl called his friend's house to tell her parents that she had a boyfriend (which she does not). He adds that the worst incident he has undergone is when someone called his girlfriend's mother about the relationship he and his girlfriend struggle to keep on the DL. Despite her precautions to leave at school the flowers and gifts that Avinash showers on her, her parents eventually found out. Although Avinash's parents have no objection to the relationship, his girlfriend knew her mother would not approve and introduced him as a friend to allay suspicion. "She actually liked me!" Avinash recalled. "She was really cool until somebody told them [we were dating]. Her mom told her to stop seeing me, so we broke up . . . for about three hours!" His girlfriend does not want to risk her chance to go away for college because of her bad behavior, so their relationship is in an ambiguous state. Avinash, who is hopelessly in love with her, implored, "Don't tell nobody because it's on the down low. It's so on the down low that I don't even know what's going on." As Avinash's and Aaliya's predicaments indicate, wanting to keep a relationship on the DL and actually accomplishing that are two very different things, especially when haters interfere. Such drama can be especially hurtful as teens attempt to preserve their reputations as they think about marriage.

ARRANGED MARRIAGE

Arranged marriage for Desis in Silicon Valley rarely means meeting one's betrothed for the first time at the wedding. Rather, it varies from parents selecting someone for their son or daughter to marry to teens choosing their spouse within set parameters of religion, caste, and language at an appropriate time in their life.[4] Arranging a marriage can begin right after high school, depending on the family and community. Even in high school, Desi teens are exposed to arranged marriage through older siblings and cousins who participate in this system. Similar to their disposition about the social value system they follow, they are not simply coerced into arranged marriage but rather value it as a means of remaining in their communities. Despite the term "arranged," youth are pleased to have the right of refusal and are grateful to not be betrothed to someone from birth. Meru clarified, "My parents aren't like, 'You *have* to get married to him.' They're, like, 'We'll show you a couple of guys. If you like him, you talk to him for a while, then if you guys like each other, then you get engaged.' " This is infinitely more comforting than having to marry someone chosen for them. Azra is confident that her parents will let her choose a suitable boy from their lineup, which she much prefers to having the choice made for her. She recalls reading a novel in which a teenage Muslim girl was married to a fifty-year-old man: "I swear I would be scared of something of that kind, but my parents can't do that." Not feeling completely cornered or trapped by this system leaves teens some space to shape their future while also ensuring their participation in communities in which they hope to build adult lives.

Staying in one's community is only part of why youth believe in arranged marriage. Some teens find encouragement in seeing their parents' marriage succeed. Ranvir reflected, "[My parents] talked to me about an arranged marriage. Actually, I like it, I want to have one. You get to choose whoever you want. I don't know, I think it's cool. My parents had one." Equally compelling is the belief that "love marriages" have a much higher chance of failing. When one finds a spouse without any familial involvement, especially if he or she is from a different caste, ethnicity, religion, or race, the risk of failure can appear overwhelming. Some Desi teens question the viability of love marriages, such as Nidhi, who flatly stated, "If it's a love marriage, there are problems, like divorce." Sharing this viewpoint, Meru suggested how the two might differ: "In love marriages, some people are like, 'If I'm with that person, it's because that's the way I am.' With an arranged marriage you learn to work with them, you learn to do this. You both learn to mold yourself around each other. And I think it's more special when you learn to love them." Meru's point of view resonates with that of other youth who think that having an arranged marriage does not amount to a life devoid of romance; rather, that it is a means to find love. Some youth liken arranged marriages to the attractive setups they see in Bollywood films, in which a boy and girl shyly meet under family supervision but moments later find themselves atop a mountain in Switzerland in a passionate embrace. While they clearly acknowledge the fantasy element in such a portrayal, the underlying optimism remains.

Marrying Outside One's Community • Marriage brings to light the otherwise invisible topic of caste in diasporic communities. Despite the lack of overt talk about caste and the way it is downplayed in everyday social interactions, it factors heavily into arranged marriages. Simran is excited to eventually get married, but takes her family's caste requirements into account. Sharing her perspective on two prominent Punjabi castes, Jatt and Saini, she exclaimed, "I'll find a perfect guy and marry him. He has to be Punjabi and Jatt. You know how it is. You know how they are, Jatt and Saini. My *chacha* (uncle) married a Saini cudi, and you can tell who the Jatt were and the Saini [at the wedding]. The Sainis were all dancing together, the men touching their wives in public. You don't touch your wife in public . . ." She stopped abruptly as it dawned on her that she might be offending me and asked, "Are you Saini?" "I'm not Punjabi," I replied." "Oh, yeah," she continued excitedly. "You can tell the difference. Jatt and Saini stay apart—they don't mix. I don't want my kids to make fun of me if I marry a Saini. So I have to marry a Jatt."

Like Simran, a handful of other teens agreed with their parents that they should marry within their caste, and that such differences mattered here, if not in any other social context. Kareena, a middle-class Sikh girl who believes she can get along with a range of people, admitted that she would miss speaking Punjabi and aspects of her family life if she married outside her caste. She remarked that caste is very important to her family, despite Sikhism's proscriptions against caste difference: "He will have to be Jatt. Even though my gurus didn't want us to divide into castes, [we] still divided." Even when teens do not agree with the ideological basis of caste, they realize the power of this system. Abhijeet's parents want him to marry a Sikh girl from his own caste. He admitted, "I wouldn't date outside. It would bring about too much trauma and cause too much trouble." Indeed, this otherwise seldom mentioned topic comes to the fore in this context.

In religiously conservative families—be it Sikh, Muslim, Hindu, or Christian—marrying within one's religion and caste is common for middle- and upper-middle-class Desis alike. Taahir, an upper-middle-class Muslim boy, declared, "I'm not going to ever date, or at least I think I'm going to hold off until after college and medical school. Whoever I want to marry has to be okay with my parents, and I think it's going to be a Pakistani Muslim person." Likewise, Joseph knows his Christian family does not condone dating and feels uncomfortable about his attending events such as the prom. He explained, "I can talk to them openly, but they are all into arranged marriage. If I did that they would be happy. Sometimes you do things that will make others happy, right?" Rather than date freely and ultimately have an arranged marriage—a path that is certainly more feasible for boys—boys like Abhijeet and Joseph choose to lay the groundwork for adulthood during their teenage years.

In conservative communities, teens who are against love marriages also speak out against interracial unions. Taahir, who plans to marry within his Muslim community, explains why he thinks interracial dating is problematic: "Like, I've seen a lot of [interracial] kids and, yeah, they look beautiful, because they are a mixture of a White person and something else, because its automatic, biologically, if you have two different people, the child is automatically going to be beautiful. But the child is *actually* really confused, when the father is the one religion and the mother is another, and the child is, like, one religion out of the two. I mean, they think they are, like, really cool, or whatever, but if you look at them they're actually really confused. They don't speak the language. Like my friend Laila, her mom is White and her dad Persian. She doesn't speak in Persian or whatever when she goes to Persian parties." This ideology of racial purity is especially strong among Desi teens like Taahir who grew up in strong, insular communities.

The desire to preserve the racial exclusivity of their community along with their religion, caste, and language is shared by teens and adults alike. In Tara's upper-middle-class Gujarati Hindu community, her friend's older sister married a Tamil Hindu man. Although the sister is happy, her friend remarked that even this is a stretch. While she might consider dating people from other races and ethnicities in college, she would prefer to marry someone from her own community. She opined, "My parents will relate to him better and I will have more in common with him than I will with a White person. That's why there are so few White people who marry Indians." Her friend immediately disagreed and asserted, "No, there are plenty of Indian and White couples," and she named a number of her older sisters' college friends.

In discussions of interracial unions, Desi-White unions are the norm; youth seldom speak of dating African Americans or Latinos. Dating members of these groups would potentially cause even more tension in their communities. While marrying a White person would still enable the type of upward mobility Desis desire, the largely silent prejudice against African American and Latino unions underscores the negative valuation of these communities and the threat they pose to preserving and improving

Desis' socioeconomic position in Silicon Valley. While most teens are not openly racist and most are progressive in their racial thinking to an extent, they draw the line at dating African Americans and Latinos. Middle-class Desi teens are most likely to embark on this type of relationship with people they meet at school. Doing so potentially earns them the disapproval of their Desi peers and a scandalous reputation in their community. The greatest tension would arise out of a Hindu-Muslim union, and youth from both these groups note the calamitous consequences that would surely ensue from such a marriage, including potentially being disowned altogether. Neetu noted, "To us, cultural differences don't matter as much, but to our parents it matters. In my family, my aunt married a Muslim, people stopped talking to her. It took a while to get back in touch. Everyone felt really awkward. It's all about educating people."

Some teens think they should be able to choose their own spouse but feel tremendous pressure from immediate and extended family from an early age. Nidhi began by telling me, "My dad is okay with me marrying a person of my choice, as long as he isn't a murderer or something . . . anyone educated." She then added, "I *want* to marry outside the Indian community really badly. I think Desi men are so controlling. . . . [But] my cousins said they would beat me up if I did." Hearing this, her friend responded, "I've thought about it, but it's out of the question. My mom says when you're ready we can go look for a guy. My dad's brothers and sisters expect me to marry anyone they pick." Although Neetu hopes to retain some control in the question of her marriage, her cousin's recent marriage to an African American man has limited her desire to step outside of the parameters set for her. She declares, "I'll choose my person, but I'll stick to the culture. I don't want to completely upset [my parents], and it is good to stick to your culture too." Other teens emphasize wanting to enjoy college and settle into a career before marriage.

Some teens, however, express far stronger objections. To Feroze, arranged marriage seems like "a trap" and is simply one more thing parents in his Bangladeshi Muslim community are trying to control in their kids' lives. He remarked that some of his friends are going through with arranged marriages "just to make their parents happy." While his parents do not ask that of him, they are extremely invested in his choosing someone Muslim. He conceded that this is a request he can comply with, as he intends to eventually settle down with a Muslim girl. Very few teens are willing to admit that they do not want their parents' help finding a spouse. Dilip, an upper-middle-class Hindu boy, contrasted his parents' vision with his ideal: "My parents don't really want me to date, they want my friends to be Indian, and they really want me to marry a nice Indian girl. Me and my sisters are totally against arranged marriage and I think my parents have accepted that, but they still want us to marry Indians. I'm not sure if that's going to happen either. I tell my parents, but they don't want to deal with it." An extreme version of this scenario is expressed by Devan, who wants absolutely no part of what he considers to be a meddlesome system. "No arranged marriage! They know that I won't let them do that," he remarked with certainty.

Proposal Time • In the midst of speculating about what they *would* do about marriage, Simran and Preeti had to decide whether or not to accept marriage proposals they received during their junior and senior years of high school, respectively. Though generally amenable to arranged marriage, the two sisters expressed to me their conflicted feelings about this situation on separate occasions. Simran recalled that it all started when her father ran into "this uncle" (unrelated to them) at the gurdwara who made note of her and her sister as potential brides for his two sons. Shortly thereafter, the uncle invited Simran's family to their house, where they had lunch. Following the meal, Simran, Preeti, and their mother accompanied the uncle's wife and daughter, who was getting married, on a shopping trip for wedding outfits. During the trip, the uncle's wife also bought outfits for Simran and Preeti. Noting the significance of the purchase, Simran exclaimed, "Red suits, with all the *pidai* [embroidery]! Engagement suits." For Simran, Preeti, and their mother, the symbolism of this act was unmistakable. Their father, however, was completely caught off guard. Simran elaborated: "It doesn't affect my dad that, 'Oh yeah, I have four girls to get married someday.'" When he caught on to what was happening, their father was stunned and wondered if his daughters were too young to marry. In their religious Sikh community, marrying young is not unheard of, and he began to seriously consider the prospect. Simran told Preeti that they should try speaking to the two boys, even though she had no clue what they would talk about.

While Simran went along with what she thought her parents wanted,

Preeti was far more conflicted: "My mom told me if I don't want to get married, don't, but it's not that easy, with all the things that go thorough your head. I was seventeen and I'm still a kid, and on top of that they wanted Simran to get married, and she didn't know *what* was going on." Despite their ambiguous feelings, neither of the girls objected, and both families began to plan the engagement. Plans were barreling ahead when a defining incident occurred. Simran recalled:

> One night, I was sleeping. I am a really heavy sleeper but sometimes I just wake up like that. It felt like there was something in my room, some *booth* [ghost] or weird spirit in my room. I was shaking and all cold. I went to my dad and my dad wears a *kirpan*, you know, he wears a sword. When he saw me he was all shocked. He's all, "What's wrong, what's wrong?" He just took the sword and put it over me and was like, "Okay go to sleep." The next morning he was like, "Whatever's happening, I'm not about to let it happen . . . it's some kind of sign." 'Cause my dad does a lot of *bakthi* [prayer] so he knows, like, a lot of stuff. He called it all off.   ·

Simran's father interpreted the dream-like apparition as a bad omen for the union. In a dramatic move, he decided to cancel the engagement altogether, much to the dismay of the uncle's family, who had already bought rings and announced the news to family and friends. Yet for Preeti and Simran, the outcome of events was a huge relief. Realizing the tension between her own desires and wanting to please her parents, Preeti recounted, "It was going so fast! I felt that if I didn't please my parents, I may break their hearts, and I didn't want to do that. All your life you want to please your parents, and then they're thinking about this great guy [for you], they think he's the one for you, and if you tell them your opinion . . ." Preeti's voice trailed off as we sat together at her usual table on the school campus and she reflected on what her life might have become. Similarly moved by the event, Simran admitted that she simply did not realize the magnitude of the situation until much later: "It still hadn't hit me that I could have been stuck with him for the rest of my life. He was a really nice guy. We were playing cards." She laughed, "Watch me spend the rest of my life playing cards with this guy! It didn't hit me." Both sisters came to realize that they would have to live with their choice long after their parents were gone and had to consider their own preferences more carefully.

Suitable Boys and Girls • The process of locating and screening suitable candidates for their son or daughter before they are introduced to one another is traditionally handled by adults and family elders, but some outspoken teens get involved. Girls tend to be far more interested in matchmaking than boys, who generally shy away from this process. When her family began searching for a match for her uncle, Umber, a middle-class Sikh girl who cannot bear to be uninvolved in anything that happens around her, immediately immersed herself in the process. She proudly showed me the picture of her uncle that was circulated to prospective brides: "This is when we found a girl for my *mama* [uncle]. I picked her and I said, 'I like her! Get them married!'" she laughed. "They were attracted to each other, so they got married." Likewise, when her family decided it was time for Janvi's oldest sister to get married at twenty-four, Janvi was integral in the process of screening candidates for her sister to meet. Janvi explained that she had a better sense of her sister's tastes than her mother did, and that she wanted to be sure she found a match who would be good to her sister. While her parents wanted these things as well, they valued Janvi's opinion to help them better understand what a modern groom with traditional values might look like.

Although it is understood that older siblings and relatives will have the final right of refusal with these prospective matches, they are often too busy with work or away at school to be involved in the day-to-day aspects of matchmaking. By contrast, teenagers are home all the time and find the search a fun diversion. Seizing on the break from the usual grind of school and homework, Ananya helps her parents size up prospective grooms for her twenty-three-year-old sister, Aparna. Some of the criteria Ananya follows are dictated by her parents, such as wanting the boy to be a doctor, "just because she is a doctor and he can't have a lower education than her." She and her parents are searching for someone who is a few years older than her sister, from Orissa like her family, who is of their caste or higher and comes from "a good family." Once these criteria are met, Ananya applies her own expertise to decide what her sister would want— insights that her parents may not have. She recalled one such instance: "There's this one guy who my parents thought was perfect, but he was, like, *so* ugly. When they sent us the picture I was the first one that said 'No, my sister will not like this guy!'" By participating in this system, youth familiarize themselves with a process that they may one day undergo.

Explaining their preferences early on to their parents and underscoring the importance of certain traits are ways youth play a role in shaping their future while following the codes of their community.

Especially telling is that teens already think and talk about how they will raise their own children—most often with the same restrictions and limits that bear upon them. Teens suggest several things they would do differently, but also much that they would not change. Many report that communicating with their children more consistently and asking about their opinions and feelings are two areas in need of change. Distrusting one's children and making rules without explanations also elicited vows of "I would *never* do that to my kid!" By and large, however, teens do not consider codes about social life, dating, and marriage to be in need of reform. The will to avoid becoming the subject of rumors motivated Meru to vow that her daughters would be "covered" slightly less than she had to be, but covered nonetheless: "I would let my daughter wear shorts and dresses, but not where her butt is hanging out." With their firsthand knowledge about American high schools, Desi teens suggest that they would be more lenient about attending events. Meru added, "I would not argue with my kids if they want to go to prom or if they want to go to dances. I had to beg my parents for three months and they said yes two weeks before." Meru's mother admitted that she and her husband finally relented when they saw no end in sight to Meru's incessant pleas to attend this event.

Although a handful of teens declare that they would let their children date openly and conduct themselves as they pleased, most indicate that they would adhere to the same standards of dress, morality, and family values that they follow. Taahir explained, "I will try to raise my kids the way my parents raised me, with strict morals. You have to do well in school. I don't think I would let them date. I don't want anyone to say bad things about them." In these ways, Desi teens express a strong belief in the codes they currently follow.

CONCLUSION

Gossip and other forces of social control are effective because most Desi youth are invested in remaining active members of their communities and hope to live in Silicon Valley as adults. Making the right choices in the eyes of their community paves the way for their future. Abstaining from dating and premarital sex, marrying within their community, and following appropriate codes for dress and interaction are not always followed to the letter, but youth rarely reject them outright. Dating on the DL is one alternative to abstinence, but it carries the risk of tarnishing a family reputation and chances of finding a suitable partner. Even Desi teens who are less interested in being adult members of their community do not want to jeopardize their parents' standing.

By emphasizing caste, religion, and other variables, Desis are interested in protecting the insular nature of their communities and, accordingly, the racial composition of this group. For upper-middle-class teens, marrying within their socioeconomic and racial group will preserve their already favorable racial standing that enables them to situate themselves in White America while still preserving their community. For middle-class Desis, strengthening their ties of religion, caste, and language does not necessarily ensure upward mobility, but it does make unions viewed as unfavorable—including those with African Americans, with Latinos, or between Hindus and Muslims—easier to avoid. Their overwhelming adherence to and belief in this system illustrate their investment in these communities as well as in the numerous mechanisms that ensure that community continues.

IN THE NEW MILLENNIUM

"[The] hardest thing about high school [is] learning how to go to class. Once you start cutting, you're [cutting] three or four classes, then you don't want to go at all. We'll go tomorrow, tomorrow, and before you know it you haven't been to school in three months." Although he is motivated to succeed financially and socially in Silicon Valley, Uday has a difficult time remaining interested in school. A middle-class boy at Greene, Uday moved from India to San Jose with his parents when he was four. His father came to the Bay Area to start working at sixteen, when he stayed with relatives and saved money, and later he got married in India and sponsored his wife and Uday. Both his parents work the same assembly line shift as inspectors for PC motherboards. Uday kicks it with his FOBby clique behind the C building and tries to resist the temptation of drugs to which his friends succumb. He asserted, "There are Indians here who sell it. It's easy to get, if you want it right now we can go get it. You call them up, they have cameras in front of the house. You can't just go over there, that dude is big, he'll kick your ass. He even has Mexicans living with him." Doing the right thing is especially difficult when Uday has constant exposure to Desi gangs who promise to take good care of him for life—a prospect that is at once tempting and terrifying.

Uday is on the fringes of the extensive Desi gang network in the Bay Area. He speculates that people join gangs because they want to be cool. Sometimes Desi gangs fight gangs of other nationalities, but lately there has been some solidarity between groups. He noted, "First they started out all Punjabis. Then [there were] more Mexicans on the Indian side. [Mexicans] come to lots of things like melas [festivals], and these people used to hate us and now they are sitting next to us eating roti and stuff. I have real close relatives who are in [gangs]. Uncles and older people, they *make kids get into this mess. They started this stuff, they're too old to [gang] bang, and now they get these kids to do it. These guys are huge. FBI: Fucking Bloody Indians. Now the youngest started AIM, All Indian Mob. He has hundreds of people behind him."* One of Uday's uncles, however, was very careful to see that Uday steered clear of drugs and gangs, and now he is thinking more positively about his future. Uday wants to set a good example for his younger brother and spends time with him and takes him to the gurdwara with him on Wednesdays. Shortly after graduating from high school he told me, *"Hopefully I will go to college. Right now my grades aren't good enough for state. I'll probably go to community college. I want to do something in networking, software technicians, something in computers."*

As teenagers look ahead to adulthood, they welcome the notion of inheriting this place in Silicon Valley that they have come to consider their own. As I have noted throughout this ethnography, Desi Land means different things to different Desi teens, and this is especially the case in a post-9/11, posttech bubble Silicon Valley. Meanings of race have notably changed for Desi teens as they enter adulthood in a post-9/11 society. In the current age of war, being Brown means being under intense scrutiny. Asian Americans from South Asia and the Middle East are now potential enemies of the state and stand apart from Asian Americans of East and Southeast Asian descent. Not unlike other moments in American history, such as the Japanese internment, when one Asian American population was singled out as a threat while others were lauded as model citizens, this most recent turn further complicates terms such as "Asian American" and its positive associations. Until 2001, upper-middle-class and middle-class families alike appeared to be model citizens in an inspiring, multicultural place of opportunity. In the somewhat bleaker times that have characterized the first decade of the new millennium, meanings of race and class are once again undergoing intense redefinition. This new generation of Desi teens challenges the static model minority stereotype and raises the question of who will define what it means to be Desi in public culture.

In the wake of the high-tech bust, the status and significance of technology have shifted. The opportunities this industry can offer and the alternatives it poses for success are different for upper-middle-class and middle-class teens. For middle-class Desis, the potential for class mobility has been severely curtailed by this downturn. The alternatives youth may now consider vary significantly; few industries have the heightened promise that high tech did during the bubble. What is the future of Desi Land and where are these youth positioned in their communities and in Amrika? Desi teens are coming of age at a formative moment in U.S. history. Their racial standing is shaped both by the potential for class mobility that has been curtailed by the high-tech industry and by their own language practices, interracial alliances with other groups, and broader discourses of what it means to be Brown in a post-9/11 Amrika.

I have argued that what teens do in high school affects their racial and socioeconomic standing afterward. The monolingual high school can position youth who do not follow its dictates in adverse ways. Even sanctioned expression during Multicultural Day is most accessible to those teens who have the cultural capital to take advantage of school resources. Community-based values also play a role in shaping teenage ideals, and aspirations to Desi bling lifestyles lead youth to pursue paths that may not necessarily involve postsecondary education. All of these things affect what it means to be Desi at the start of the millennium. The ways in which youth are positioned by their high schools and the types of decisions they make about their careers, social lives, and living in Silicon Valley affects the future of Desi Land.

RACE IN A POST-9/11 AMRIKA

In the 1990s, before the rhetoric of multiculturalism was replaced by narrower ideologies of patriotism and when the high-tech industry offered opportunities for middle-class youth to transcend their parents' occupational status, the differences within this so-called model minority seemed less stark. In the new millennium, however, the inequalities that divide this diasporic population have become more present. Although the 2000 Census reports that Asian Americans are overtaking Latinos as the largest immigrant group in a White minority California, being successful still equals being White. Upper-middle-class Desi teens succeed in ways that do not challenge the White hegemony of U.S. society. About this trend, Nazli Kibria (1998: 72) argues that Desis are "ideologically disengaged from the U.S. racial order. . . . When confronted with the fact of their nonwhite ambiguity, South Asian Americans can turn to alternative conceptions of race to interpret their identity" (see also Mazumdar 1989; Singh 1996). This is especially true for upper-middle-class youth who are

195

upwardly mobile and are poised to follow the paths of their professional parents. Upper-middle-class Hindu and Sikh youth are by and large still poised to make a place for themselves in upper-middle-class California neighborhoods alongside Whites, other Asian Americans, and other wealthy minorities as they finish their undergraduate degrees and begin graduate school or upwardly mobile careers. While they certainly stand out as Brown, they are not marked in the same way as middle-class Desis or Muslim youth (whom I discuss shortly). Middle-class Desis and Muslims, on the other hand, may be fitting into very different places in the shifting racial order of the United States at the new millennium. Whether they will undergo the same discourses of Whitening is far less certain.

Now that the tech bubble has burst and opportunities are less robust, middle-class youth appear to have far less racial flexibility. Mary Waters (1999) asserts that while "ethnic options" are a possibility for some, others are not able to "choose" how to position themselves in a racist order that does the selecting for them. Desi teens who do not perform up to model minority standards are often grouped in with Latinos and other students who are perceived to require greater assistance. This assessment, along with their Latino social alliances, makes racial status for some Desis move further from Whiteness.

It remains to be seen whether upper-middle-class Desis will continue to skew this population toward Whiteness or if the variation of middle-class Desis will diversify the racial classification of this group. While upper-middle-class Desis have the cultural capital to align with White America, all of them may not chose to do so. Additionally, middle-class Desi youth who do not conform to the model minority stereotype are left to contend with what it means to be Brown in California. The neighborhoods they share with working- and middle-class Latinos, along with the affinities they find with Latino peers at school, indicate the possibility for more meaningful social alliances to come. Latino and Asian American relations that have long been a part of America's history, and their meaning has been a site of productive inquiry (De Genova 2006). While middle-class Desis may continue to preserve their exclusively Desi communities in their Latino neighborhoods and schools, increased interaction and social alliances between these groups appears to be an eventual, if not immediate possibility.[1]

Being Desi after 9/11 • In the 1990s, racializing processes for Desis were predominantly shaped by concerns of class mobility; since 2001, they are further complicated by a new need to define what it means to be Brown in a post-9/11 society. In a time of increasing hostility toward Muslims and others of South Asian and Middle Eastern descent, social positioning, meanings of race and class, and how life in school affects life after it become all the more central to understanding diaspora. The events of September 11, 2001, spawned numerous incidents of bias against South Asians in the United States (see Grewal 2005). Discourses of multiculturalism have been replaced by those of fear and suspicion, and being Brown can be a major liability. Some Desi communities, including Sikhs and Muslims, have become especially marked. Instead of turbans and skullcaps signifying diversity, they incite a xenophobia similar to that witnessed at the turn of the twentieth century. The first waves of Sikh immigrants who arrived in the Pacific Northwest were socially outcast for their beards, turbans, and other religious signs and were generally disenfranchised and barred from citizenship; some Desis now find themselves in very much the same position nearly a century later. Indeed, in a post-9/11 world, "the activities of diasporic peoples have been seriously curtailed, and a once applauded hybrid creativity seems meek and mild in the face of an aggressive neo-liberal conservatism" (Kalra, Kaur, and Hutnyk 2005: 1). In the aftermath of 9/11, it is evident how quickly the political and social climate can shift, to cast previously ideal groups as unpatriotic, disloyal, and ultimately unwelcome members of society. Desis, once grouped with other Asian Americans, are now being watched more closely as potential enemies of the state.

Such shifts are evident in post-9/11 Silicon Valley life. Recall that the pacifist ballad "Imagine" replaced the Operation Desert Storm theme song "God Bless the USA" for the problematic finale of "Multicultural Day" at Mercer in April 2001. At the time of my last visit to the school in 2005, Mercer students were again singing "God Bless the USA." With the country at war, speaking out against such choices could easily be mistaken for being unpatriotic—a stance that many students of color, Desis especially, cannot afford to take.

Likewise, English monolingualism has only gained strength in the increasingly xenophobic post-9/11 climate. In May 2006, the U.S. Senate finally voted in favor of an amendment designating English the "national language," a proposal introduced in 1981. Such a move will undoubtedly impact language use in high schools and other public venues. Some Desis have also faced increased discrimination in their neighborhoods. Harminder, a middle-class Sikh boy, remarked that he and his father told their turbaned, bearded grandfather to be extra cautious and limit his appearances in public places for a few weeks following those events after learning of family friends who encountered public hostility. Simran, a middle-class Sikh girl, recounts that her turbaned father was repeatedly harassed immediately after the terrorist attacks, but as local Desi community groups worked to raise awareness about the differences between Sikhism and Islam, his fear subsided. American flags posted on Sikh businesses in San Jose and public education campaigns that differentiate Arab headwear from Sikh turbans have been effective.

Other youth have had to come to terms with being viewed differently, especially if they have moved to regions with fewer Desis and Muslims in general. Rafiq, an upper-middle-class Muslim boy who now thinks of himself as an "American Muslim" and chooses which Islamic rules to follow and which to disregard, explains his post-9/11 life away from Desi Land, in a place far less diverse. In a March 2007 e-mail correspondence with me, he wrote:

> In the Midwest, claiming to be an outright traditional Muslim is not in one's best interest, especially since many families have sons or daughters fighting in the Middle East. The only form of discrimination I feel prevalent after 9-11 is people asking why terrorists do what they do. How the hell should I know, and why the hell should I know? Just because we follow the same religion at times should not lead to the conclusion that I can ever begin to understand why and how things happen. Muslims in these radical organizations have a very different perception of life than me. . . . Their life revolves around religion whereas my life can adopt religion when I choose. My theories or beliefs about any of this have no value and can never be substantiated . . . yet no matter how many times I explain this, it seems like the questions reoccur.

While similar misconceptions circulate in Silicon Valley, less diverse areas present a far more intense dynamic of hostility.

Discrimination has been particularly challenging for those whose citizenship is still pending. Consider the experiences of Aaliya's family, who are Fijian Muslims living in the United States for about twelve years. A few years ago, Aaliya and her parents moved out of her sister's family's home in San Jose to their own place, which cost a fraction of the price in Stockton, a town about a hundred miles away. During my conversation with Aaliya and her father, Mohammed Khan, in June 2005, Mr. Khan described an incident that occurred late in 2001 (in what follows, "Aunty" refers to his wife, and "she" refers to a female FBI agent): "FBI come here. Come here like a friend. In this house! She come talk to me, talk to Aunty. You know they want to take information. I don't know anything! You know, I tell them the fact. I come from the Pacific . . . about terrorists, I have no story about this. I don't know anything. They stay here for about an hour, hour and a half, and finally say, okay, you two good citizen." In this and his subsequent conversations with me, Mr. Khan emphasized that he is not resentful only about being suspected of terrorist activity, but also about being devalued as a potential citizen and productive member of American society because he is Muslim. He recounted the last two security jobs that he held, in which he was repeatedly asked to shave his beard off and had to remind his employer of his right to religious expression.

Despite flying a large American flag in front of his house, being Muslim has positioned Mr. Khan in opposition to Christian America. He strongly disagrees with this characterization and offered the following counterpoint about how Christianity's Abraham, Islam's Ibrahim, and America's Abraham Lincoln intersect in his life. Motioning to his beard, he explained, "See, Ibrahim have this. . . . Abraham Lincoln, also have this. You know, Abraham Lincoln have this, why they don't want me to have this?" Noting that his current employer and coworkers tried to reduce the alienation he felt after the FBI visit, he continued, "My boss, the CEO, he say you look like Abraham! They put my photo on the money. They say I'm *Ibrahim* Lincoln. So I say, yeah, I like that name, because that man . . . released the slaves. That president released the slaves!" Pointing to a laminated bill with his face pasted in the middle, he gestured, "You see Abraham Lincoln at the back here," and then to his photo, "Here, Ibrahim. So give me citizenship, man!" Mr. Khan's case underscores how being Desi is once again connected to racially charged ideologies of religion, class, and comportment.

The post-9/11 treatment of South Asian Muslims like Mr. Khan draws attention to the complicated nature of race in diasporic communities and how it affects the future of adults and their children alike. Subsequent to this FBI visit, Mr. Khan's citizenship case, which was nearly completed before the visit, is now delayed indefinitely. The five years of waiting to be sworn in has also prevented his daughter Aaliya from becoming a permanent resident and thus acquiring a driver's license and finding legal employment. For Aaliya, the current decade could not have been more different from what she imagined when she was in high school in the 1990s. As long as her father's citizenship case is denied, she cannot legally seek employment or even drive herself around, which keeps her entirely dependent on her father for money and transportation at age twenty-four. She recounted, "My last name, Khan, is too common. People hear it and immediately become suspicious. That's why the FBI came to our house. They don't understand that we're Muslims from Fiji, and that we're not connected to bin Laden or al Qaeda." As a perennial student who feels ambivalent about school and is eager to work, she is biding her time as she waits to become a permanent resident so that she can begin a career, which she hopes can still be as bright as she had imagined.

THE PROMISE OF TECHNOLOGY

"You were here in the computer boom. Now no one does that," one girl informed me when I revisited Silicon Valley in 2005. When this era came to an abrupt end in April 2000, the reality and fallout of the crash was not immediately apparent. Over the ensuing months and years, the deflated promise of technology took hold. Desi families who permanently resided in Silicon Valley watched those on temporary work visas return to the homeland. Especially among middle-class Desis, sympathy for the departed would soon dissipate as they saw the very jobs that conferred such promise in Silicon Valley being outsourced to South Asia.

Upper-middle-class families and teens have not been as dramatically affected. For those Desi teens imbued with the cultural capital to succeed in schools, technology is the latest in a long line of upwardly mobile careers available to them. After high school, upper-middle-class teens by and large attended the University of California at Los Angeles, Berkeley, Davis, Irvine, and San Diego and competitive private universities. Some attended nearby Stanford University, Santa Clara University, and San Jose State University from home. Tara, an upper-middle-class girl from Mercer, was thrilled to compete in Bollywood dance performances at UCLA and enjoyed her time in a Desi sorority. She is now working as an accountant in Fremont, where she grew up. Her friends have also graduated and are in different parts of the country, going to dental school or medical school or working in the biomedical field. Some are studying political science or law.

Jaspreet and Amanpreet from Greene and their friends studied biology, accounting, and similar fields. Jaspreet is marrying her college boyfriend, also a Sikh Punjabi, and Amanpreet is attending fashion design school and has competed in beauty pageants. Abhijeet, who enjoys bhangra dancing and had a wide variety of friends at Waverly, went on to excel at UC Berkeley and continues with his dancing. The former Greene student body president Rafiq majored in history and minored in political science at UCLA and is now completing law school. He explained, "I started out as an electrical engineering major, which was only to satisfy my father's long-lived dream of adhering [to] the acceptable mold that South Asians have come to perceive as a measure of success. But with the dot-com collapse, along with many of my hometown 'competitors' jobless, I think my father is not really regretting my decision to enter law." Once he pays off his law school debt through a corporate law job, he would like to work for the city of San Jose. Like Rafiq, other upper-middle-class youth who moved away from Silicon Valley to study or work express a strong interest in returning to this region to settle down.

Middle-class youth and their families have had a far less even time in the post-bubble economy. While most middle-class adults in my study were fortunate to hold steady jobs until the crash and have limited their unemployment to short stints since then, the lack of career advancement for these parents underscores the importance of strong community support, values, and social life outside of work. Their extended time and service at their job, coupled with their home appreciation, affords some security during these economic lulls. During the high-tech boom, community social networks were instrumental in not only instilling in teens these alternative narratives of success and progress, but also in facilitating opportunities and entrees into such jobs. Desis were poised to succeed by working collaboratively to take advantage of new opportunities in the high-tech industry. After the bust, there was no longer a clear place to turn for such work. Youth and their families appreciate the irony of outsourcing, which is steadily taking work opportunities they had relied upon and sending them overseas, often to their homeland.

For middle-class Desi teens, the world after high school has been a mixed experience. A few went to competitive schools such as UC Davis or the University of San Francisco. Meru, a popular middle-class girl at Waverly, found USF challenging but ultimately rewarding; she is now in medical school overseas. Other middle-class teens, especially some FOBs who were more careful about their grades, attended California State universities like Hayward, San Francisco, and San Jose, as well as local community colleges. Most of these youth still live at home and will likely do so until they get married. Some focus on a career in the health sciences such as nursing or physical therapy, while others take classes at a community college part time while working and do not have a specific path of study in mind. Charanpal, a FOBby boy who used to kick it behind the C building at Greene, works part time in a liquor store while taking classes at Evergreen Community College. His friend Ranvir was also at Evergreen but stopped after a year to accept his parents' offer to buy him a Jiffy Lube oil change franchise in Stockton; like Aaliya's family, Ranvir's could not afford to buy new property in Silicon Valley. Other friends of Charanpal work at the mall, DJ, or do temp work. Aaliya's family moved to Stockton, where she has been taking classes while awaiting citizenship. She and Devan broke up after high school but still keep in touch. He has completed DeVry and is one of the few who went on to work in high tech.

Teens who had a difficult time in school are relieved to find other means of success. Renu dropped out of community college as well as fashion design school and is now trying to acquire an online degree in business administration. She hopes to work at an equity company that has recognized her years of experience working her way up at Great America theme park and may offer her a position. Avinash, who had been stuck in ELD classes and bored with school in general, eventually dropped out and completed a GED. He went on to automotive school and works in a garage. Especially since his high school girlfriend broke up with him when she got to UC Santa Cruz, his love of cars has only grown. For these and many other middle-class youth, life after high school has meant finding jobs that keep their interest and trying to earn a better living than their parents have.

For middle-class Desi teens, the once cherished promise of technology has been replaced by growing cynicism about that field and an eye toward other industries. Harminder, a middle-class boy from Greene, reflected, "Computers were big in the 1990s. By 2000 it maxed out. It was, like, a fad! Even I said it, 'I'm going into computers, make a lot of money.' Bullshit!" While none are currently working on assembly lines, they are having a difficult time finding the kind of opportunities the tech industry offered when they were in high school. When those opportunities dwindled, youth who had relied on the tech industry began to explore other avenues. Since he graduated from Greene High School, Uday, from the start of this chapter, has worked part time at various places, none of which has brought him closer to his high school aspirations of succeeding in high tech. In 2005, he shared his new views on this topic, which have changed considerably from his thinking as a teen: "Nobody wants to focus on tech because it's gone down so bad. There's jobs out there, but you have to have eight to ten years of experience under your belt, they're looking for someone more mature than someone right out of college. That's how difficult it is right now."

It has been challenging for Uday, like many of his friends, to become invested in college. He has had to find other means of securing his future. He reflected, "I took care of high school, it was nothing bad. But when I went to college and took those classes, I just knew it, this isn't for me. I was studying business and management. I went two years and just couldn't understand anything in these books, so I took another road and bought a liquor store last September." He laughed. "Now I'm just making my living out of there, like every other Indian." A few short years ago "every other Indian" was trying to make their fortune in the high-tech industry. As Uday indicates, that era has had a sharp decline. Though he is not in his dream job, he does see some potential in his future as a small business owner, and prefers this to what friends in his old clique are doing: stints in retail, temp work, or other odd jobs to pass the time while they search for something more promising to pursue.

Other youth who had not planned on a career in technology have felt the collateral effects of the high-tech bust. Simran, one of four sisters in a middle-class Sikh family, has been interested in health care since I met her during her junior in high school. She had always expected her passable grades to be adequate for nursing school admission since there was so little competition. Yet the lack of opportunity elsewhere has caused a sudden upsurge of interest in this and other medical fields. As we sat in her living room in 2005, she recalled, "People *were* doing computer training, that ain't happening nowhere no more. There's no jobs. Everyone's trying to get into the medical profession. That's the next big, huge thing." After the tech economy crashed, she found that her once open pre-nursing classes were now overenrolled. She has now been wait-listed two years in a row and continues to reapply. Meanwhile, she is taking additional courses to bring up her GPA while working part time as an EMT to earn money, and she has to balance this with her familial obligations. She explained that her parents are thankful to have retained their assembly line jobs at the microfilm company they have worked at for over a decade, but this leaves her entirely in charge of caring for her two younger sisters every day after school. This situation leaves Simran wondering how she will ever actually become a nurse.

The Realities of Post-Bubble Life • While the everyday lives of Desis have certainly been affected by this economic turn, so too has the broader category of being "Desi." Most notably, the ability of middle-class teens to find a means of economic mobility through the tech industry has been all but eliminated. This complicates the pervasive legacy of the model minority stereotype for Desis in Silicon Valley. Until this point, the prosperity of Silicon Valley veiled the socioeconomic cleavages of Desi Land so that Desis appeared to be uniformly model. Vijay Prashad (1998) argues that the model minority is premised on celebrating Asian family values and contrasting them to African Americans and other minority groups that are labeled "dysfunctional." Such a schema ignores decades of prejudice and discrimination mounted against African Americans that would otherwise require the state to provide social services to improve their plight. In a neoliberal framework, this type of self-help and internal financial support within Desi communities is measured against populations who are failing to bring themselves up by their own bootstraps.

Immigrants from South Asia who arrived after 1965 quickly lived up to the self-sufficient, neighborly, socially agreeable stereotype that has arguably eased their transition into American society. In 1940, only 4 percent of Desis held professional positions and 85 percent held blue-collar jobs (Gibson 1988: 41); the primary wave of post-1965 immigrants were by and large professionals whose educational qualifications positioned them well in a U.S. economy in need of highly skilled workers. This was quite serendipitous for Desis who sought a place in White upper-middle-class America in a racist social order.

While the model minority stereotype has undoubtedly aided a gentle incorporation of Desis into neighborhoods, universities, and corporate America, socioeconomic differences in Silicon Valley are once again open to redefinition. South Asians increasingly find themselves in higher risk jobs or perilous situations where they are subject to racial discrimination (Mathew 2004; Rudrappa 2004). This is certainly the case in Silicon Valley, where assembly line and other jobs are become scarcer and maintaining a steady household income is increasingly challenging. As a new generation of Desis struggles to find a place in this uneven economy while upwardly mobile Desis turn a blind eye to their difficulty, there are no guarantees that they too will not be considered "dysfunctional" in some way. Community support networks provide some assurance against this, but the ever rising cost of living in Silicon Valley coupled with job insecurity create conditions for less than model paths.

The Next Tech Bubble? • Although high tech is not currently a booming industry, its residual influence continues to color the public imagination of this region. Glenna Matthews (2003: 1) has written, "The mythology of high-tech success has been so powerful that despite many serious attempts to depict 'the dark side of the chip,' the Valley's aura of representing the culmination of the California Dream remained nearly undiminished until the dot-com downturn at the dawn of the twenty-first century." Some youth acknowledge the strong presence of this industry in their hometown, even though they have chosen to pursue other paths. Rafiq, who is happy with becoming a lawyer, opined, "High tech is still promising. As long as companies know properly how to obtain funding from the private equity market and how to properly appease the hedgies (slang for hedge funds), then these small technology companies are still a powerful engine of commerce. As for hiring fresh recruits from San Jose State, its seems like the high-tech age is over." Adults and school faculty I spoke with echo this sentiment, agreeing that people have "managed to survive" this downturn, and while there is no "dramatic turnaround" the slow improvement coupled with the steady position of many large companies keeps the area afloat. Some teens I worked with have gravitated toward teaching, biotechnology, and the health sciences, while others are awaiting the next bubble.

Indeed, some believe that this is a temporary setback and that the next wave is imminent. Market analysts suggest that recently the tech market has began to bubble up once again. *Businessweek Online*, for instance, announced, "It feels like 1998 all over again,"[2] and alluded to the potential upturn in the market as foreshadowing the next bubble. While industry mavens debate whether this is actually a bubble or should more modestly be termed a boom, Web 2.0 is here with lower cost Internet start-ups, better infrastructure than a decade ago, and even more online consumers. Speculation that this growth spurt is poised to crash is quickly quelled by these types of analyses: "The Great Bubble may have destroyed fortunes and jobs when it burst. But the history of Silicon Valley is replete with many small bubbles that served to motivate entrepreneurs and investors without causing widespread harm."[3] While the high-tech industry offers fewer Silicon Valley residents the chance to excel, it continues to maintain its hegemony over this region and has sustained its lasting relationship with Asia. The chapter in which it created windows of opportunity for middle-class youth who sought a better life through the promise of technology, however, appears to be closed.

THE FUTURE OF DESI LAND

For Desi teens, especially those in conservative communities, the early twenties can signal the start of marriage and family life. Many communities consider this an ideal time to arrange marriages for their daughters and even sons. Several girls from Muslim and Sikh families got engaged shortly after college or in their early twenties. When she was twenty-two, Amahl, whose Pakistani American fiancé lives in a neighboring California town, was the first of the FOBulous Six to marry. Since then, several of her Muslim friends have followed suit. Middle-class Sikh girls also embark on this process in their early twenties. Janvi got married at twenty-two to a boy residing in Punjab. She is excited to show him all that she loves about California and is considering temporarily relocating to southern California, where her older sister lives. Watching her older sister manage the competing demands of her parents and her in-laws, she speculates that it will be easier for the young couple to have some time to get settled into married life apart from their families. In a few years, though, she wants to move back to San Jose.

At times youth disagree with this system and opine that their siblings and peers are getting married for the wrong reasons. Four years after her father called off her arranged marriage, Preeti decided it was time to get married and told her parents she wanted to meet potential suitors. She had stopped attending community college after a semester and was unclear about what to do with her life. Her family found a suitable boy whom she liked and the married couple now lives in southern California. As we watched Preeti's wedding video when I visited her childhood home in 2005, her younger sister Simran confided that she thought Preeti got married simply because she could not figure out what else to do with her life. Rather than establish herself professionally, the way Simran was trying to do as a nurse, Preeti opted for marital life after high school. Simran noted that escaping her own engagement at fifteen inspired her to do as much as possible before getting married.

Likewise, not all of Janvi's friends approve of her marriage. One of her formerly close friends who is now engaged to her high school boyfriend is angry that Janvi is getting married to please her parents rather than because she fell in love with someone on her own. Janvi no longer speaks to this friend and says she is happy with her fiancé. Moreover, she is confident that she made a better choice than her other friend Raminder. Renu explains that Raminder got married right after high school to the son of a family friend: "[Janvi's] older sister was to marry this guy, but she bailed one month before the wedding. Because she backed out so close to the date, so that no shame comes to the family, Raminder stepped in and married him." While girls who are to marry early cringe at Raminder's story, they nonetheless keep an open mind toward the matchmaking that is occurring on their behalf. Renu remarks that her older sister is her role model because she chose someone her parents introduced her to and is now happily married and has a child. Her grandmother is currently searching for a groom for her.

While girls like Amahl, Raminder, and Janvi married in their early twenties, other girls plan to wait until later in their twenties. Desi teens from upper-middle-class Hindu families who have lived away from home try to fit in other experiences after finishing college. Ananya explained that she wants to finish graduate school before considering marriage, and her parents are amenable to this. Likewise, although Meru's parents initially wanted her to get married after college, her decision to go to medical school has proven to be a good reason to postpone. However, her younger sister Jasbir had an arranged marriage a few years after high school.

In contrast to the many girls who marry early, boys tend to get married around age twenty-five or later, when they have finished school and are more established in their career. Uday, who wants to get married when he is twenty-five, remarked that he will ask his parents to find him someone if he hasn't found someone on his own. For boys and girls, however, keeping their choice of marriage partner within their religion and community remains an important concern.

This is the case because, even as Desi teens approach adulthood, they have remained invested in the communities in which they were raised. These growing communities have been marked by further demographic changes, most notably the rise of Asian immigration. Media stories have featured headlines that reinforce the model minority stereotype, much to the dismay of some local Asian American residents. An NPR report, for example, focused on the process of Asian repopulation that Fremont and other parts of the Bay Area have experienced. It noted the shift from the mid-1980s, when students in this district were almost all White, to today, when they are almost all Chinese, Japanese, and Indian.[4]

Such backlash, not unlike the public outcry that has erupted about University of California campuses where Asian American students are the majority, suggests that this racial group might be garnering hostility in other ways. Indeed, the characterization of South Fremont as "an enclave of Asian privilege and power" sets it apart from equally wealthy White neighborhoods and underscores the perilous position of this racial group.[5] While other groups are critiqued for their perceived failures, Asian Americans are here chastised for their success. Along these lines, a Wall Street Journal article entitled "The New White Flight" reports that Whites are leaving the area, not, as in other areas, to avoid African American and Latino populations, but because Asians have made Silicon Valley schools too academically driven and narrowly focused on math and science at the cost of liberal arts and extracurriculars. In other words, the schools have become "too Asian." Asian American parents are called "too competitive," and local residents complain that this previously White area is now overwhelmingly Asian, even though Asians make up only 4 percent of the country's overall population.[6]

As more Asian families arrive in Silicon Valley, very few have left. They remain in the same homes they lived in at least a decade ago. Families who have sold their home to buy a larger home elsewhere and girls who leave to live with their husband are the exception rather than the norm. This is especially noteworthy as housing prices in Silicon Valley have steadily increased even when the regional economy has not. New housing and retail are built at increasingly astronomical prices. In 2005, as Amanpreet and I sat at one of the half-dozen new Starbucks coffee shops within five miles of her house and cars whizzed by on a once sleepy roadway in front of us, she reflected, "Where we are sitting now used to be orchards." Indeed, there is barely any land that has not been transformed by developers. Despite new construction, the housing market continues to escalate, so much so that Desi youth wonder how they will be able to settle close to their communities. Most concede that even though the Bay Area has become very expensive and overcrowded, they would still like to remain here.

For Desi teens, being successful as teens has paved the way for becoming successful adults. For some this means higher education and upwardly mobile careers; for others it involves lucrative opportunities that enable a Desi bling lifestyle while participating in the closely knit community networks in which they were raised. Throughout my research I was made aware of just how complicated the term "success" can be, and the following incident early in my fieldwork has guided my analysis of this highly subjective term.

One day, as I was taking leave of Taahir and his mother after a lengthy interview, I met Taahir's father, Mr. Malik, who was returning from work. As we stood on his front steps chatting, what began as a friendly conversation about my project turned into an inquisition. After a torrent of questions about my research, Mr. Malik embarked on an irate discourse about how my interviews with teens should be two-way processes in which I should fulfill my duty of telling teens to achieve high SAT scores, get into competitive colleges, and make a lot of money. When I indicated that the interview did not include any advice from me, Mr. Malik expressed his deep dissatisfaction by roaring, "You mean you're not telling them anything? What kind of interview is that? You have a responsibility!" I tried to explain that it was not my method to tell students what to do, but this accomplished little. Eager to end the conversation, I thanked him and said I would think about his suggestion.

I have since carefully considered Mr. Malik's message. I knew I had responsibilities, but Mr. Malik and I defined them quite differently. While I was respectful to teenagers and their parents, observed their privacy, and listened to their ideas, telling teens how to live their lives seemed to be at cross-purposes with learning about what they think about the world and their future. Moreover, it would have placed me in the same category as everyone else who tells them to live differently, and they would probably have stopped speaking to me altogether. My exchange with Mr. Malik ultimately did not lead me to change how I approached youth, as I fundamentally believe it is not my place to tell them how to live.

This is not, however, to say that I do not have a vested interest in their well-being and Desis succeeding in America, but it is the nature of that success that concerns me. With no interest in society beyond their own material accumulation, upwardly mobile Desis get wealthier while less wealthy Desis and other social groups are struggling to stay afloat. I wondered what type of civic example this would set for the upcoming generation of Desi teens, and whether spending time thinking about society and one's place in it would not also play a role in being a successful community member and citizen. This exchange with Mr. Malik and other events have pushed me to carefully consider what really matters to Desi parents in Silicon Valley, and what is beginning to matter to teens as they become adults.

In February 2007, MTV Desi's short life came to a halt, and now its future is uncertain; Desi Land, however, continues to thrive. As it becomes further divided along class lines, racial meanings of Desi will shift. How these youth will fare as adults, and how their children will manage the challenges of finding an advantageous position in the racial order of the United States, will undoubtedly change what it means to be Desi. Thus far they are maintaining their ethnically and religiously insular communities. How this may change as more youth find life partners and their children make different choices remains to be seen. Either way, their sense of themselves and of being Desi resides here in Desi Land, and they are an indelible part of the California landscape.

POSTSCRIPT

Like most anthropologists, I found it impossible to stop visiting my field site. My most recent visit to Silicon Valley in July 2007 was primarily to attend my cousin's wedding, but I managed to visit a handful of middle-class families who wanted to meet my eighteen-month-old son. When I visited in 2005, most teens had changed somewhat since high school; two years later they had clearly entered adulthood. This unofficial shift was marked less by their age or occupation and more by their disposition and outlook on the world. Janvi, who got married the year prior, was expecting her own child in a few weeks while frantically trying to wrap things up at her accounting job. The girl I met as a sixteen-year-old, marginalized FOBby girl had transformed into a happy, accomplished woman who radiated a sense of self-confidence and satisfaction I had not seen in her before.

Likewise, Simran and her younger sister greeted me at their home and proudly showed off pictures of their older sister Preeti's baby, now two years old. Although Simran had chastised her for marrying early, she now admits that it was Preeti's choice and that she is happy for her. More importantly, Simran is happy with her own life. She is working in a hospital and had not lost sight of her goal to become a nurse, though plans for study are not fully formed. When I visited the Kapoor family, newly married Jasbir was still awaiting the immigration of her husband, while her older sister was taking her medical exams elsewhere. These teens shared news of their friends Avinash and Uday, who are still living at home with their parents and searching for work, and Renu, who is married and now set on starting a family.

In all these cases, unpopular teens who were cheerful and optimistic when I knew them seemed to finally be finding their place in the world. They exuded a happiness and an assurance that years of searching in high school and college did not afford them. It is a wonderful thing that being so marginalized in high school did not deflate their excitement for life. In fact, bonding together in the back corners of the school and staying the course they thought best seem to have worked well. Some were perhaps too good for this world, and are no longer here. Two of the most articulate and thoughtful boys, Taahir and Harminder, died in car accidents while in college or shortly thereafter. Their passing came as a deep shock to their parents, communities, and friends, who cannot fathom such young lives already over.

Desi Land continues to grow and thrive, with new housing developments and Starbucks at every turn. There is a cautious yet palpable optimism in the air, signaling a willingness to give high tech another chance. Living in a perpetual state of "orange alert" has gradually eased people's anxiety about conflating racial difference with potential terrorism, although INS cases, such as Mr. Khan's hope for citizenship, show no signs of improvement. Most striking of all, although it should come as no surprise, is that the families in this ethnography still live in Desi Land. They live in the same homes, and their now adult children either live with them or in nearby rental apartments. With Desi Land going strong with this new generation, meanings of race, class, community, and success can only diversify and change over time. It is my hope that this ethnography has raised questions and provided a context for further examination of these issues as residents of Desi Land, California, contribute to its transformation in the new millennium.

APPENDIX 1

STUDENT INTERVIEW

- Name
- Date of birth
- Place of birth
- Grade level
- Name of high school

Family Background

- Parents' names
- Parents' place of birth
- If your parents were not born in the U.S., do you know when they moved here?
- How long have you been living in San Jose? Where else have you lived, and for how long?
- Do you have any brothers or sisters? If so, what are their ages? If older, where do they go to college?

- What languages other than English do you speak?
- Where do you speak these languages?
- With whom do you speak them? If you use them with friends, what kinds of things do you talk about when you use them?
- Do your siblings use them?
- Why do you speak them?

Family Life

- Describe your relationship with your parents.
- Do you get along well with them? What does that mean to you?
- Describe your parents' expectations of you: Academically? About college and your career? Socially?
- Do your parents place any type of restrictions on your social life?

- Do you have any other relatives in the area? In the country? How often do you see them? What kinds of things do you do with them?
- Does your family have a circle of friends in the area? What kinds of things do they do together?
- Describe how religion fits into your life. What about your family?
- Do you go to any religious places of worship, classes, etc.?
- What other kinds of things do you do as a family? Vacations, dinner parties, etc.

- How often do you visit India/Pakistan/etc.?
- Who have you gone with in the past?
- Describe what your time is like there.
- Do you look forward to going there?

Social Life

- Describe your friends at school—grade level, ethnic background, etc.
- How long have you had these friends (e.g., just high school, since elementary, etc.)?
- What kinds of things do you do together at school?
- Do you spend time together outside of school? If not, who are your friends outside of school?
- What kinds of things do you do with your friends outside of school?
- Where do you go? Do you meet up with other people? Do you have a curfew?
- Do you go places/meet up with people without your parents' knowing about it?
- Do you have your own car? Was it bought especially for you when you got your license?

- If you don't have one, how do you get around? How does this affect your social life?

Dating and Marriage

- Do you date?
- Do your parents let you date?
- Can you talk about dating openly with them?
- What are your thoughts on arranged marriage?
- Did your parents have one?
- Do they want you to have one?
- Do you think you will have one?
- Is marriage a focus in your life? What about your parents'?
- How would your parents ideally imagine your future family life?
- What do you think about dating/marrying outside of your community?
- How do you imagine it?

Media and Technology

- Do you watch TV? If so, what kinds of shows and how often?
- Do you watch movies? What kinds? Where do you watch them? With whom do you watch them?
- Do you watch Hindi movies?
- Do you speak Hindi?
- Do you understand Hindi?
- If it is not the language your family speaks, where did you learn it?
- Where do you watch movies: theater, home, friend's or relative's houses?
- With whom do you watch movies?
- Do you listen to songs from Hindi movies? What kinds of things do you do with them?

- Does your family own a TV, VCR, DVD, stereo system, video camera, camera, digital camera, computer (with Internet access)?
- Which of them do you use on a regular basis?

- Do you use computers:
- At school? Where? For what?

- Out of school? Where? For what?
- To do reports/assignments? To get information? To play games?
- To connect with other people (email, chat, IM, etc.)? Describe.
- With whom do you email? IM?
- Do you chat with people you don't know/meet online?
- Is it local or international?
- Do you keep in touch with friends and family worldwide?
- How much time per day (or week) do you spend online?

- Do you have a pager? Who pages you?
- Do your friends have pagers?
- If so, do you have pager codes with which you communicate?
- Do you have a cell phone? Who do you talk to on it?

High School

- What do you think about your high school?
- Are there cliques at your school? Describe the cliques.
- Why do you think they are like that?
- Do you think that racism is a problem there? Among students? Among staff?
- Are there acts of racism at school?
- Do you think there are problems that deserve attention?

- How would you define your race/ethnicity?
- What are some of the stereotypes about this ethnicity?
- Which of them do you think are true? Which ones would you like to change?
- Is there a group with which you feel most comfortable at school? What about outside school?
- Do you feel like you belong to any community?
- What types of events/activities do you do with them?
- What makes you a member?
- Are there any thoughts or issues you have about being an Indian/Pakistani teenager living in Silicon Valley? What are some of the positive aspects? What are some of the challenges?
- How do you think people perceive you?

Current and Future Activities

- What are your present hobbies and interests?
- Do you want to go to college? Where and what kind?
- What are your career goals? What do you want to do?
- What made you choose this? Did your parents have a say in it? What do they think about it?
- Describe your ideal future: where you would like to live, what you would like to be doing, what your house and lifestyle will look like, etc.

APPENDIX 2

FACULTY INTERVIEW

Personal Information

- Tell me a little bit about yourself: where you were born and raised, where you went to college, what led you to the field of school administration, and when you joined YOUR SCHOOL.
- What exactly are you responsible for in your position?
- With whom do you work most closely?

Student Body

- General impressions of the student body at YOUR SCHOOL?
- Describe some of the changes you have seen, demographically and socioeconomically.
- Describe the range of students that you see: high/low achievers, gang members, etc.
- Do many of the students here work after school and on weekends? Do you know if it is to contribute to family earnings, for college, for their own shopping and expenses?
- How do name brands and other commodities affect the way students view and relate to one another?

Ethnic/Race Relations

- How do you think various ethnic groups get along at YOUR SCHOOL?
- Students tend to socialize mainly with their own ethnic group. Any thoughts on why?
- Is most of the fighting within an ethnic group, or across groups?
- Compared to ten years ago, what kind of changes have you seen at the schools, especially around ethnic groups?

Desi Students

- Do many of them live near the school?
- Do you sense any tension or pressure between the expectations of the parents and what the students do at school?
- Are you aware of any social problems affecting these students?
- I have heard stories from various teachers and students about Indian students, both about those who do well and those who have difficulty. Can you relate any similar experiences you have had?
- As a teacher/administrator, what kinds of judgment calls have you had to make regarding students?
- Given the changing demographics of the area, in what ways do you envision the school changing over the next several years?
- What changes would you like to make?

APPENDIX 3

PARENT AND RELATIVE INTERVIEW

- Full name
- Place of birth
- When did you move to the U.S.? How long have you lived here?
- Where did you live before?
- How did you decide to move to the Bay Area?
- Do you have family out here?
- Were you sponsored to come here?
- Have you sponsored anyone?
- Are you a citizen or thinking about citizenship?

- How many other children do you have and what do they do?
- What is your profession? Spouse's profession?
- Where did you go to school and what did you study? Level of education? Spouse's?

Family Life

- What other kinds of things do you do as a family? Vacations, dinner parties, etc.
- Do you have any other relatives in the area? In the country? How often do you see them? What kinds of things do you do with them?
- Does you have a circle of friends in the area? What kinds of things do they do?

- Socially, what do you do for entertainment?
- Do you watch Hindi movies?
- Do you speak Hindi? Do you understand Hindi?
- Where do you watch movies: theater, home, friend's or relative's houses?
- Do you listen to songs from Hindi movies? What kinds of things do you do with them?

- Describe how religion fits into your life. What about your family?
- Do you go to any religious places of worship, classes, etc.?
- Do you belong to any cultural or religious organizations?

- How often do you visit India/Pakistan/Fiji?
- What has it been like taking your kids there?
- What kinds of ties do you keep with family worldwide: phone, email, letters?

- What are some of your impressions of the U.S.?
- What are some of the challenges you've faced since moving to this country, in terms of your own career and settling down here?
- Do you have any close friends who are not of your own ethnic group?

Children

- What is your relationship like with your children?
- Did you want to impart your language and culture to your children? How have they responded?
- Are there hobbies or interests you encouraged for your kids?
- Describe some expectations of your children socially?
- What types of things do you let them do? What types of boundaries do you set?
- What are some of the challenges you've faced with your children?

- What is your worst fear regarding your children?
- What do you expect of them academically?
- Do you want them to go to college? Will they be allowed to go away for college?
- What career would you like them to choose? Do you think they will do this?

- Do you want your children to have an arranged marriage?
- What are your thoughts about their marrying outside their community?
- Did you have an arranged marriage?
- At what age do you want your kids to get married?
- How would you imagine your child's future family life?

- What are your thoughts or issues on being Indian/Pakistani living in Silicon Valley? What are some of the positive aspects? What are some of the challenges?

APPENDIX 4

STUDENT SURVEY

This is an abbreviated version of the survey. A slightly longer version formatted over four pages was distributed to students.

1. Name
2. Year of birth
3. Place of birth
4. What country is your family originally from (e.g., Pakistan, India, Fiji)? What city or region of that county (e.g., Karachi, Gujurat)?
5. What languages does your family speak at home? Do you speak them? To whom do you speak them?
6. What year did your family immigrate? Where have they lived in the United States? What do your parents do?
7. List the names of your close friends at school. Do you spend time together outside of school? What language(s) do you use to speak with your friends at school? Outside of school?
8. Do you have a computer at home? Can you get online? How often do you go online, and what do you do online? What types of websites do you visit most? What languages do you use to communicate online? Whom do you talk to?
9. Do you have a cell phone or pager? Whom do you use it to keep in touch with? Do you and your friends have a pager code? Do you use the pager or cell phone regularly with your parents?

10. Where do you like to shop? What types of things do you buy? Whom do you go shopping with? Who pays for the things you buy?

11. Do your parents let you go out with friends? Date? Do you have a curfew?

12. What type of career do you want to pursue? Are you planning to go to college?

13. Do your parents want you to have an arranged marriage? Do you want to have one?

14. Do you want to stay in Silicon Valley when you become an adult?

NOTES

Introduction: Welcome to Desi Land

1.   Desi teens in my study rarely used this term in earnest, but did deploy it sarcastically on occasion. Kiran Narayan (2004) similarly notes that few Desi youth she spoke with actually use the term ABCD. One of her interviewees cleverly suggested that the "C" should stand for "cool" instead of "confused." Likewise, Khyati Joshi (2006: 6) found differences between earlier and later born second-generation Desi youth, grouping them as "Second Generation A" (born between 1965 and 1978) and "Second Generation B" (born between 1979 and 1992), and notes the increased presence of religious establishments, Desi classmates, markers of Desi culture, Bollywood and Desi satellite TV, and ethnic organizations in the lives of this latter group.

2.   Studies have reported Desi college students' affinity for remixed bhangra music as a means of displaying ethnicity or their engagement with hip-hop as a way to access blackness (Maira 2002; Sharma 2004, respectively), but neither of these musical cultures are especially meaningful for Desi teens in Silicon Valley. Bhangra music is used for Punjabi dance performances and remixed songs are enjoyed at community and teen parties, but not in a way that privileges this genre over others. Likewise, identifying with hip-hop culture and seeking racial solidarity with Blacks is not common for these Desi teens. In San Jose, the predominant racial groups are Latinos, Whites, and Asian Americans. Desi teen culture, then, is largely influenced by these populations, Bollywood, and other types of media and commodities, and varies according to class.

3. My thanks to Micaela di Leonardo for challenging me to clarify my definition of class in Silicon Valley during a February 2007 conversation.

4. While I believe the term "middle-class" better describes these Desis, I do
not want to suggest that there are not other important similarities connecting these Desis with working-class Desi communities elsewhere. There may
well be points of articulation, even though other communities did not likely
have analogous opportunities for class mobility.

5. Some scholars of migration may wish to understand this phenomenon in
terms of "segmented assimilation" (see Alba and Nee 2003; Kao and
Thompson 2003; Levitt and Jaworsky 2007; Portes and Rumbaut 2001; Zhou
1997b). My analysis is not presented in this framework because I choose to
focus on the processes through which meanings about race and class are
formed rather than the end results alone. This ethnography does not reduce
the diversity encompassed within this population of Desi teens in order to
speak to assimilation models; rather, it welcomes the inconsistencies and
atypical aspects of migration as being the very qualities that imbue a concept
like assimilation with the multifaceted meaning it entails in everyday life.
While there are certainly productive points of articulation between dominant
sociological paradigms of migration and anthropology (see Brettell 2000),
these frameworks are less illustrative of the topics I discuss here.

6. Occasionally this category can be useful to 1.5 individuals themselves (see
Park 1999), but I did not find this to be the case in my study.

7. The high schools in which I conducted research were chosen from six
finalists after preliminary visits to about fourteen high schools during the
summer of 1998. Of the approximately fifty high schools in the Silicon
Valley area, these were selected based on census data obtained from the
Santa Clara County and Alameda County Boards of Education. Additional
input was drawn from participant observation that summer at community
events, after which I visited schools based on community recommenda-
tions. Each of these schools gave me permission to conduct research before
I started. Upon locating schools with high numbers of students listed on
the census as "Asian-Other," I visited schools to speak with faculty and
administrators about their school's South Asian population, to inquire
whether they had a South Asian student club, and to try to eyeball the
population during lunch and breaks. This unscientific methodology yielded
some surprisingly useful results as well as some inaccurate assessments
that ultimately added to the depth and complexity of this study.

I was particularly interested in finding teens from different socioeconomic backgrounds. Finding an upper-middle-class high school with a high population of Desi teens was not difficult, and I actually located one in San Jose that I decided not to include because they requested full access to my field notes. Instead, I found a school in Fremont that proved to have just as large and dynamic a Desi population. The school I had expected to have middle-class students had both middle- and upper-middle-class teens. The school I thought would have only middle-class teens also had a considerable number of upper-middle-class students attending a premed academy.

Initially I conducted open-ended interviews with fifty-five students who were primarily fourteen to eighteen years of age, thirty teachers and administrators, and twenty parents and relatives. I got to know many more teachers, students, siblings, and relatives on an informal basis. About thirty hours of spontaneously occurring conversations were taped-recorded in school during breaks and lunch periods. Supplementing these data, I surveyed one hundred Desi students (approximately one-fourth overlapped with the interview sample) about various aspects of their family background, social life, academic and extracurricular activities, and future plans. See the appendixes for interview and survey instruments used between 1999 and 2001. Since then, I have kept in contact with numerous youth on an ongoing basis through email, instant messenger chats, telephone, and visits in July 2002, June 2005, and July 2007. During my 2005 visit, I conducted thirty open-ended follow-up interviews with youth as well as school faculty to gauge changes in their lives and in Silicon Valley.

Chapter 1   California, Here We Come

1. Bhangra is a popular folk dance from Punjab that is widely performed in the Desi diaspora, especially in competitions.

2. My thanks to Andrew Ross for bringing to my attention the similarities of these two areas. For a detailed comparison between these regions, see Everett Rogers and Judith Larsen (1984) and Martin Kenney and Richard Florida (2000).

3. A. Aneesh (2006) identifies May 1998 through July 1999 as an especially dynamic period in the high-tech industry due to free-flowing capital and the increased demand for Y2K programmers. During this time, 63,900 HI-B workers came from India to become 47.5 percent of the "specialty occupa-

tion workers" in the United States. This number increased from October 1999 to September 2000, when 124,697 workers represented 48.4 percent of HI-B workers. During fiscal years 2000 and 2001, 57.1 percent and 58.2 percent, respectively, of all HI-B workers came to work in computer-related occupations (Aneesh 2006: 172–73).

4. It is beyond the purview of this work to offer detailed discussions about the racialization of Mexican Americans in Northern California, or the differences between terms such as "Latino," "Chicano," and "Mexican American" (see Norma Mendoza-Denton [2007] for elaboration). For perspectives on this important topic, see Stephen Pitti (2003) for historical and contemporary discussions of Mexican Americans in Silicon Valley and Christian Zlolniski (2006) for analyses of labor and activism among Mexican immigrants in low-wage high-tech jobs.

5. Jessica Barnes and Claudette Bennett, "The Asian Population: 2000." Issued February 2002, see http://www.census.gov/population/www/cen2000/briefs .html.

6. "Curry on Home," *San Jose Mercury*, March 31, 2001.

7. Karen Leonard's (1992) groundbreaking study of California's Punjabi Mexican population presents the stories of a number of individuals and their modern-day descendants. I encountered a handful of youth who identified as being of mixed Punjabi-Mexican descent, but these teens were difficult to trace, as they no longer had South Asian surnames due to generations of intermarrying.

8. Parminder Bhachu (1996) describes a phenomenon she calls "twice" or "thrice" migrants to account for the multiple moves made by those who originally migrated from the Indian Subcontinent. One such trajectory is from India to East Africa in the late nineteenth century, then to Britain in the late 1960s, then to the United States, Australia, and parts of Europe in the 1980s and 1990s. I met only a few families who had such a migration trajectory. For further discussion, see Vertovec (2000).

9. Since the late 1990s and into the current decade, the redrawing of Fremont school district boundaries has caused a massive uproar among Asian Americans who relocated specifically because of this school district and high school. Many felt this was an anti-Asian issue. See Wei Li and Edward Park (2006) for further discussion.

10. Magnet programs are prevalent in many northern California school districts. Each school in a district serves as a magnet for a particular profes-

sional field, such as medicine, journalism, media, and business. Instead of being required to enroll in the school they are zoned to attend, students may apply to a magnet school in that district.

11. When I conducted my fieldwork, the gurdwara was located on Quimby Road. In 2004, a large new gurdwara replaced it. It is located on a tract of land in the Evergreen hills and is no longer within walking distance of most Sikhs in my study.

12. Studying twentieth-century labor patterns, Glenna Matthews (2003) notes continuities between the agricultural and high-tech era, in that women have played a key role in the production of both fruit and electronics. See also Rogers and Larsen (1984: 145) and Ann Markusen (1985: 39).

13. This issue is compellingly portrayed in the documentary *Secrets of Silicon Valley* (2001).

14. "Systems operators" (also called "sysops") manage servers to which individual machines are connected. Likewise, network administrators manage users who are logged into a network and handle matters of network security. Larger companies hire systems operators and network administrators as part of their permanent staff, while smaller businesses generally employ them on a consultant basis.

Chapter 2 Defining Desi Teen Culture

1. An example of this is the 1973 film *Bobby*.

2. In 2000, most teenagers who used pagers owned the basic one-way numeric model with a 2 x ½ inch LCD display window, which were available in a variety of colors and translucent styles. Smaller, more stylish pagers ranged from $30 to $60; the basic models cost about $10 and even came with free monthly service, which was otherwise about $10 per month. Cell phones remain far more costly to acquire and maintain. Although cell phones have now become ubiquitous in high schools, teens use the text messaging feature far more than the voice feature during the school day—a method that is more complex than, but essentially the same as, using pager codes.

3. One advantage of a communities of practice model is a move away from Paul Willis's (1977) lads as "historical individuals." As Penelope Eckert's (1989) social categories of "jocks" and "burnouts" illustrate, these are dynamic roles that shift according to social actors. This latter approach is especially useful as I look at language-based practices that solidify social

groups. It is important to bear in mind that communities of practice, while voluntary, are still rife with dynamics of power and inequality (Barton and Tusting 2005).

4. An especially poignant portrayal of social categories in high school can be found in *Freaks and Geeks*, Judd Aptow's short-lived television series of the late 1990s. In an all-American, predominantly White midwestern high school, jocks and popular teens ruled the school while freaks collected on the margins, behind buildings and in places no one else wanted to be. They rarely if ever participated in school rallies, sporting events, and arts and academic enrichment programs. Geeks owned this last area, but their lack of popular cultural knowledge and physically diminutive stature usually made them a target for all types of mockery. What Aptow depicts so well is the complex and contradictory nature of these categories in action, and how seemingly rigid boundaries are often crossed, thereby disrupting the very categories that define youth. Such boundary crossing also occasionally occurred in my research, especially when one group needed another's help.

5. An ongoing debate ensues about the term "geek" versus "nerd." Youth in my study used the term "geek" much more frequently and specifically, applying "nerd" momentarily to any person exhibiting studious tendencies. For a more detailed discussion of differences between these terms, see Ron Eglash (2002).

6. Justin Lin's provocative film *Better Luck Tomorrow* (2002) illustrates this point. Youth who appear to be studious teens who follow the rules are actually involved in various illegal activities.

Chapter 3   Living and Desiring the Desi Bling Life

1. Rob Walker, in his *New York Times* article "The Brand Underground" (July 30, 2006) makes a similar point and discusses a handful of designers from the "brand underground" who report that their brand itself is the message, rather than the brand indexing some other social meaning.

2. Unlike some Desi youth who have musical aspirations to become hip-hop artists (see N. Sharma 2004), youth in my study primarily adopted the material dimensions of hip-hop culture.

3. Silicon Valley has several different malls that cater to clientele of various class backgrounds. Eastridge and Oakridge are the main malls in San Jose, Oakridge being the more upscale of the two, and are frequented by kids at

Waverly and Greene. "Gangsta' " styles are especially available at Eastridge Mall, which contains several stores that cater to this market, and in general fit middle-class budgets. Kids from Mercer sometimes go to the New Park Mall, which has some popular stores but is down-market compared to the Stoneridge Galleria, about twenty miles away in Pleasanton. With its high-end chain stores and superior cosmetic selection, including Sephora, it is the favorite of many of the upper-middle-class teens. These kids also go to the Valley Fair Mall in Santa Clara, in the heart of the Silicon Valley and among the most upscale in the Bay Area. The Great Mall, formerly the Ford Auto plant in nearby Milpitas, has earned the unfortunate nickname of "The Not-So-Great Mall." Despite its proximity to both San Jose and Fremont, it is often overlooked.

4. A lehenga is a blouse, skirt, and scarf outfit, common in parts of North India.

5. See Amy Best (2000) for a detailed discussion of proms.

6. A bindi is a dot placed in the middle of a woman's forehead as a symbol of Hinduism.

7. Charles Peirce (1955) originally discussed indexicality in the context of the sign, but not language exclusively; thus indexicality has been used to discuss words or things, but rarely in conjunction. The indexical uses of language can, along with commodities, signal meanings beyond either commodities or language alone.

8. It may seem paradoxical that middle-class Desis displayed their mass-produced commodities, which would soon be replaced by newer models, more overtly than potentially unique items that had endured generations. On this point, Annette Weiner (1992: 155) astutely notes that despite capitalism's driving need for obsolescence, people still aim to form inalienable relationships with objects, even mass-produced ones. Igor Kopytoff (1986: 90) remarks on this phenomenon as well and asserts that while works of art and other distinctive objects are sure to have histories, homogenized commodities still have biographies and are classified and reclassified according to categories that shift with changes in context.

9. "Lowering" cars and adding other custom features was and continues to be a very popular trend in California, especially among Latinos and Asian Americans.

10. In her fieldwork in London, one of Dhooleka Raj's (2003) research participants offers this observation in response to her study of Punjabi culture: "At

the essence," he stressed, "Punjabis are consumers, there is nothing to study." To prove his point he added, "If you went to a temple the women would be discussing their saris or the price of gold and the men on the other side would be talking about business and how much they had paid for their Mercedes Benz" (14). I found this remark particularly noteworthy as an indication that what I discuss here is quite possibly occurring in Desi diasporic communities elsewhere.

Chapter 4   Desi Fashions of Speaking

1. Other studies rely on speakers' self-reports of their language practices and link these to notions of ethnic attachment (Fong 2004; Hong and Min 1999). Self-reports are illustrative but necessarily partial, for they do not examine what else people do that may contradict what they say they are doing.

2. Although the British did not attempt to eradicate local language, they did censor local literature, especially literature that spoke out against their colonizing presence.

3. Joanne Hong and Pyong Gap Min (1999) observe that Korean American children have an advantage over Indian and Filipino communities because Koreans have only one language, their media is in that language, and their churches offer language programs. While Muslim and Sikh children could also take advantage of this through their musjid or gurdwara schools, this was less of an option for Hindus, who encompassed a very broad range of language backgrounds.

4. Bilingualism has also facilitated connections between teens and their parents and helped immigrants take advantage of social connections in their ethnic communities (Zhou and Bankston 1995, cited in Zhou 2004: 26).

5. See Monica Heller (1988) for a discussion of the differences between code-switching and code-mixing, as well as how these differences are not always self-evident.

6. I am grateful to Norma Mendoza-Denton and Bambi B. Schieffelin for their personal communication of August 2003.

7. Such wordplay has been examined in those learning a second language (Tarone, Gass, and Cohen 1994).

8. Although I could participate in conversation in Hindi-speaking households, it was far more difficult for me in Punjabi-speaking homes. Although my comprehension increased over the course of my research, I often did not

understand why something was funny until it was explained to me. As this humor rarely translated into English, some families began to teach me words and phrases to help me understand double entendres. Like their children who taught me how to curse in their heritage language, their parents taught me how to say things with loaded meaning and jokingly tried to get me to say them in inappropriate contexts.

Chapter 5 Being FOBulous on Multicultural Day

1. Waverly High School also had an International Night program, but all interested participants were welcome. As the event was held at night and admission was charged, it drew a smaller crowd. Since Waverly students did not face the same constraints as the other two schools, I have chosen to focus on Mercer and Greene high schools for this discussion.

2. The faculty was nearly all White, so this selection was typical.

3. MEChA is a statewide movement of Chicano groups on California campuses. For a detailed discussion, see Cirenio Rodriguez and Enrique Trueba (1998).

4. *Taal* is a popular movie about a dancer played by beauty contest winner Aishwarya Rai, a favorite actress among many kids. The word *taal* means "beat" or "rhythmic cycle," and the songs from this film were a popular choice for many performances.

5. *Filmi* is a common adjective used by Hindi film viewers to describe a song, dance, or attribute resembling a Bollywood movie.

6. These are ethnic clothes from North India, used both for daily wear and festivals.

7. Vijay Prashad (2000: 113) notes about India in particular, "Multiculturalism draws its own idea of India from U.S. orientalism and sees it as fundamentally spiritual. . . . Religion is seen as the subcontinent's cultural essence."

8. "God Bless the USA" was recorded and released by Lee Greenwood in 1984 but regained popularity in 1991 after Operation Desert Storm, and again in 2001 after the attacks of September 11.

Chapter 6 Remodeling the Model Minority Stereotype

1. Although schools offered to make student records available to me, I declined because I am not concerned with their grades and do not offer any

quantitative assessments of academic achievement. Rather, I discuss success in terms of how Desi teens themselves regard their education, how they form relationships with their schools as institutions, and how their everyday practices in schools position them in ways that affect their future. Differences in academic ability most definitely exist, but my daily interactions with so-called low achievers indicate that many of them could improve greatly with sustained mentoring and guidance. For these reasons, I avoid referring to students as low achievers and high achievers—terms that are widely used in academic literature and everyday conversations among teachers and faculty—because they can become self-fulfilling prophesies of student progress. My thanks to Purnima Mankekar, who in her early review of this manuscript suggested that I think more carefully about my own use of these terms.

2. John Brademas is quoted by Asia Society president Robert B. Oxnam, cited in David Palumbo-Liu (1999: 195).

3. See Margaret Gibson and John Ogbu (1991) for more examples of this process.

4. For a similar discussion, see Mia Zhou and Jennifer Lee (2004: 15).

5. In the South Asian educational context, school rankings are paramount as they determine the type of postsecondary education students can pursue. Top-ranked students can expect to gain admission into engineering and science colleges, followed by business and commerce a rung lower, and social science and humanities further down on this hierarchy. While this order is changing somewhat in post–neoliberal globalization South Asia, the high value on science remains intact.

6. Several notable similarities emerge between my work with middle-class Sikh Punjabi communities and those in Margaret Gibson's (1988) study from the early 1980s in a small Californian city called Valleyside. Adults in her study also had little understanding of the school system and rarely visited the school or helped with homework or course selection. Gibson remarks that this "non-interventionist" parental strategy is a norm in Punjab, but that despite this, many students in her study managed to excel academically. While it is difficult to speculate on why youth in my study had a different experience, one factor certainly seems to be the hypercompetitive, overcrowded Silicon Valley high schools in which students who needed extra attention rarely received it. Notably, some students in my study also got tracked in ESL and felt it held them back.

7.   The four main questions in the Greene survey are: Which language did your son or daughter learn when he/she first began to talk; what language does your son or daughter use most frequently at home; what language do you use most frequently to speak to your son or daughter; and name the languages in the order most often spoken by adults at home. See Norma Mendoza-Denton (2007) for a discussion of the effects of the Home Language Survey for Latina youth in California.

Chapter 7   Dating on the DL and Arranged Marriages

1.   "The down low" is also used to reference secret gay relationships among African American men.

2.   See Marie Gillespie (1995) for a discussion of izzat (respect) in a Punjabi community in Southall, England. I have chosen to use the terms "reputation" and "respect" in place of "izzat," as not all youth in my study used this term.

3.   Early in my fieldwork, I unwittingly struck up a conversation with two teenage boys I often spoke with at Greene High School while waiting in line for lungar at the gurdwara. Oblivious to their discomfort and the stares of irate adults on the verge of reprimanding me, I was thankfully corrected by their female friend, who told me I should not talk to them here. Although I initially regarded the interaction as no different from those we had in their high school, community elders and others who did not know me witnessed an open flouting of codes of conduct that applied to all unmarried people. I was careful not to repeat my mistake.

4.   Rayna Rapp (1982) notes that the literature on working-class families is filled with accounts of how young women use love as an escape from oppressive family conditions. The result is most often adolescent pregnancy and childbirth, which places limits and challenges on upward class mobility. In this Desi community, however, early pregnancy and childbirth are widely avoided through overlapping systems of peer and community surveillance that are geared toward supporting arranged marriage. The arranged marriage system defers reproduction until after marriage, in most cases until a woman's twenties.

Chapter 8   In the New Millennium

1.   While I can suggest that there is potential for synergy between Latinos and Desis in Silicon Valley and saw evidence of individual and group youth alliances, the limitations of my study precluded any systematic examination of the relationship between these two groups. Further research in this area is needed.

2.   Justin Hibbard and Heather Green, "It Feels Like 1998 All Over Again," BusinessWeek Online, May 22, 2006, http://www.businessweek.com/maga zine/content/06_21/b3985051.htm?campaign_id=bier_tcm.

3.   Ibid.

4.   Claudio Sanchez, "Part One: Immigrants Weigh Splitting from California School System," Morning Edition, November 29, 2004, http://www.npr.org/ templates/story/story.php?storyId=4190129; and Claudio Sanchez, "Part Two: Children of Immigrants Seek to Define Their Identity," Morning Edition, November 30, 2004, http://www.npr.org/templates/story/story.php?s toryId=4192018.

5.   In Claudio Sanchez, "Part One: Immigrants Weigh Splitting from California School System," Morning Edition, November 29, 2004, http://www.npr.org/ templates/story/story.php?storyId=4190129.

6.   Suein Hwang, "The New White Flight: In Silicon Valley, Two High Schools with Outstanding Academic Reputations Are Losing White Students as Asian Students Move In. Why?" Wall Street Journal, November 19, 2005.

GLOSSARY OF HINDI AND PUNJABI TERMS

Amrika—America

behen—sister

behen chod—sister fucker

bhangra—a type of Punjabi folk dance and music (Punjabi)

bindi—dot worn on a woman's forehead, usually a sign of Hinduism

chacha—paternal uncle

chai—tea

cudi—girl (Punjabi)

daal—cooked lentils

filmi—an adjective that references aspects of Bollywood films

garba—a Gujarati folk dance

gurdwara—Sikh temple

hajj—pilgrimage to Mecca

jahil—illiterate

Jatt—caste name (Punjabi)

langar—free meal at the gurdwara prepared and served by volunteers (Punjabi)

lehenga—a woman's outfit consisting of a skirt, top, and cloth worn as a sash

ma—mother

mader chod—mother fucker

maiya—a Sikh prewedding custom where the bride and groom do not leave their houses a few days before the wedding (Punjabi)

mama—maternal

mehendi—henna applied to hands and feet in an intricate design, generally for weddings

Glossary of Hindi and Punjabi Terms

mela—community festival (Punjabi)

musjid—mosque

roti—unleavened bread made from wheat flour on a stove-top

Saini—caste name (Punjabi)

samosas—fried pastries stuffed with vegetable filling

sherwani—a man's outfit consisting of a long shirt, pajamas, and vest or jacket

subzi—vegetable curry

zari—gold thread embroidery

BIBLIOGRAPHY

Abraham, Margaret. 2000. *Speaking the Unspeakable: Marital Violence among South Asian Immigrants in the United States.* New Brunswick, N.J.: Rutgers University Press.

Abu-Lughod, Lila. 1995. "The Objects of Soap Opera: Egyptian Television and the Cultural Politics of Modernity." In *Worlds Apart: Modernity through the Prism of the Local,* ed. D. Miller, 190–210. London: Routledge.

Agarwal, Priya. 1991. *Passage from India: Post 1965 Indian Immigrants and Their Children: Conflicts, Concerns and Solutions.* Palos Verdes, Calif.: Yuvati Publications.

Agha, Asif. 1998. "Stereotypes and Registers of Honorific Language." *Language in Society* 27:151–93.

———. 2003. "The Social Life of Cultural Value." *Language and Communication* 23:231–73.

Ahmad, Fauzia. 2003. "Still 'in Progress'—Methodological Dilemmas, Tensions, and Contradictions in Theorizing South Asian Muslim Women." In *South Asian Women in the Diaspora,* ed. Nirmal Puwar and Parvati Raghuram, 43–65. Oxford: Berg.

Alba, Richard, and Victor Nee. 2003. *Remaking the American Mainstream: Assimilation and Contemporary Immigration.* Cambridge, Mass.: Harvard University Press.

Allesandrini, Anthony. 2001. " 'My Heart's Indian for All That': Bollywood Film between Home and Diaspora." *Diaspora* 10(3): 315–40.

Anderson, Benedict. 1991. *Imagined Communities.* London: Verso.

Aneesh, A. 2006. *Virtual Migration.* Durham, N.C.: Duke University Press.

Angel, David. 2000. "High-Technology Agglomeration and the Labor Market: The

Case of Silicon Valley." In *Understanding Silicon Valley: An Anatomy of an Entrepreneurial Region*, ed. M. Kenny, 124–40. Stanford: Stanford University Press.

Appadurai, Arjun. 1986. "Introduction: Commodities and the Politics of Value." In *The Social Life of Things: Commodities in Social Perspective*, ed. Arjun Appadurai, 3–63. Cambridge: Cambridge University Press.

———. 1993. "Heart of Whiteness." *Callaloo* 16:797–808.

———. 1996. *Modernity at Large: Cultural Dimensions of Globalization*. Minneapolis: University of Minnesota.

Aronowitz, Stanley, and Henry Giroux. 1991. *Postmodern Education: Politics, Culture, and Social Criticism*. Minneapolis: University of Minnesota Press.

Askew, Kelly. 2002. "Introduction." In *The Anthropology of Media: A Reader*, ed. K. Askew and R. Wilk, 1–13. London: Blackwell.

Auer, Peter. 1998. *Code-Switching in Conversation: Language, Interaction, and Identity*. London: Routledge.

Axel, Brian. 2004. "The Context of Diaspora." *Cultural Anthropology* 19(1): 26–60.

Bacon, Jean. 1996. *Lifelines: Community, Family, and Assimilation among Asian Indian Immigrants*. New York: Oxford University Press.

Bahrami, Homa, and Stuart Evans. 2000. "Flexible Recycling and High-Technology Entrepreneurship." In *Understanding Silicon Valley: An Anatomy of an Entrepreneurial Region*, ed. M. Kenney, 165–89. Stanford: Stanford University Press.

Barthes, Roland. 1972. *Mythologies*. New York: Noonday Press.

Barton, David, and Karin Tusting, eds. 2005. *Beyond Communities of Practice: Language, Power, and Social Context*. New York: Cambridge University Press.

Basch, Linda, Nina Glick-Schiller, and Christina Szanton-Blanc. 1994. *Nations Unbound: Transnational Processes, Postcolonial Predicaments, and Deterritorialized Nation-States*. Langhorne, Pa.: Gordon and Breach.

Basso, Keith. 1996. *Wisdom Sits in Places*. Albuquerque: University of New Mexico Press.

Baudrillard, Jean. 1988. *Selected Writings*. Stanford: Stanford University Press.

Baxter, Janeen, and Mark Western, eds. 2001. *Reconfigurations of Class and Gender*. Stanford: Stanford University Press.

Best, Amy. 2000. *Prom Night: Youth, Schools, and Popular Culture*. New York: Routledge.

Bhabha, Homi. 1994. *The Location of Culture*. London: Routledge.

Bhachu, Parminder. 1994. "New Cultural Forms and Transnational South Asian

Women: Culture, Class, and Consumption among British South Asian Women in the Diaspora." In *Nation and Migration: The Politics of Space in the South Asian Diaspora*, ed. P. van der Veer, 222–44. Philadelphia: University of Pennsylvania Press.

———. 1996. "The Multiple Landscapes of Transnational Women in the Diaspora." In *Re-Situating Identities: The Politics of Race, Ethnicity, and Culture*, ed. Vered Amit-Talai and Caroline Knowles, 283–303.

Bhardwaj, Surinder, and N. Madhu Sudana Rao. 1990. "Asians in the United States: A Geographic Appraisal." In *South Asian Overseas: Migration and Ethnicity*, ed. Colin Clarke, Ceri Peach, and Steven Vertovec, 197–216. New York: Cambridge University Press.

Bhatia, Sunil. 2007. *American Karma: Race, Culture, and Identity in the Indian Diaspora*. New York: New York University Press.

Bhatt, Rakesh. 2001. "World Englishes." *Annual Review of Anthropology* 30:527–50.

Bhattacharjee, Ananya. 1992. "The Habit of Ex-Nomination: Nation, Woman and the Indian Immigrant Bourgeoisie." *Public Culture* 5: 19–46.

Bocock, Robert. 1993. *Consumption*. London: Routledge.

Bourdieu, Pierre. 1977. *Outline of a Theory of Practice*. Cambridge: Cambridge University Press.

———. 1984. *Distinction: A Social Critique of the Judgment of Taste*. Cambridge, Mass.: Harvard University Press.

———. 1985. "The Forms of Capital." In *Handbook of Theory and Research for the Sociology of Education*, ed. J. Richardson, 241–258. New York: Greenwood.

Bourdieu, Pierre, and Jean-Claude Passeron. 1990 [1977]. *Reproduction in Education, Society, and Culture*. London: Sage.

Brah, Avtar. 1996. *Cartographies of Diaspora: Contesting Identities*. London: Routledge.

Brake, Mike. 1980. *The Sociology of Youth Culture and Youth Subcultures*. London: Routledge and Kegan Paul.

Braziel, Jana, and Anita Mannur. 2003. "Nation, Migration, and Globalization: Points of Contention in Diaspora Studies." In *Theorizing Diaspora: A Reader*, ed. Jana Braziel and Anita Mannur, 1–22. Malden, Mass.: Blackwell.

Brettell, Caroline. 2000. "Theorizing Migration in Anthropology." In *Migration Theory*, ed. Caroline Brettell and James Hollifield, 97–136. New York: Routledge.

Brodkin Sacks, Karen. 1994. "How Did Jews Become White Folks?" In *Race*, ed. Steven Gregory and Roger Sanjek, 78–102. New Brunswick, N.J.: Rutgers University Press.

Brown, Judith. 2006. *Global South Asians: Introducing the Modern Diaspora.* New York: Cambridge University Press.

Bucholtz, Mary. 2002. "Youth and Cultural Practice." *Annual Review of Anthropology* 31: 525–52.

Cameron, Deborah. 1998. "Performing Gender Identity: Young Men's Talk and the Construction of Heterosexual Masculinity." In *Language and Gender: A Reader,* ed. Jennifer Coates. 270–84. Cambridge, Mass.: Blackwell.

Cammarota, Julio. 2004. "The Gendered and Racialized Pathways of Latina and Latino Youth: Different Struggles, Different Resistances in the Urban Context." *Anthropology and Education Quarterly* 35(1): 53–74.

Castells, Manuel. 1985. "High Technology, Economic Restructuring, and the Urban-Regional Process in the United States." In *High Technology, Space, and Society,* ed. M. Castells, 11–40. Beverly Hills, Calif.: Sage.

——. 1996. *The Rise of Network Society.* Cambridge, Mass.: Blackwell.

Cavanaugh, Jillian R. 2005. "Accent Matters: The Material Consequences of Sounding Local in Northern Italy." *Language and Communication* 25(2): 127–48.

Chang, Shenglin. 2006. *The Global Silicon Valley Home: Lives and Landscapes within Taiwanese American Trans-Pacific Culture.* Stanford: Stanford University Press.

Chiang-Hom, Christy. 2004. "Transnational Cultural Practices of Chinese Immigrant Youth and Parachute Kids." In *Asian American Youth: Culture, Identity, and Ethnicity,* ed. Jennifer Lee and Min Zhou, 143–58. New York: Routledge.

Chow, Rey. 1993. *Writing Diaspora: Tactics of Intervention in Contemporary Cultural Studies.* Bloomington: Indiana University Press.

Chun, Elaine. 2001. "The Construction of White, Black, and Korean American Identities through African American Vernacular English." *Journal of Linguistic Anthropology* 11(1): 52–56.

——. 2004. "Ideologies of Legitimate Mockery: Margaret Cho's Revoicings of Mock Asian." *Pragmatics* 14 (2/3): 263–90.

Clarke, John, Stuart Hall, Tony Jefferson, and Brian Roberts. 1976. "Subcultures, Cultures, and Class." In *Resistance through Rituals: Youth Subcultures in Post-war Britain,* ed. Stuart Hall and Tony Jefferson, 9–74. London: Hutchinson, in association with the Centre for Contemporary Cultural Studies, University of Birmingham.

Clifford, James. 1994. "Diasporas." *Cultural Anthropology* 9: 302–38.

Cohen, Phil. 1997. "Subcultural Conflict and Working Class Community." In *The Subcultures Reader,* ed. Ken Gelder and Sarah Thornton, 86–93. London: Routlege.

Cohen, Stephen, and Gary Fields. 2000. "Social Capital and Capital Gains: An

Examination of Social Capital in Silicon Valley." In *Understanding Silicon Valley: An Anatomy of an Entrepreneurial Region*, ed. Martin Kenney, 190–217. Stanford: Stanford University Press.

Cohn, Bernard. 1985. "The Command of Language and the Language of Command." *Subaltern Studies* 4: 276–329.

Conner, W. 1986. "The Impact of Homelands on Diasporas." In *Modern Diasporas in International Politics*, ed. Gabriel Sheffer, 16–46. London: Croom Helm.

Coupland, Nikolas. 2001. "Dialect Stylization in Radio Talk." *Language in Society* 30(3): 345–75.

Crawford, James. 1992. *Language Loyalties: A Source Book on the Official English Controversy*. Chicago: University of Chicago Press.

———. 2000. *At War with Diversity: U.S. Language Policy in an Age of Anxiety*. Clevedon: Multilingual Matters.

Darrah, Charles. 2001. "Techno-Missionaries Doing Good at the Center." *Anthropology of Work Review* 22(1): 4–7.

Das Gupta, Monisha. 2006. *Unruly Immigrants: Rights, Activism, and Transnational South Asian Politics in the United States*. Durham, N.C.: Duke University Press.

de Certeau, Michel. 1984. *The Practice of Everyday Life*. Berkeley: University of California Press.

De Genova, Nicholas. 2005. "Introduction: Latino and Asian Racial Formation at the Frontiers of U.S. Nationalism." In *Racial Transformations: Latinos and Asians Remaking the United States*, ed. Nicholas De Genova, 1–20. Durham, N.C.: Duke University Press.

Devine, Fiona, and Mike Savage. 2005. "The Cultural Turn: Sociology and Class Analysis." In *Rethinking Class: Culture, Identities, and Lifestyles*, ed. Fiona Devine, Mike Savage, John Scott, and Rosemary Crompton, 1–23. New York: Palgrave Macmillan.

DeWind, Josh, and Philip Kasinitz. 1997. "Everything Old Is New Again? Processes and Theories of Immigrant Incorporation." *International Migration Review* 31(4): 1096–1111.

di Leonardo, Micaela. 1984. *The Varieties of Ethnic Experience: Kinship, Class, and Gender among Californian Italian Americans*. Ithaca, N.Y.: Cornell University Press.

Douglas, Mary, and Baron Isherwood. 1996. *The World of Goods: Toward an Anthropology of Consumption*. New York: Routledge.

Drew, J. 1987. "Modes of Marginality: Sociological Reflections on the Worldwide Indian Diaspora." In *Studies in Third World Societies* 39:81–96.

D'Souza, Dinesh. 1998. *Illiberal Education: The Politics of Race and Sex on Campus*. New York: Free Press.

Bibliography

Dudrah, Rajinder Kumar. 2006. *Bollywood: Sociology Goes to the Movies*. New Delhi: Sage.

Eckert, Penelope. 1989. *Jocks and Burnouts: Social Categories and Identity in High School*. New York: Teachers College Press.

Eckert, Penelope, and Sally McConnell-Ginet. 1992. "Think Practically and Look Locally: Language and Gender as Community Based Practice." *Annual Review of Anthropology* 21: 461–90.

Eglash, Ron. 2002. "Race, Sex, and Nerds: From Black Geeks to Asian American Hipsters." *Social Text* 20(2 71): 49–64.

Eisenlohr, Patrick. 2006. *Little India: Diaspora, Time and Ethnolinguistic Belonging in Hindu Mauritius*. Berkeley: University of California Press.

Eisenstadt, Samuel. 1956. *From Generation to Generation*. New York: Free Press.

English-Lueck, Jan. 2002. *Cultures@Silicon Valley*. Stanford: Stanford University Press.

Ernst, Gisela. 1994. "Beyond Language: The Many Dimensions of an ESL Program." *Anthropology and Education Quarterly* 25: 317–35.

Fader, Ayala. 2007. "Reclaiming Sacred Sparks: Linguistic Syncretism and Gendered Language Shift among Hasidic Jews in New York." *Journal of Linguistic Anthropology* 12(1): 1–22.

Farr, Marcia. 2006. *Rancheros in Chicagoacan: Language and Identity in a Transnational Community*. Austin, Tex.: University of Texas Press.

Feld, Steven, and Keith Basso, eds. 1996. *Senses of Place*. Santa Fe, N.M.: School of American Research Press.

Fong, Vanessa. 2004. "Filial Nationalism among Chinese Teenagers with Global Identities." *American Ethnologist* 31(4): 631–48.

Fordham, Signthia. 1996. *Blacked Out: Dilemmas of Race, Identity, and Success at Capital High*. Chicago: University of Chicago Press.

Foucault, Michel. 1979. *History of Sexuality*. New York: Vintage.

Frankenburg, Ruth. 1993. *White Women, Race Matters: The Social Construction of Whiteness*. Minneapolis: University of Minnesota Press.

Freeman, James. 1989. *Hearts of Sorrow: Vietnamese-American Lives*. Stanford: Stanford University Press.

Gal, Susan. 1987. "Code-Switching and Consciousness in the European Periphery." *American Ethnologist* 14: 637–53.

Gal, Susan, and Kathryn Woolard, eds. 2001. *Language and Publics: The Making of Authority*. Manchester, England: St. Jerome.

Ganti, Tejaswini. 2002. "And yet my heart is still Indian": The Bombay Film

Industry and the (H)Indianization of Hollywood." In *Media Worlds: Anthropology on New Terrain*, ed. Faye Ginsburg, Lila Abu-Lughod, and Brian Larkin, 281–300. Berkeley: University of California Press.

———. 2004. *Bollywood: A Guidebook to Popular Hindi Cinema*. New York: Routledge.

Garcia, Ofelia. 1997. "New York's Multilingualism: World Languages and Their Role in a U.S. City." In *The Multilingual Apple: Languages in New York City*, ed. Ofelia Garcia and Joshua Fishman, 3–52. New York: Mouton de Gruyer.

Gelder, Ken, and Sarah Thornton, eds. 1997. *The Subcultures Reader*. London: Routledge.

Gell, Alfred. 1998. *Art and Agency: An Anthropological Theory*. Oxford: Clarendon Press.

George, Rosemary. 1997. "From Expatriate Aristocrat to Immigrant Nobody: South Asian Racial Strategies in the Southern California Context." *Diaspora* 6: 31–60.

George, Sheba. 2005. *When Women Come First: Gender and Class in Transnational Migration*. Berkeley: University of California Press.

Gibson, Margaret. 1988. *Accommodation without Assimilation: Sikh Immigrants in an American High School*. Ithaca, N.Y.: Cornell University Press.

Gibson, Margaret, and John Ogbu, eds. 1991. *Minority Status and Schooling: A Comparative Study of Immigrant and Involuntary Minorities*. New York: Garland.

Gillespie, Marie. 1995. *Television, Ethnicity and Cultural Change*. London: Routledge.

Gilroy, Paul. 1993. *The Black Atlantic: Modernity and Double Consciousness*. Cambridge, Mass.: Harvard University Press.

Ginsburg, Faye, Lila Abu-Lughod, and Brian Larkin, eds. 2002. *Media Worlds: Anthropology on New Terrain*. Berkeley: University of California Press.

Glazer, Nathan, and Daniel Moynihan. 1963. *Beyond the Melting Pot*. Cambridge, Mass.: MIT Press.

Goldberg, David. 1994. "Introduction: Multicultural Conditions." In *Multiculturalism: A Critical Reader*, ed. David Goldberg, 1–44. Oxford: Basil Blackwell.

Gopinath, Gayatri. 1995. " 'Bombay, U.K., Yuba City': Bhangra Music and the Engendering of Diaspora." *Diaspora* 4: 303–21.

Grewal, Inderpal. 2005. *Transnational America: Feminisms, Diasporas, and Neoliberalisms*. Durham, N.C.: Duke University Press.

Grewal, Inderpal, and Caren C. Kaplan, eds. 1993. *Scattered Hegemonies: Postmodernities and Transnational Practices*. Minneapolis: University of Minnesota Press.

Gupta, Akhil, and James Ferguson. 1997a. "Culture, Power, Place: Ethnography at the End of an Era." In *Culture, Power, Place: Explorations in Critical Anthropology*, ed. Akhil Gupta and James Ferguson, 1–32. Durham, N.C.: Duke University Press.

———. 1997b. "Beyond 'Culture': Space, Identity, and the Politics of Difference." In *Culture, Power, Place: Explorations in Critical Anthropology*, ed. Akhil Gupta and James Ferguson, 33–51. Durham, N.C.: Duke University Press.

Hall, Kathleen. 2002. *Lives in Translation: Sikh Youth as British Citizens.* Philadelphia: University of Pennsylvania Press.

Hall, Stuart. 1990. "Cultural Identity and Diaspora." In *Identity, Community, Culture, Difference*, ed. Jonathan Rutherford, 222–37. New York: Lawrence and Wishart.

———. 1996. "Who Needs 'Identity'?" In *Questions of Cultural Identity*, ed. Stuart Hall and Paul du Gay, 1–17. London: Sage.

Halle, David. 1984. *America's Working Man.* Chicago: University of Chicago Press.

Harris, Roxy. 2006. *New Ethnicities and Language Use.* New York: Palgrave Macmillan.

Harvey, David. 1990. *The Condition of Postmodernity.* London: Blackwell.

Hebdige, Dick. 1979. *Subculture: The Meaning of Style.* London: Methuen.

Heller, Monica. 1988. "Introduction." In *Code-switching: Anthropological and Sociolinguistic Perspectives*, ed. Monica Heller, 1–24. Berlin: Mouton de Gruyter.

———. 1999. *Linguistic Minorities and Modernity: A Sociolinguistic Ethnography.* New York: Addison Wesley Longman.

Helweg, Arthur, and Usha Helweg. 1990. *An Immigrant Success Story: East Indians in America.* Philadelphia: University of Pennsylvania Press.

Hess, Gary. 1976. "The Forgotten Asian Americans: The East Indian Community in the United States." In *The Asian American: The Historical Experience*, ed. N. Hundley Jr., 157–77. Santa Barbara, Calif.: Clio Books.

Hong, Joann, and Pyong Gap Min. 1999. "Ethnic Attachment among Second Generation Korean Adolescents." *Amerasia* 25(1): 165–78.

Hull, Glynda. 1993. "Hearing Other Voices: A Critical Assessment of Popular Views on Literacy and Work." *Harvard Educational Review* 63(1): 20–49.

———. 2001. "Constructing Working Selves: Silicon Valley Assemblers Meet the New Work Order." *Anthropology of Work Review* 22:17–22.

Hutnyk, John. 1999–2000. "Hybridity Saves? Authenticity and/or the Critique of Appropriation." *Amerasia* 25(3): 39–58.

Hwang, Henry David 1979. *FOB.* NY: Theater Communication Group Inc.'s Plays in Process.

Ignatiev, Noel. 1996. *How the Irish Became White.* London: Routledge.

Ima, Kenji. 1995. "Testing the American Dream: At-Risk Southeast Asian Refugee Students in Secondary Schools." In *California's Immigrant Children: Theory, Research, and Implications for Educational Policy*, ed. Ruben Rumbaut and Wayne Cornelius, 191–209. San Diego: University of California, Center for U.S.-Mexican Studies.

Inkelas, Karen. 2006. *Racial Attitudes and Asian Pacific Americans: Demystifying the Model Minority*. New York: Routledge.

Irvine, Judith. 1989. "When Talk Isn't Cheap: Language and Political Economy." *American Ethnologist* 16(2): 248–67.

Jacobsen, Knut, and P. Pratap Kumar. 2004. "Introduction." In *South Asians in the Diaspora: Histories and Religious Traditions*, ed. K. Jacobsen and P. Kumar, ix–xxiv. Boston: Brill.

Jameson, Fredric. 1991. *Postmodernism, or, the Cultural Logic of Late Capitalism*. Durham, N.C.: Duke University Press.

Jensen, Joan. 1988. *Passage from India: Asian Indian Immigrants in North America*. New Haven: Yale University Press.

Jeon, Mihyon. 2001. "Avoiding FOBS: An Account of a Journey. *Working Papers in Educational Linguistics* 17(1–2): 83–106.

Joseph, John. 2006. *Language and Politics*. Edinburg: Edinburg University Press.

Joshi, Khyati. 2006. *New Roots in America's Sacred Ground: Religion, Race, and Ethnicity in Indian America*. New Brunswick, N.J.: Rutgers University Press.

Kachru, Braj. 2000. "The Alchemy of English." In *Routledge Language and Cultural Theory Reader*, ed. L. Burke, T. Crowley, and A. Girvin, 31–29. London: Routledge.

Kalra, Virinder, Raminder Kaur, and John Hutnyk. 2005. *Diaspora and Hybridity*. London: Sage.

Kao, Grace, and Jennifer Thompson. 2003. "Racial and Ethnic Stratification in Educational Achievement and Attainment." *Annual Review of Sociology* 29:417–42.

Karamcheti, Indira. 1992. "The Shrinking Himalayas." *Diaspora* 2(2): 261–76.

Kaur, Raminder, and Ajay Sinha, eds. 2005. *Bollyworld: Popular Indian Cinema through a Transnational Lens*. London: Sage.

Keane, Webb. 2003. "Semiotics and the Social Analysis of Material Things." *Language and Communication* 23(3–4): 409–25.

Kenney, Martin. 2000. "Introduction." In *Understanding Silicon Valley: An Anatomy of an Entrepreneurial Region*, ed. Martin Kenney, 1–12. Stanford: Stanford University Press.

Kenney, Martin, and Richard Florida. 2000. "Venture Capital in Silicon Valley: Fueling New Firm Formation." In *Understanding Silicon Valley: An Anatomy of an Entrepreneurial Region*, ed. M. Kenney, 98–123. Stanford: Stanford University Press.

Khan, Aisha. 2004. *Callaloo Nation: Metaphors of Race and Religious Identity among South Asians in Trinidad*. Durham, N.C.: Duke University Press.

Khandelwal, Madhulika. 1995. "Indian Immigrants in Queens, New York City: Patterns of Spatial Concentration and Distribution 1965–1990." In *Nation and Migration: The Politics of Space in the South Asian Diaspora*, ed. P. van der Veer, 178–96. Philadelphia: University of Pennsylvania Press.

——. 2002. *Becoming American, Being Indian: An Immigrant Community in New York City*. Ithaca, N.Y.: Cornell University Press.

Khanna, Dan. 1997. *The Rise, Decline, and Renewal of Silicon Valley's High Technology Industry*. New York: Garland.

Khubchandani, Lachman. 1983. *Plural Languages, Plural Cultures: Communication, Identity and Sociopolitical Change in Contemporary India*. Honolulu: University of Hawaii Press.

Kibria, Nazli. 1998. "The Racial Gap: South Asian American Racial Identity and the Asian American Movement." In *A Part, Yet Apart: South Asians in Asian America*, ed. Lavina Shankar and Rajini Srikanth, 69–78. Philadelphia: Temple University Press.

Kim, Sun Seog. 2004. "The Experiences of Young Korean Immigrants: A Grounded Theory of Negotiating Social, Cultural, and Generational Boundaries." *Issues in Mental Health Nursing* 25:517–37.

Kopytoff, Igor. 1986. "The Cultural Biography of Things: Commoditization as a Process." In *The Social Life of Things: Commodities in Social Perspective*, ed. Arjun Appadurai, 64–94. Cambridge: Cambridge University Press.

Kripalani, Coonoor. 2006. "Trendsetting and Product Placement in Bollywood Film: Consumerism through Consumption." *New Cinemas: Journal of Contemporary Film* 4(3): 161–76.

Kroskrity, Paul. 2000. "Identity." *Journal of Linguistic Anthropology* 9: 111–14.

Kumar, Amitava. 2000. *Passport Photos*. Berkeley: University of California Press.

Kumsa, Martha Kuwee. 2006. " 'No! I'm not a Refugee!' The Poetics of Be-Longing among Young Oromos in Toronto." *Journal of Refugee Studies* 19(2): 230–55.

Kymlicka, Will. 1996. *Multicultural Citizenship: A Liberal Theory of Minority Rights*. New York: Oxford University Press.

Labrador, Roderick. 2004. " 'We Can Laugh at Ourselves': Hawai'i Ethnic Humor, Local Identity, and the Myth of Multiculturalism." *Pragmatics* 14 (2/3): 291–316.

LaDousa, Chaise. 2005. "Disparate Markets: Language, Nation, and Education in North India." *American Ethnologist* 32(3): 460–78.

Langman, Lauren. 1992. "Neon Cages: Shopping for Subjectivity." In *Lifestyle Shopping: The Subject of Consumption*, ed. Rob Shields, 40–82. London: Routlege.

Larkin, Brian. 1997. "Indian Films, Nigerian Lovers: Media and the Creation of Parallel Modernities." *Africa* 67: 406–40.

Lash, Scott, and John Urry. 1987. *The End of Organized Capitalism*. Madison: University of Wisconsin Press.

Latour, Bruno. 1993. *We Have Never Been Modern*. Cambridge, Mass.: Harvard University Press.

Lave, Jean, and Etienne Wenger. 1991. *Situated Learning in Communities of Practice*. Washington, D.C.: American Psychological Association.

Lave, Jean, Paul Duguid, and Nadine Fernandez. 1992. "Coming of Age in Birmingham." *Annual Review of Anthropology* 21: 257–82.

Lavie, Smadar, and Ted Swedenburg, eds. 1996. *Displacement, Diaspora and Geographies of Identity*. Durham, N.C.: Duke University Press.

Lee, Chong-Moon, William Miller, Marguerite Hancock, and Henry Rowen. 2000. "The Silicon Valley Habitat." In *The Silicon Valley Edge: A Habitat for Innovation and Entrepreneurship*, ed. Chong-Moon Lee, William Miller, Marguerite Hancock, and Henry Rowen, 1–15. Stanford: Stanford University Press.

Lee, Christopher. 2005. "Diaspora, Transnationalism, and Asian American Studies: Positions and Debates." In *Displacements and Diasporas: Asians in the Americas*, ed. Wanni Anderson and Robert Lee, 23–38. New Brunswick, N.J.: Rutgers University Press.

Lee, Jennifer, and Min Zhou. 2004. "Conclusion: Reflection, Thoughts, and Directions for Future Research." In *Asian American Youth: Culture, Identity, and Ethnicity*, ed. Jennifer Lee and Min Zhou, 314–24. New York: Routledge.

Lee, Stacey. 1996. *Unraveling the "Model Minority" Stereotype: Listening to Asian American Youth*. New York: Teacher's College Press.

——. 2004. "Up Against Whiteness: Students of Color in Our Schools." *Anthropology and Education Quarterly* 35(1): 121–25.

——. 2005. *Up Against Whiteness: Race, School, and Immigrant Youth*. New York: Teacher's College Press.

Leonard, Karen. 1992. *Making Ethnic Choices: California's Punjabi Mexican Americans*. Philadelphia: Temple University Press.

———. 1997. "Finding One's Own Place: Asian Landscapes Re-visioned in Rural California." In Culture, Power, Place: Explorations in Critical Anthropology, ed. Akhil Gupta and James Ferguson, 118–36. Durham, N.C.: Duke University Press.

Leslie, Stuart. 2000. "The Biggest 'Angel' of Them All: The Military and the Making of Silicon Valley." In Understanding Silicon Valley: An Anatomy of an Entrepreneurial Region, ed. M. Kenney, 48–67. Stanford: Stanford University Press.

Lessinger, Johanna. 1996. From the Ganges to the Hudson: Indian Immigrants in New York City. Boston: Allyn and Bacon.

Levitt, Peggy, and Nadya Jaworsky. 2007. "Transnational Migration Studies: Past Developments and Future Trends." Annual Review of Sociology 33:129–56.

Levitt, Peggy, and Mary Waters. 2002. Introduction. In The Changing Face of Home: The Transnational Lives of the Second Generation, ed. Peggy Levitt and Mary Waters, 1–30. New York: Russell Sage.

Lew, Jamie. 2004 "The 'Other' Story of Model Minorities: Korean American High School Dropouts in an Urban Context." Anthropology and Education Quarterly 35(3): 303–23.

Li, Wei, and Edward Park. 2006. "Asian Americans in Silicon Valley: High Technology Industry Development and Community Transformation." In From Urban Enclave to Ethnic Suburb, ed. Wei Li 119–33. Honolulu: University of Hawaii Press.

Liechty, Mark. 1995. "Media, Markets and Modernization: Youth Identities and the Experience of Modernity in Kathmandu, Nepal." In Youth Cultures: A Cross-Cultural Perspective, ed. Vered Amit-Talai and Helena Wulff, 166–201. London: Routledge.

———. 2003. Suitably Modern: Making Middle-class Culture in a New Consumer Society. Princeton: Princeton University Press.

Lippi-Green, Rosina. 1997. English with an Accent. London: Routledge.

Lipsitz, George. 2006. The Possessive Investment in Whiteness: How White People Profit from Identity Politics. Philadelphia: Temple University Press.

Lo, Adrienne. 1999. "Codeswitching, Speech Community Membership, and the Construction of Ethnic Identity." Journal of Sociolinguistics 3/4:461–79.

Lo, Adrienne, and Angela Reyes. 2004. "Language, Identity, and Relationality in Asian Pacific America: An Introduction." Pragmatics 14(2/3): 115–26.

Loomis, Terrence. 1990. Pacific Migrant Labour, Class, and Racism in New Zealand. Aldershot, England: Avebury Gower Publishing Company.

Low, Setha. 1996. "The Anthropology of Cities." Annual Review of Anthropology 25: 383–409.

Lowe, Lisa. 1996. *Immigrant Acts: On Asian American Cultural Politics*. Durham, N.C.: Duke University Press.

Maira, Sunaina. 2000. "Henna and Hip Hop." *Journal of Asian American Studies* 3(3): 329–69.

——. 2002. *Desis in the House: Indian American Youth Culture in New York City*. Philadelphia: Temple University Press.

Maira, Sunaina, and Elizabeth Seop, eds. 2005. *Youthscapes: The Popular, The National, The Global*. Philadelphia: University of Pennsylvania Press.

Mankekar, Purnima. 2002. " 'India Shopping': Indian Grocery Stores and Transnational Configuration of Belonging." *Ethnos* 67: 75–98.

——. 1999. *Screening Politics, Viewing Culture: Ethnography of Television, Womanhood, and Nation in Postcolonial India*. Durham, N.C.: Duke University Press.

Marcus, George, ed. 1995. *Connected: Engagements with Media*. Chicago: University of Chicago Press.

Markusen, Ann. 1985. "High-Tech Jobs, Markets, and Economic Development Prospects: Evidence from California." In *Silicon Landscapes*, ed. Peter Hall and Ann Markusen, 35–48. Boston: Allen and Unwin.

Mathew, Biju. 2004. *Taxi! Cabs and Capitalism in New York City*. New York: New Press.

Matthews, Glenna. 2003. *Silicon Valley, Women, and the California Dream: Gender, Class, and Opportunity in the Twentieth Century*. Stanford: Stanford University Press.

Mazumdar, Sucheta. 1989. "Race and Racism: South Asians in the United States." In *Frontiers of Asian American Studies*, ed. Gail Normura, 25–39. Pullman: Washington State University Press.

Mazzarella, William. 2003. *Shoveling Smoke: Advertising and Globalization in Contemporary India*. Durham, N.C.: Duke University Press.

McCarthy, Cameron, and Arlette Willis. 1995. "The Politics of Culture: Multicultural Education After the Content Debate." In *Beyond Comfort Zones in Multiculturalism: Confronting the Politics of Privilege*, ed. Sandra Jackson and Jose Solis, 67–88. Westport, Conn.: Greenwood.

McCracken, Grant. 1991. *Culture and Consumption: New Approaches to the Symbolic Character of Consumer Goods and Activities*. Bloomington: Indiana University Press.

McLaren, Peter. 1994. "Multiculturalism and the Postmodern Critique: Toward a Pedagogy of Resistance and Transformation." In *Between Borders: Pedagogy and the Politics of Cultural Studies*, ed. Henry Giroux and Peter McLaren, 192–224. New York: Routledge.

Bibliography

McRobbie, Angela. 1991. *Feminism and Youth Culture: From Jackie to Just Seventeen.*
London: Routledge.

Mendoza-Denton, Norma. 1996. " 'Muy Macha': Gender and Ideology in Gang-
Girls' Discourse about Makeup." *Ethnos* 61: 47–63.

———. 2007. *Homegirls: Language and Cultural Practice among Latina Youth Gangs.*
Malden, Mass.: Blackwell.

Miller, Daniel. 1987. *Material Culture and Mass Consumption.* New York: Blackwell.

———. 1995. "Consumption Studies as the Transformation of Anthropology." In
Acknowledging Consumption: A Review of New Studies, ed. Daniel Miller, 264–95.
London: Routledge.

———. 1998a. *A Theory of Shopping.* Ithaca, N.Y.: Cornell University Press.

———. 1998b. "Why Some Things Matter." In *Material Cultures: Why Some Things
Matter,* ed. Daniel Miller, 3–21. Chicago: University of Chicago Press.

———, ed. 2001. *Car Cultures.* Oxford: Berg.

Milroy, Lesley, and Peter Muysken. 1995. *One Speaker, Two Languages: Cross-
Disciplinary Perspectives on Code-Switching.* Cambridge: Cambridge University
Press.

Min, Pyong Gap, and Rose Kim, eds. 1999. *Struggle for Ethnic Identity: Narratives by
Asian American Professionals.* Walnut Creek, Calif.: Alta Mira Press.

Mohammad-Arif, Aminah. 2002. *Salaam America: South Asian Muslims in New York.*
London: Anthem Press.

Moorti, Sujatha. 2006. "Uses of Diaspora: Indian Popular Culture and the NRI
Dilemma." *South Asian Popular Culture* 3(1): 49–62.

Morely, David. 1995. "Media and Consumption." In *Acknowledging Consumption,* ed.
Daniel Miller, 296–328. London: Routledge.

Mukhi, Sunita S. 2000. *Doing the Desi Thing: Performing Indianness in New York City.*
New York: Garland.

Myers, Fred. 2001. "Introduction: The Empire of Things." In *The Empire of Things:
Regimes of Value and Material Culture,* ed. Fred Myers, 3–64. Santa Fe: School of
American Research Press.

Naficy, Hamid. 1993. *The Making of Exile Cultures: Iranian Television in Los Angeles.*
Minneapolis: University of Minnesota Press.

Narayan, Kirin. 1993. "How Native Is a 'Native' Anthropologist?" *American
Anthropologist* 95:671–85.

———. 2004. "Haunting Stories: Narrative Transmissions of South Asian Identities
in Diaspora." In *South Asians in the Diaspora: Histories and Religious Traditions,* ed.
K. Jacobsen and P. Kumar, 415–34. London: Brill.

Niranjana, Tejaswini. 2006. *Mobilizing India: Women, Music, and Migration between India and Trinidad*. Durham, N.C.: Duke University Press.

O'Dougherty, Maureen. 2002. *Consumption Intensified: The Politics of Middle-Class Daily Life in Brazil*. Durham, N.C.: Duke University Press.

Okihiro, Gary. 1994. *Margins and Mainstreams: Asians in American History and Culture*. Seattle: University of Washington Press.

Omatsu, Greg. 1994. "The 'Four Prisons' and the Movements of Liberation: Asian American Activism from the 1960s to the 1990s." In *The State of Asian America*, ed. Karin Aguilar-San Juan, 19–70. Boston: South End Press.

Omi, Michael, and Howard Winant. 1994. *Racial Formation in the United States*. New York: Routledge.

Ong, Aihwa. 1993. "On the Edge of Empires: Flexible Citizenship among Chinese in Diaspora." *Positions* 1: 745–78.

——. 1996. "Cultural Citizenship as Subject-Making: Immigrants Negotiate Racial and Cultural Boundaries in the United States." *Current Anthropology* 37(5): 737–62.

Ortner, Sherry. 2003. *New Jersey Dreaming: Culture, Capital, and the Class of '58*. Durham, N.C.: Duke University Press.

Palumbo-Liu, David. 1999. *Asian/American: Historical Crossings of Racial Frontier*. Stanford: Stanford University Press.

Park, Kyeyoung. 1999. " 'I Really Do Feel Like I'm 1.5!' The Construction of Self and Community by Young Korean Americans." *Amerasia* 25(1): 139–63.

Patico, Jennifer. 2002. "Chocolate and Cognac: Gifts and the Recognition of Social Worlds in Post-Soviet Russia." *Ethnos* 67(3): 345–68.

——. 2005. "To be Happy in a Mercedes: Tropes of Value and Ambivalent Visions of Marketization." *American Ethnologist* 32(3): 479–96.

Peirce, Charles. 1955. *Philosophical Writings of Peirce*. New York: Dover.

Pellow, David Naguib, and Lisa Sun-Hee Park. 2002. *The Silicon Valley of Dreams: Environmental Injustice, Immigrant Workers, and the High-Tech Global Economy*. New York: New York University Press.

Pennycook, Alistair. 2007. *Global Englishes and Transcultural Flows*. London: Routledge.

Perry, Pamela. 2002. *Shades of White: White Kids and Racial Identities in High School*. Durham, N.C.: Duke University Press.

Pitti, Stephen. 2003. *The Devil in Silicon Valley: Northern California, Race, and Mexican Americans*. Princeton: Princeton University Press.

Portes, Alejandro. 1995. "Children of Immigrants: Segmented Assimilation and

Its Determinants." In *The Economic Sociology of Immigration: Essays on Networks, Ethnicity, and Entrepreneurship*, ed. Alejandro Portes, 248–80. New York: Russell Sage Foundation.

———, ed. 1996. *The New Second Generation*. New York: Russell Sage.

———. 1998. "Social Capital: Its Origins and Applications in Modern Sociology." *Annual Review of Sociology* 24: 1–24.

Portes, Alejandro, and Ruben Rumbaut. 1996. *Immigrant America: A Portrait*. 2nd ed. Berkeley: University of California Press.

———. 2001. *Legacies: The Story of the Immigrant Second Generation*. Berkeley: University of California Press.

Prashad, Vijay. 1998. "Crafting Solidarities." In *A Part, Yet Apart: South Asians in Asian America*, ed. L. Shankar and R. Srikanth, 105–26. Philadelphia: Temple University Press.

———. 2000. *The Karma of Brown Folk*. Minneapolis: University of Minnesota Press.

———. 2002. *Everybody Was Kung Fu Fighting: Afro-Asian Connections and the Myth of Cultural Purity*. Boston: Beacon Press.

Punathambekar, Aswin. 2005. "Bollywood in the Indian American Diaspora: Mediating a Transitive Logic of Cultural Citizenship." *International Journal of Cultural Studies* 8(2): 151–73.

Purkayastha, Bandana. 2005. *Negotiating Ethnicity: Second-Generation South Asian Americans Traverse a Transnational World*. New Brunswick, N.J.: Rutgers University Press.

Puwar, Nirmal. 2003. "Melodramatic Postures and Constructions." In *South Asian Women in the Diaspora*, ed. Nirmal Puwar and Parvati Raghuram, 21–41. Oxford: Berg.

Pyke, Karen, and Tran Dang. 2003. " 'FOB' and 'Whitewashed': Identity and Internalized Racism among Second Generation Asian Americans." *Qualitative Sociology* 26(2): 147–72.

Radhakrishnan, R. 1996. *Diasporic Mediations: Between Home and Location*. Minneapolis: University of Minnesota Press.

———. 2003. "Ethnicity in an Age of Diaspora." In *Theorizing Diaspora: A Reader*, ed. J. Braziel and A. Mannur, 119–31. Malden, Mass.: Blackwell.

Raj, Dhooleka. 2003. *Where Are You From? Middle Class Migrants in the Modern World*. Berkeley: University of California Press.

Rampton, Ben. 1995. *Crossing: Language and Ethnicity among Adolescents*. New York: Longman.

———. 1999. "Styling the Other: Introduction." *Journal of Sociolinguistics* 3/4:421–27.

Rangaswamy, Padma. 2000. *Namaste America: Indian Immigrants in an American Metropolis*. State College: Pennsylvania State University Press.

Raphael-Hernandez, Heike, and Shannon Steen, eds. 2006. *AfroAsian Encounters: Culture, History, Politics*. New York: New York University Press.

Rapp, Rayna. 1982. "Family and Class in Contemporary America: Notes toward an Understanding of Ideology." In *Rethinking the Family: Some Feminist Questions*, ed. Barrie Thorne and Marilyn Yalom, 168–87. New York: Longman.

Ray, Manas. 2000. "Bollywood Down Under." In *Floating lives: The Media and Asian Diasporas*, ed. Stuart Cunningham and John Sinclair, 136–84. Brisbane: University of Queensland Press.

Rayaprol, Aparna. 1997. *Negotiating Identities: Women in the Indian Diaspora*. Delhi: Oxford University Press.

Reyes, Angela. 2002. "Are You Losing Your Culture? Poetics, Indexicality, and Asian American Identity." *Discourse Studies* 4(2): 183–99.

———. 2007. *Language, Identity, and Stereotype among Southeast Asian American Youth*. Mahwah, N.J.: Lawrence Erlbaum Associates.

Rodriguez, Cirenio, and Enrique Trueba. 1998. "Leadership, Education, and Political Action: The Emergence of New Latino Ethnic Identities." In *Ethnic Identity and Power*, ed. Yali Zou and Enrique Trueba, 43–66. New York: State University of New York Press.

Rogers, Everett, and Judith Larsen. 1984. *Silicon Valley Fever: Growth of High-Technology Culture*. New York: Basic Books.

Rosaldo, Renato, and William Flores. 1997. "Identity, Conflict, and Evolving Latino Communities." In *Latino Cultural Citizenship: Claiming Identity, Space, and Rights*, ed. William Flores and Rina Benmayor, 57–96. Boston: Beacon Press.

Rudrappa, Sharmilla. 2004. *Ethnic Routes to Becoming American: Indian Immigrants and the Cultures of Citizenship*. New Brunswick, N.J.: Rutgers University Press.

Rumbaut, Ruben. 1997. "Assimilation and Its Discontents: Between Rhetoric and Reality." *International Migration Review* 31(4): 923–60.

———. 2002. "Severed or Sustained Attachments? Language, Identity, and Imagined Communities in the Post-Immigrant Generation." In *The Changing Face of Home: The Transnational Lives of the Second Generation*, ed. P. Levitt and M. Waters, 43–95. New York: Russell Sage.

Rumbaut, Rumbaut, and Wayne Cornelius, eds. 1995. *California's Immigrant Children: Theory, Research, and Implications for Educational Policy*. San Diego: Center for U.S.-Mexican Studies, University of California.

Rutz, Henry, and Benjamin Orlove, eds. 1989. *The Social Economy of Consumption*. Lanham, Md.: University Press of America.

Bibliography

Rymes, Betsy. 2001. *Conversational Borderlands: Language and Identity in an Alternative Urban High School*. New York: Teachers College Press.

Safran, William. 1991. "Diasporas in Modern Societies: Myths of Homeland and Return." *Diasporas* 1: 83–99.

Sahlins, Marshall. 1981. *Historical Metaphors and Mythical Realities: Structure in the Early History of the Sandwich Islands Kingdom*. Ann Arbor: University of Michigan Press.

Sandhu, Sabeen. 2004. "Instant Karma: The Commercialization of Asian Indian Culture." In *Asian American Youth: Culture, Identity, and Ethnicity*, ed. J. Lee and M. Zhou, 131–41. New York: Routledge.

Saran, Parmatma. 1985. *The Asian Indian Experience in the United States*. Rochester, Vt.: Schenkman Books.

Sassen, Saskia. 1991. *The Global City: New York, London, Tokyo*. Princeton: Princeton University Press.

Saussure, Ferdinand de. 2000 [1916]. "The Nature of the Linguistic Sign." In *The Routledge Language and Cultural Theory Reader*, eds. Lucy Burke, Tony Crowley, and Alan Girvin, 21–32. London: Routledge.

Saxenian, AnnaLee. 1985. "Silicon Valley and Route 128: Regional Prototypes or Historic Exceptions?" In *High Technology, Space, and Society*, ed. Manuel Castells, 81–105. Thousand Oaks, Calif.: Sage.

Schieffelin, Bambi, Kathryn Woolard, and Paul Kroskrity, eds. 1998. *Language Ideologies*. New York: Oxford University Press.

Sengupta, Somini. 1996. "To Be Young, Indian and Hip: Hip-hop Meets Hindi Pop as a New Generation of South Asians Finds Its Own Groove." *New York Times*, section 13, p. 1, June 30.

Shankar, Shalini. 2001. "Languages of Youth Connectivity." *SAMAR (South Asian Magazine for Action and Reflection)* (fall/winter): 44–48.

——. 2003. "Windows of Opportunity: South Asian American Teenagers and the Promise of Technology in Silicon Valley." PhD diss., New York University, Department of Anthropology.

——. 2004a. "FOBby or Tight? 'Multicultural Day' and Other Struggles in Two Silicon Valley High Schools." In *Local Actions: Cultural Activism, Power and Public Life*, ed. Melissa Checker and Maggie Fishman, 184–207. New York: Columbia University Press.

——. 2004b. "Reel to Real: Desi Teens' Linguistic Engagements with Bollywood." *Pragmatics* 14(2–3): 317–36.

——. 2006. "Metaconsumptive Practices and the Circulation of Objectifications." *Journal of Material Culture* 11(3): 293–317.

Sharma, Nitasha. 2004. "Claiming Space, Making Race: Second Generation South Asian American Hip Hop Artists." PhD diss., University of California at Santa Barbara.

Sharma, Sanjay, John Hutnyk, and Ashwani Sharma, eds. 1996. *Dis-Orienting Rhythms: The Politics of the New Asian Dance Music*. London: Zed.

Shields, Rob. 1992. "Spaces for the Subject of Consumption." In *Lifestyle Shopping*, ed. Rob Shields, 1–20. London: Routledge.

Shukla, Sandhya. 1997. "Building Diaspora and Nation: The 1991 'Cultural Festival of India.'" *Cultural Studies* 11: 269–315.

——. 1999–2000. "New Immigrants, New Forms of Transnational Community: Post-1965 Indian Migrations." *Amerasia Journal* 25(3): 19–36.

——. 2001. "Locations for South Asian Diasporas." *Annual Review of Anthropology* 30: 551–72.

——. 2003. *India Abroad: Diasporic Cultures of Postwar America and England*. Princeton: Princeton University Press.

Silverstein, Michael. 1993. "Metapragmatic Discourse and Metapragmatic Function." In *Reflexive Language: Reported Speech and Metapragmatics*, ed. John Lucy, 33–58. Cambridge: Cambridge University Press.

——. 1996a. "Monoglot 'Standard' in America: Standardization and Metaphors of Linguistic Hegemony." In *The Matrix of Language: Contemporary Linguistic Anthropology*, ed. Donald Brennis and Ronald Macauley, 284–306. Boulder: Westview Press.

——. 1996b. "Shifters, Linguistic Categories, and Cultural Description." In *Language, Culture, and Society*, ed. Ben Blount, 187–221. Prospect Heights, Ill.: Waveland Press.

——. 2003. "Indexical Order and the Dialectics of Sociolinguistic Life." *Language and Communication* 23(3–4): 193–230.

Singh, Amritjit. 1996. "African Americans and the New Immigrants." In *Between the Lines: South Asians and Postcoloniality*, ed. Deepika Bahri and Mary Vasudeva, 93–110. Philadelphia: Temple University Press.

Siu, Lok. 2001. "Diasporic Cultural Citizenship: Chineseness and Belonging in Central America." *Social Text* 19(4 69): 7–28.

Skeggs, Beverly. 2005. "The Re-branding of Class: Propertising Culture." In *Rethinking Class: Culture, Identities, and Lifestyles*, ed. Fiona Devine, Mike Savage, John Scott, and Rosemary Crompton, 46–68. New York: Palgrave Macmillan.

Sollors, Werner. 1986. *Beyond Ethnicity*. New York: Oxford University Press.

——. 1989. "Introduction: The Invention of Ethnicity." In *The Invention of Ethnicity*, ed. W. Sollors, xiv–xvi. New York: Oxford University Press.

Song, Min. 1998. "Pahkar Singh's Argument with Asian America: Color and the Structure of Race Formation." In *A Part, Yet Apart: South Asians in Asian America*, ed. Lavina Shankar and Rajini Srikanth, 79–104. Philadelphia: Temple University Press.

Spitulnik, Deborah. 1993. "Anthropology and Mass Media." *Annual Review of Anthropology* 22: 293–315.

——. 1996. "The Social Circulation of Media Discourse and the Mediation of Communities." *Journal of Linguistic Anthropology* 6(2): 161–87.

Srinivas, Lakshmi. 1998. "Active Viewing: An Ethnography of the Indian Film Audience." *Visual Anthropology* 11(4): 323–53.

Stam, Robert, and Ella Shohat. 1994. "Contested Histories: Eurocentricism, Multiculturalism, and the Media." In *Multiculturalism: A Critical Reader*, ed. David Goldberg, 296–324. Oxford: Basil Blackwell.

Steinberg, Stephen. 1981. *The Ethnic Myth*. Boston: Beacon Press.

Sturgeon, Timothy. 2000. "How Silicon Valley Came to Be." In *Understanding Silicon Valley: An Anatomy of an Entrepreneurial Region*, ed. M. Kenney, 15–47. Stanford: Stanford University Press.

Suarez-Orozco, Carola, and Marcelo Suarez-Orozco. 1995. *Transformations: Migration, Family Life and Achievement Motivation among Latino Adolescents*. Stanford: Stanford University Press.

Takaki, Ronald. 1995. *India in the West: South Asians in America*. New York: Chelsea House Publishers.

——. 2001. "Multiculturalism: Battleground or Meeting Ground?" In *Color-Line to Borderlands: The Matrix of American Ethnic Studies*, ed. Johnella Butler, 3–17. Seattle: University of Washington Press.

Talmy, Steven. 2004. "Forever FOB: The Cultural Production of ESL in a High School." *Pragmatics* 14(2/3): 149–72.

Tarone, Elaine, Susan Gass, and Andrew Cohen. 1994. *Research Methodology in Second-Language Acquisition*. Mahwah, N.J.: Lawrence Erlbaum.

Taylor, Charles. 1992. *Multiculturalism and "The Politics of Recognition."* Princeton: Princeton University Press.

Thai, Hung. 1999. " 'Splitting Things in Half Is So White!' Conceptions of Family Life and Friendship and the Formation of Ethnic Identity among Second Generation Vietnamese Americans." *Amerasia* 25(1): 53–88.

Thornton, Sarah. 1997. "The Social Logic of Subcultural Capital." In *The Subcultures Reader*, ed. Ken Gelder and Sarah Thornton, 184–92. New York: Routledge.

Tilley, Christopher. 1999. *Metaphor and Material Culture*. Oxford: Blackwell.

Ting-Toomey, Stella. 1981. "Ethnic Identity and Close Friendship in Chinese-American College Students." *International Journal of Intercultural Relations* 5: 383–406.

Tololyan, Khaching. 1991. "The Nation-State and Its Others." *Diasporas* 1: 3–7.

Tuan, Mia. 1998. *Forever Foreigners or Honorary Whites? The Asian Ethnic Experience Today*. New Brunswick, N.J.: Rutgers University Press.

Turner, Terence. 1994. "Anthropology and Multiculturalism: What Is Anthropology That Multiculturalists Should Be Mindful of It?" In *Multiculturalism: A Critical Reader*, ed. David Goldberg, 406–25. Oxford: Basil Blackwell.

Urchiuoli, Bonnie. 1999. *Exposing Prejudice: Puerto Rican Experiences of Language, Race, and Class*. Boulder: Westview Press.

van der Veer, Peter, ed. 1995. *Nation and Migration: The Politics of Space in the South Asian Diaspora*. Philadelphia: University of Pennsylvania Press.

Veblen, Thorstein. 1953. *The Theory of the Leisure Class*. New York: Mentor.

Vertovec, Steven. 2000. *The Hindu Diaspora: Comparative Patterns*. New York: Routledge.

Vertovec, Steven, and Robin Cohen, ed. 2002. *Conceiving Cosmopolitanism: Theory, Context, and Practice*. Oxford: Oxford University Press.

Visweswaran, Kamala. 1993. "Diaspora by Design: Flexible Citizenship and South Asians in U.S. Racial Formations." *Diaspora* 6: 5–29.

Voloshinov, V. N. 1973. *Marxism and the Philosophy of Language*. New York: Seminar Press.

Wallace, Michele. 1994. "Multiculturalism and Oppositionality." In *Between Borders: Pedagogy and the Politics of Cultural Studies*, ed. Henry Giroux and Peter McLaren, 180–91. New York: Routledge.

Wallerstein, Immanuel. 1990. "Culture as the Ideological Battleground of the Modern World-System." In *Global Culture: Nationalism, Globalization, and Modernity*, ed. Mike Featherstone, 31–56. London: Sage.

Waters, Mary. 1990. *Ethnic Options: Choosing Identities in America*. Berkeley: University of California Press.

Werbner, Pnina. 1997. "Afterword: Writing Multiculturalism and Politics in the New Europe." In *The Politics of Multiculturalism in the New Europe: Racism, Identity, and Community*, eds. Tariq Modood and Pnina Werbner, 261–267. New York: Macmillan.

Weiner, Annette. 1992. *Inalienable Possessions: The Paradox of Keeping-while-giving*. Berkeley: University of California Press.

Weiss, Marc. 1985. "High-Technology Industries and the Future of Employment." In *Silicon Landscapes*, ed. Peter Hall and Ann Markusen, 80–93. Boston: Allen and Unwin.

Wenger, Etienne. 1999. *Communities of Practice: Learning, Meaning, and Power*. New York: Cambridge University Press.

Werbner, Pnina, and Tariq Modood, eds. 1997. *Debating Cultural Hybridity: Multicultural Identities and the Politics of Anti-Racism*. London: Zed Books.

Whorf, Benjamin. 1956. "The Relation of Habitual Thought and Behavior to Language." In *Language, Thought, and Reality: Selected Writings of Benjamin Lee Whorf*, ed. J. Carroll, 134–59. Cambridge, Mass.: MIT Press.

Wilk, Richard. 1995. "Learning to Be Local in Belize: Global Systems of Common Difference." In *Worlds Apart: Modernity through the Prism of the Local*, ed. Daniel Miller, 110–33. London: Routledge.

Williams, Raymond. 1988. *Religions of Immigrants from India and Pakistan*. Cambridge: Cambridge University Press.

Willis, Paul. 1977. *Learning to Labor: How Working Class Kids Get Working Class Jobs*. New York: Columbia University Press (Morningside Edition, 1981).

Winant, Howard. 1997. "Behind Blue Eyes: Whiteness and Contemporary U.S. Racial Politics." In *Off White: Readings on Race, Power, and Society*, ed. Michelle Fine, 40–56. New York: Routledge.

Wong, Bernard P. 2006. *The Chinese in Silicon Valley: Globalization, Social Networks, and Ethnic Identity*. Lanham, Md.: Rowman and Littlefield.

Woolard, Kathryn. 1995. "Gendered Peer Groups and the Bilingual Repertoire in Catalonia." *SALSA* 2: 200–220.

——. 1999. "Simultaneity and Bivalency as Strategies in Bilingualism." *Journal of Linguistic Anthropology* 8(1): 3–29.

Wulff, Helena. 1995. "Introducing Youth Culture in Its Own Right: The State of the Art and New Possibilities." In *Youth Cultures: A Cross-Cultural Perspective*, ed. Vered Amit-Talai and Helena Wulff, 1–18. London: Routledge.

Zentella, Ana Celia. 1997. *Growing Up Bilingual: Puerto Rican Children in New York*. Malden, Mass.: Blackwell.

Zhou, Min. 1997a. "Growing Up American: The Challenge Confronting Immigrant Children and the Children of Immigrants." *Annual Review of Sociology* 23: 63–95.

——. 1997b. "Segmented Assimilation: Issues, Controversies, and Recent Research on the New Second Generation." *International Migration Review* 31: 975–1008.

——. 2004. "Coming of Age at the Turn of the Twenty-First Century: A

Demographic Profile of Asian American Youth." In *Asian American Youth: Culture, Identity, and Ethnicity*, ed. Jennifer Lee and Min Zhou, 33–50. New York: Routledge.

Zhou, Min, and Carl L. Bankston. 1996. "Social Capital and the Adaptation of the Second Generation: The Case of Vietnamese Youth in New Orleans." In *The New Second Generation*, ed. Alejandro Portes, 197–220. New York: Russell Sage Foundation.

Zhou, Min, and Jennifer Lee. 2004. "Introduction: The Making of Culture, Identity, and Ethnicity among Asian American Youth." In *Asian American Youth: Culture, Identity, and Ethnicity*, ed. Jennifer Lee and Min Zhou, 1–30. New York: Routledge.

Zlolniski, Christian. 2006. *Janitors, Street Vendors, and Activists: The Lives of Mexican Immigrants in Silicon Valley*. Berkeley: University of California Press.

Films

American Desi. 2001. Dir. Piyush Pandya.

Bend It Like Beckham. 2002. Dir. Gurinder Chadha.

Better Luck Tomorrow. 2002. Dir. Justin Lin.

Bobby. 1973. Dir. Raj Kapoor.

Dil To Paagal Hai (The Heart Is Crazy). 1997. Dir. Yash Chopra.

Dilwale Dulhuniya Le Jayenge (The Bravehearted Will Take the Bride). 1995. Dir. Aditya Chopra.

Ghost World. 2001. Dir. Terry Zwigoff.

Kabhi Alvida Naa Kehna (Never Say Goodbye). 2006. Dir. Karan Johar.

Kaho Naa . . . Pyaar Hai (Say This Is Love). 2000. Dir. Rakesh Roshan.

Kal Ho Naa Ho (Tomorrow May Never Come). 2003. Dir. Nikhil Advani.

Kuch Kuch Hota Hai (Something Is Happening). 1998. Dir. Nikhil Advani.

Moulin Rouge. 2001. Dir. Baz Luhrmann.

Pardes (Foreign Land). 1997. Dir. Subhash Ghai

Refugee. 2000. Dir. J. P. Dutta.

Secrets of Silicon Valley. 2001. Dir. Deborah Kaufman and Alan Snitow.

Taal (Rhythm). 1999. Dir. Subhash Ghai.

SHALINI SHANKAR

is an assistant professor of
anthropology and Asian American studies
at Northwestern University.

Library of Congress Cataloging-
in-Publication Data
Shankar, Shalini
Desi land : teen culture, class, and success
in Silicon Valley / Shalini Shankar.
p. cm.
Includes bibliographical references and
index.
ISBN 978-0-8223-4300-4 (cloth : alk. paper)
ISBN 978-0-8223-4315-8 (pbk. : alk. paper)
1. South Asian American teenagers—
California—Santa Clara Valley (Santa Clara
County)—Social conditions. 2. South Asian
American teenagers—California—Santa
Clara Valley (Santa Clara County)—Ethnic
identity. 3. South Asian Americans—
California—Santa Clara Valley (Santa Clara
County)—Social conditions. 4. South Asian
Americans—California—Santa Clara Valley
(Santa Clara County)—Ethnic identity.
5. Ethnicity—California—Santa Clara Valley
(Santa Clara County) 6. Subculture—
California—Santa Clara Valley (Santa Clara
County) I. Title.
E184.S69S55 2008
305.235089'914079473—dc22
2008028432